50

TIPS, TRICKS, AND SECRETS FOR THE SUCCESSFUL IB STUDENT

50

TIPS, TRICKS, AND SECRETS FOR THE
SUCCESSFUL IB STUDENT

MARTIN RUZICKA
INESSA KULBARISOVA
KENNETH CHRISTOPHER HENDRA
AHSAS YEUOZ

ZOUEY PUBLISHING

This book is printed on acid-free paper.

Copyright © 2025. All rights reserved.

No part of this book may be used or reproduced in any manner whatsoever without written permission, except in the case of brief quotations embodied in critical articles or reviews.

Published 2025
ZOUEV PUBLISHING

ISBN 978-0-9934187-6-1, hardcover.

*Dedicated to you –
the student.*

Introduction		5
1.	Is the IB For Me?	9
2.	IB vs AP	14
3.	Irrational IB Fear	20
4.	Subject Choice [Part I]	24
5.	Subject Choice [Part II]	29
6.	Do the Basics Right	35
7.	Student-Teacher Relations	39
8.	Maximizing Productivity at School	47
9.	The Importance of IA	55
10.	Managing Stress	66
11.	Procrastination in the IB	75
12.	IB Friendships	80
13.	Time Management	84
14.	IB Efficiency and Self-Improvement	89
15.	Improving Memory	96
16.	Writing IB Essays	99
17.	Mastering the IB Presentation	103
18.	IB Exam Revision [Part 1]	106

19.	IB Exam Revision [Part 2]	111
20.	IB Exam Revision [Part 3]	115
21.	The Power of Past Papers	125
22.	The Power of Past Papers [Part II]	134
23.	Examination Technique [Part I]	140
24.	Examination Technique [Part II]	145
25.	Acing the Literature (Group 1) Exam	149
26.	IO Tips and Tricks	165
27.	Blasting Through Language B	172
28.	The Group 3 Struggle	179
29.	Engineering A 7 In Hl Economics	185
30.	Hacking History	195
31.	Beating Biology	213
32.	Cracking Chemistry	219
33.	Figuring Out Physics	222
34.	The Group 4 Project	228
35.	Mastering HL Maths	233
36.	Mastering the Math IA [part I]	242
37.	Mastering the Math IA [Part II: Example]	252
38.	Hacking Your GDC	259

39.	Acing Visual Art	263
40.	Excel at the Extended Essay [Part I]	284
41.	Excel at the Extended Essay [Part II]	299
42.	Excel at the Extended Essay [Part III]	308
43.	Tackling TOK: The Essay	313
44.	Tackling TOK: The Presentation	330

45. How to get a 45	338
46. Conquering CAS	384
47. Applying Artificial Intelligence	393
48. The Power of Technologies in the IB	397
49. Academic Dishonesty	407
50. Appeals and Re-takes	412
Life After IB	415
Conclusion	417
Contributors	420
Special Thanks	420

Introduction

Before we dive into the substantive part of this guidebook, I wish to spend a few pages explaining who I am, and my motivation for compiling and writing this book. This is not my first IB guidebook, but it will (hopefully) be my last, in the sense that I wish to exhaust every piece of crucial advice that I have. I hope that this endeavour will be more structured and reflective than my previous IB guidebooks, and I certainly hope it reaches and helps as many students as possible.

Before diving into the world that I like to call "stress-free IB" you may want to ask yourself the question "who am I to listen to some stranger's advice on how to do well on my IB?" At least I hope you are asking yourself this question. After all, I have never officially worked at an IB school, nor am I in any way affiliated with the organisation. Moreover, in recent years, the market for IB 'help' material has become greatly saturated with both recommendable and also some avoidable books being published. Thus, before going into the details of how to maximize your IB points total, let me put your mind at ease by providing a little background on myself and my own academic experiences.

I graduated with the International Baccalaureate Diploma Program totalling 43 points in 2007, setting a school record at the time and finishing top in most of my classes. The next few years were spent at Oxford University where I completed my BA in Economics and Management, while simultaneously starting to tutor students over Skype from my dorm room. It was during the summer breaks of these years that I completed my first IB guidebook, *Three*, which dealt with the 3 'bonus point' (Extended Essay and Theory of Knowledge) component of the diploma.

Upon graduating from Oxford, I pursued an MSc in Financial Mathematics from the Cass Business School in London. During this year, I completed my second IB guidebook, *I Think Therefore IB*, which incidentally serves as the inspiration for this book. It was around this time that I was also one of the first tutors to work for EliteIB (www.eliteib.co.uk – now bought out by Lanterna/Kognity) which has now grown to be one of the largest IB tutoring agencies in the world.

I left EliteIB to set up my own freelancer IB tutoring practice – IBTutorOnline (www.ibtutoronline.com). It was here that I honed my skills as an Economics and Mathematics tutor, specializing in helping students with their Internal Assessments. I was busy with IBTutorOnline for over five years and in that time oversaw hundreds of Extend Essays, TOK assignments, and helped over two hundred students in their IB studies. My students improved their grades, on average, by 2.3 points and I even had the pleasure of tutoring several 45/45 students.

In 2015, I set up a small publishing house (www.zouevpublishing.com) that specializes in publishing IB guidebooks, written by former students and aimed at current students. We have published books that cover subjects such as History and Physics, as well as general IB and IA guidebooks.

So over the last 20 years I have become somewhat of *the IB Guru* (as my friends jokingly call me). I have been an active contributor on IB forums, and I have probably personally and directly helped nearly 10,000 IB students over the last two decades. I truly believe that as far as being a consultant on the broader IB goals of achieving success, I am probably the best at what I do – which leads us to the creation of this book.

Reading this book is probably the most efficient method of earning a 40+ grade in your International Baccalaureate Diploma. Whether you are a student in need of guidance, a teacher looking to find new teaching techniques, or simply an interested reader – hopefully you will find that this extensive treasure-chest of advice meets all of your expectations. If you follow the advice put forth in this book correctly and put in some effort and determination, I firmly believe that you can obtain a point total of 40 or above – irrespective of any 'natural' intelligence.

Those of you still curious to know, the two points I missed out on to get a 45 were due to a 6 in Physics (Standard Level) and a 6 in English (Standard Level). Looking back I do blame myself for not following my own advice enough to get that 7 in Physics, however the English I have no regrets about; I tried my best and did what I could, but did not get a 7. Unfortunately, and despite the title, this book will not teach you how to get a perfect score of 45/45 and place you into the top 0.01% of candidates. I know plenty of people who have obtained this amazing feat; however, almost all admit to having had a slice of good fortune somewhere along their path to perfection. With most university offers capped at around 40 points, there is also no need to get a perfect score - unless you are the ultimate perfectionist.

There is no effortless way to achieve the grades that you want. There are however ways that will save you time, effort, and money, yet still let you reach your maximum potential and get the grades you dream of. For those of you reading to find any tips on plagiarism, cheating or any other non-ethical method to get a higher grade, you will have to look elsewhere. My tips and techniques are 100% in line with the rules and regulations of the IB guidelines. Understandably, there will be critics amongst parents and teachers who suggest that a lot of what I endorse is in some ways unethical and not in accordance with what the IB preaches. These arguments lack merit. Countless students are getting the top grades and succeeding without actually succumbing to becoming lifeless bookworms. One needs to understand and appreciate that there is "cheating" and then there are "tactical and efficient study techniques", and there is a thick line separating the two concepts. This book will ultimately teach you to become masters of manipulating the resources at your disposal efficiently and tactically, without having to resort to anything that can be regarded as 'cheating'.

What is essential before we begin is that you throw away all preconceived notions about the IB as being something scary, elitist, incredibly demanding and impossible to crack. I was once amongst you, but after finding out that the IB is just as easy to decipher as the A-levels, the AP programs, or the SATs – I became fearless. This is an essential stepping-stone in your long road to IB success. Yes, your non-IB friends will call you an overachieving geek. Yes, you may find you have more assignments and tests than the other "normal" kids. And yes, there will be times when you wonder why your parents/teachers would ever want to put you through so much traumatising pain. However, one should not fear. The techniques in this book will ensure that your two-year ride in the IBDP will be amongst the most memorable and fun two years of your life.

It certainly was for me.

1. Is the IB for Me?

Before you even embark on your IB adventure, you need to decide if the IB is for you. By that I mean, is the IB diploma the bridge you need to get to the next point in your life – whatever that may be?

Depending on where you are located geographically, what your future career ambitions are, and what school choices are on offer, you may be faced with the task of deciding whether the IB is worth it in your individual situation. Let's start by briefly looking exactly what the IB Diploma Program entails:

Founded nearly 50 years ago, the IB organization is a non-profit institution that offers an international education to students at over 3,500 IB World schools in 145 countries. The Diploma Program includes an advanced academic curriculum and several core requirements, including the Extended Essay (a kind of senior thesis), Theory of Knowledge (an epistemology course that emphasizes the IB philosophy), and CAS (extracurricular activities highlighting "creativity, action, and service" that counterbalance academic studies). Your IB final examination scores and fulfilment of above requirements determine whether you earn the IB diploma.

If that sounds like a lot of work – it's because it is. There is a good reason that the IB program has such a notoriously difficult and rigorous reputation around the world. The upside is that you are encouraged to think independently and learn how to think. You also become more culturally aware as you develop a second language, and you will be able to engage with people in an increasingly globalized and rapidly changing world.

US Scenario

It's widely considered that American students rarely take on the IB diploma to attend university outside of the States, but rather to earn as many college-transferable credits as possible (to "get ahead" in completing General Education requirements in college) or increase their college application marketability by boasting the IB diploma as an achievement on their resume.

Advanced Placement courses have long been considered the go-to option for U.S. high schoolers who desire more challenging work than what's offered in the standard curriculum. But IB students may have more options for getting an academic challenge. An increasing number of American high schools offer the IB program which, like the AP program, offers a rigorous set of courses. Moreover, the SATs and your GPA seem to still be the dominant factors which US universities look at when deciding on applicants. Thus, it would make sense for US-based students to find out if their 'dream' university will be more likely possible if they take the IB. This could even mean you need to call up the universities and talk to their admissions offices.

More importantly, students can earn college credits by taking certain IB subjects. This is very important to consider because rather than taking the full diploma, you may be inclined to take IB certificates instead. If a student chooses to pursue the IB certificate route and not the full lB Diploma he/she does not have to complete the Theory of Knowledge course, the Extended Essay, or the 150 hours over two years of CAS. Taking IB Certificates is similar to taking AP courses. Those students enrolled as just certificate students could also choose to take the AP tests and, therefore, double dip with IB and AP credit on their transcript.

There is also the cost to consider: IB exams are more expensive than AP. There is a $160 registration fee each year plus $110 fee per exam. AP exams are 92$ without an additional fee. Many schools however have financial aid and fee-waiver programs. If financing is an issue for you, you should contact your school and see if help is available. Talk with a counsellor at your school to find out about testing costs.

I know it seems crazy to be thinking about all of this when you are 15 years old and don't even know much about university and what you wish to study, but the IB is a huge decision and one you should not take lightly. The main advice here is to do your research. I can only give general help, each case will vary on the specifics, so pick up that phone and start calling potential universities to find out their recognition of the IB Diploma.

UK Scenario

In the UK (and some parts of Europe), the choice is altogether different. Here you are required to choose between the traditional A-levels and the IB. Although the IB has only been around since 1968, it has grown substantially in the UK and is finding itself offered at more schools, often alongside the A-levels.

If your school offers both, then it's relatively agreed upon which students do more work. Over the two years, IB students will get up to half as much teaching as their A-level counterparts. On top of that, they have to adopt a more inquiring approach than A-level students. There is also this myth that because IB students can only do two sciences (and A-level students could potentially do three), they have less chance of getting into medical school. This has been proven false as IB students are as successful (if not more) and the IB lets students do biology and chemistry (which is essential for medicine) alongside maths.

Prospective IB students should take comfort in the fact that the IB has become more and more appreciated by UK universities. As a rule of thumb, an IB score of 7 earns 130 UCAS points, while an A* is worth 140 points, and an A-grade 120.

Arguments for students opting for A-levels instead of IB usually focus around the principal objection that the IB burdens students with subjects which they may have no interest or aptitude for. The A-level system allows students who aren't very good at maths, or hate languages, to abandon these weaknesses once their GCSEs are over – but the IB requires you take on these challenges for two more years.

Rest of the World

Non-US/UK students face different scenarios altogether. I can't possibly go into the details for each individual country, but basically it boils down to what choices you have on offer in your national education system, and where you wish to go once you finish high school. I have met plenty of students who wanted to go straight into a trade job once completing high school, or someone who wanted to enter the family business as soon as possible. In these situations, I can understand why the two years of the IB Diploma would seem like a time waste.

Ultimately (and I may be slightly biased in this assessment) the IB Diploma does in fact develop well-rounded, inquisitive and global learners. I would strongly argue that it's the best high school education a student can get, and it opens the door to so many diverse opportunities. The skillset you acquire upon completion of the program is going to set you up for a very successful future career.

The IB Diploma is not for everyone. Although it is a wonderfully challenging program that has gained incredible worldwide recognition, you need to look at your individual scenario and decide if the program is right for you and for where you want to be in a few years.

2. IB vs AP

Due to the rising popularity of the IB program in America, we decided to include a specific chapter to deal with how US-based students should approach their IB (as most of the information available caters to European audiences).

It's true, the International Baccalaureate Diploma Program is daunting. Certainly, a formidable opponent, monstrous with its intent on obstructing your journey to a happier destination. Coming from a less-than-adequately-funded school in urban America, I've seen quite a few of my friends shrink away at the thought of tackling the academic juggernaut. However, like most of life, the greater the challenge, the greater the reward. I can't speak with authority on universities outside of the United States, though I'm sure they're quite similar, but I can assure you that the most prestigious American universities look upon an International Baccalaureate Diploma with immense respect and appreciation.

Some context for you: my high school was and is the poorest public educational facility in the immediate district and most of the surrounding area. It also happens to be the most diverse school in the entire state of Washington with over 65 languages spoken, about as international as it gets here in America. More than 60% of the student body receives financial aid in the form of "free or reduced lunch". The school offers only 15 International Baccalaureate classes, 8 of which are Standard Level only and many of which were only added within the past year. This contrasts with the 40+ subjects provided by the Programme, the clear majority of which are available in both Standard and Higher Level.

With all that in mind please trust me when I say, within reason, everybody willing to put in the effort can graduate the Programme with flying colors.

A very good friend of mine, an illegal immigrant and from a poor background, was accepted into a Top 20 American university with a full ride scholarship, all thanks to the International Baccalaureate Diploma Programme. Your two years in this esteemed Programme will be hellish. You will stress, you will question your decision and yes, you will consider dropping out. But your two years in this Programme will be worth it. It will prepare you for university, it will prepare you for your career and yes, it will prepare you for your future. So why Choose IB over AP?

1) Preparation for College

Though it may be true that AP Students get much more college credit than their fellow IB counterparts, the IB does infinitely more in preparing you for the workload you will receive in college. What makes the IB such a daunting program is the fact that it throws so much information at you. Students that do well in the IB can effectively manage this information, learn it efficiently, and at the same time maintain healthy, balanced lives. In college, similarly, you're going to be bombarded with all kinds of information, both academic and non-academic. You're going to have to make choices on prioritizing your work over going to a frat party, about whether you can afford to join another extracurricular activity, or whether staying up all night to finish that paper is worth it. In this sense, the IB offers you invaluable experience and you should treat everything it throws at you as a learning curve for college. Last time I checked, AP students didn't have to write a 4000-word research paper, question their own existence, and manage CAS activities whilst having to juggle six subjects. Truth be told, the

IB will make the college transition very smooth and you'll go in feeling like a rockstar.

2) Broader Perspective

Let's be honest: The APs have always been primarily geared to provide an American Education, possessing very few courses such as AP World History that critically examine society from a global perspective. Before I get bullets fired at me for challenging the greatest nation in the world, let me add that this is completely fine: The APs prepare you very well for college and ensure you learn loads of material. However, I personally feel the IB offers you something much more rich and substantial. Indeed, the IB turns you into a scholar of the world: you're forced to examine things from multiple different perspectives, challenge assumptions, and this leads you to become a well-rounded, critical thinker. Sure, you can argue that this global mumbo-jumbo isn't necessary, and that the point of a high-school program should be to simply gain knowledge in subjects you're interested in (hence why you don't have as many subjects if you do the APs). But the way I see it, the IB is in a way that 'study abroad' experience that so many people claim is invaluable. Think of yourself as Dora the Explorer, always questioning everything around you, and wanting to delve further into your intellectual pursuits.

3) Alumni Love

This doesn't seem like a real reason, but hear me out. Nothing quite compares to being in college, meeting someone new, and then realizing that both of you are IB Alumni! You suddenly feel as if you have known each other for many, many years and can relate to each other. The pain, the misery, the grade boundaries—oh, what bliss! It's like you're family. No, you ARE family.

4) Creativity, Action, Swag

Though the IB is a lot of work, it ensures that you pursue worthwhile and enjoyable activities outside the classroom. You're going to graduate high school having done activities that you previously would never have thought of doing, and the most exciting part is that one of these activities might end up being something you love to do! Take it from me: I unwillingly decided to learn chess to fulfil my Creativity Section, after my mother went out and spent money on buying a chess board. Hundreds of hours later, chess has become one of my favourite hobbies, one that I pursue even in college! See, the AP Program aims to simply focus on the courses that you take. The IB, as hard as it may sound to believe, wants you to go outside and discover the amazing opportunities that are available.

5) Work Ethic

Granted, the average IB student will have more work to do than the average AP student. You take more subjects, have a lot to do outside the classroom, and oh god, there's just so much writing to do! But whilst doing all of this, you start to develop a strong work ethic. Even if you procrastinate, you realize that you just must get your work done. Unless you want very little sleep, you start to become much more efficient with your work and know how to prioritize your day. You know whether you can afford to go out with your friends, or should rather stay in to do some revision. Conversely, you realize that having a social life is also important to maintaining a balanced lifestyle, and thus you make time to hang out with your friends.

These are invaluable skills not only to hone for college, but also for the rest of your life. With each day, you start to work smarter, you start to feel like a champion.

6) Research and Investigation Skills

If you've ever been interested in doing research (or even if you haven't) the IB is an excellent program to cultivate investigative qualities. The IAs that you must write for your sciences ensure that you develop skills in data analysis, know how to work with uncertainties, and are comfortable combining both quantitative and qualitative elements to form a cogent paper. The Internal Assessments that you must write for your Humanities, especially Economics, allow you to combine real-life information and theory to craft a compelling argument. The Math Internal Assessment is an amazing way to understand the practicalities of Math in the real world, and allow you to consolidate your fundamentals in specific areas. The Extended Essay that you must write gives you real-hand experience on drafting a paper of such large volume. And of course, who can forget scourging the Internet for all those precious past papers and their markschemes.

7) A Powerful Resume

Think about it for a second. In a world where colleges expect you to do a billion activities, ask you to go above and beyond both within and outside the classroom, and even want you to do research, isn't the IB marvellous? Your CAS leads to all those Extra-Curricular Activities, you get to put down your EE as 'research' (I for sure did), and your TOK endeavours demonstrate intellectual curiosity. Aren't you, by simply doing the IB, building up an awesome portfolio for applying to college? All the stuff that you learn, that you do, and that you're able to get deeply involved in will look fantastic on your application, for both college and prospective internships.

8) Way of Thinking vs Curriculum Readiness

The APs will ensure that once you get to college, you know the curriculum that is going to be covered and that you've had some sort of experience dealing with it beforehand. That's in part why the AP Program warrants so many college credits. However, what the IB program will do is that it will force you to develop a dynamic way of thinking that is tailored to new situations. That is, you may not have seen the material presented to you, but you will be fantastically equipped to deal with it. You will recognize patterns, structure your revision effectively, look at details from different perspectives; essentially, you'll have a mental toolkit ready to tackle all sorts of new problems. To me, that's something that is much more important than simply gaining enough college credits or having familiarity with the curriculum. Life is all about adapting to new situations, solving new problems, and the IB is what is going to prepare you for the best.

3. Irrational IB fear

Perhaps one of the first and most important topics to address is this widespread belief that the IB programme is elitist, unrealistically difficult, and a two-year burden on your teenage life. You need to throw away all your negative preconceptions and fears about the IB diploma and start believing in yourself. No matter who you are and what kind of academic record you have had up to this point in your life, the IB diploma program is an opportunity for you to start anew.

I have known students that have come from C grade averages to end up with high 30s on their IB diploma. I was quite the high-school slacker and troublemaker until I realised that my IB grades could decide a large part of my near future. The key here is that natural intelligence and 'book-smart' are not essential to achieving IB success. What is essential however is the willpower and self-belief that you can survive and succeed in the most academically intense high school degree program and come out with flying colours.

Consider your two-year IB experience as something of a sporting event. The final exams are the grand finale, and everything before is your preparation and training for that event. I use this sporting analogy because it highlights the importance of planning and mental preparedness that is needed to perform at the highest level. Even the greatest athletes cannot do their best unless they master the skill of visualizing their own success.

Without getting too philosophical, I do want to stress how important this 'visualization' exercise is. Unless you can imagine yourself getting the top marks and achieving a total of

40+ points, it will be very difficult to do so in reality. This is not a 'self-help' book per se, nor do I fully agree with the ideas that some self-help books tend to promote – most famously The Secret's notion that anything is possible if you keep thinking about it. However, although I don't think that visualization alone is sufficient for success, I do think that it is necessary.

When someone tells you that the IB program is 'difficult', you need to appreciate that difficulty is always relative. Yes, perhaps compared to the A-Levels or the AP program, the IB is more academically challenging and there is more work to be done. However, this does not mean that the IB is the hardest task any 16-18 year olds across the world must face. Trust me, there will be much more demanding and stressful challenges as you get older. Don't let this 'IB fear' become a scapegoat for underperformance. I see this happen all the time. Students get lost in this illusion of the IB as something impossible, and subsequently lose any motivation to do well because they think it is beyond their reach. This is where mental strength is of utmost importance.

The first few weeks of the IB program are relatively tranquil. Use this 'easing-in' period as an opportunity to prove to yourself that you can conquer and beat anything the IB program throws at you. Only once you overcome your mental fear of the IB program can you begin to deal with the challenges of the program itself. It is imperative that your first few weeks of the program go as smoothly as possible. If you start to fall behind early, any preconceived fears you may have had will soon turn into a reality. So at least for the first month or so make sure you meet all of the deadlines and perform at your highest level. Once you have proven to yourself that you can overcome the first month, any fear left will gradually dissolve.

Now that we've got the fear aspect out of the way, the question becomes: how should you best spend the few months leading up to your first day in the IB program? Unfortunately, there is no concrete answer, and you will hear a variety of responses when asking who has been through it all. However, there are certainly some things you can do that are more beneficial than others.

Summertime is here and you must relax, so for a few weeks forget that you are even in the IB. I suggest doing this at the start of summer. I also strongly recommend travelling and relaxing with friends and family. Take this as an opportunity to reset, and go fresh into the IB next year.

Now say 2-3 weeks are left before the IB starts or restarts, what do you do? You get back to work and you work hard! Ok, but what do you work on? Firstly, be sure that there is nothing you don't understand from the previous year. Make sure to patch up all your weak points. If there is something you don't understand in Chemistry, go over it, review it and then test yourself.

Do not be afraid to send a few emails to your teachers, they will find it incredible that you are working during your summer. If you have also noticed that you are not good at a particular type of assignment, for example you seem to score poorly on certain types of English essays, research into them, rewrite a few essays and then ask your teacher to look over them.

Say you have patched up all your areas of weakness, what now? It's time to get ahead of the game. Look over the assignments you will have to do next year and start preparing for those. If you can't do that, then look over certain particularly difficult topics you will be doing next year and go over them. In all honesty you will probably not have much time to get ahead, most of your 2-3 weeks will be consumed with review work and patching any weakness in your knowledge. On that note, enjoy the summer and best of luck to you.

4. Subject Choice [Part I]

Although to most of you this chapter will have little relevance, to those who are yet to decide which subjects you want to take – this chapter is of great importance. I find that choosing your subjects is, rather unfortunately, underestimated in importance. You are deciding what you will learn in depth for the next two years of your life. So, just as you would take time to choose a college degree, an occupation or a spouse, you should sit down and think about what interests you - even slightly. There are a few factors that you should consider and I have outlined these below:

Interest

As with almost everything you do, you will tend to succeed more and find it easier if you are doing something you have an interest for and enjoy. The same goes for IB subjects. Although this is of less importance in choosing a group 1 or 2 language, it has great importance in choosing your group 4 science and group 3 subject. If you know for a fact that you have absolutely no passion and interest for memorizing human anatomy and studying Biology, then you can cross that off. If, on the other hand, you want your IB to have as little maths as possible, then you probably would not be too interested in studying Physics. If you are strongly passionate about a certain subject and are already reading external material concerned with it, then by all means go ahead and take it into consideration.

However, one should be careful not to confuse interest with vague curiosity. If you always thought that graffiti is cool, it would not be wise choosing HL Visual Art solely based on that observation. Similarly, don't let a childhood obsession with spaceships be the deciding factor for choosing HL Physics. This is where a slight familiarity with the course content can greatly help. Take the time to glance over the syllabus of the course you are interested in, and only then check to see if it matches your interests.

Ability

Obviously if you are clearly naturally gifted in a certain subject then you should thank your natural abilities and take it. Of course, there are limitations to this rule of thumb. I used to be obsessed with drawing and graphic design, and for many years believed I would be studying Art at Diploma level. However, as the time came for me to make my final decision, I did a little research (with the statistics that the IB provides on their webpage) and talked to many seniors who had previously done Art as a subject. The general feeling seemed to be that if I wanted to go for a subject that I enjoyed, excelled at, and wouldn't be under too much stress then I should choose Art instead of another Group 3 topic. Having done that research also showed me that it seemed very few get 7s in Art (especially in my school), no matter how passionate or how good the candidate is (perhaps due to the nature of the final exam and luck of the draw).

Since I was more concerned with obtaining a 7 than following my passion for Art and gambling with the grade, I chose geography (which I also had a reasonable ability for). The message I'm trying to get across is that often students get confused about how great their abilities are in a certain subject. Just because you got A's in English in Elementary School does not mean that you should expect to jump into a Higher Level English exam and effortlessly produce a grade 7 piece of work.

Be honest with yourself when assessing your own ability in a certain subject.

Future

Please don't get me wrong. When I say future I don't mean that the subjects you choose for your IB diploma will reflect in any way where you will be in ten years and what sort of occupation you will have (although, funnily enough, they have for me). Nevertheless, you do need to take into consideration what you want to do at university level if you plan on pursuing a university education. It's unfortunate that you need to be thinking about your post-school decision from almost the age of 16 when university is probably the last thing on your mind but that's the reality of it. Too often I have seen students wanting to study medicine at a top UK university be rejected because, despite taking Biology as a subject, they did not take Chemistry, which is often a requirement to study medical science. The same can be said for students wanting to study Economics. Taking Mathematics Studies severely limits your chances of ending up at a top Economics course – in most cases.

Thus, if you're one of those students that has his/her heart set on a specific course at a specific university by the age of 16, then you should do some research and find out which courses are essential, and which will help you in getting closer to your goal. For those of you thinking of studying abroad, you may want to reconsider which foreign languages you want to take, if your school offers a wider variety.

Although this is important to take into consideration, don't worry too much about it. In most cases offers from universities are given based on a final score, rather than subject-specific.

Also, I have seen people go on to get PhDs in Economics without having taken Economics as an IB subject. So, with regards to the long-term future, subject choice is probably not the most important factor to consider.

Teachers

This is a tough one. I hate to say it but there is such a thing as a "bad teacher" even in the glamorous top-of-the-line world of the IB Diploma. Trust me; I have seen the best of both worlds. Some of the teachers I have worked with were masters at what they did, with more than a decade of first-hand IB experience. Then there were those who probably couldn't spell International Baccalaureate – let alone teach it. Most students tend to believe this idea where the teacher is the one factor that will make or break the subject. They think that the teacher has a greater influence on the final grade than they do themselves.

I do not agree. Even if your teacher is utterly useless at what they are hired to do, this does not mean you should spend two years moaning only to ultimately fail the subject and live your whole life cursing that teacher. Believe me, I have seen some of the worst of the worst. But even despite the poor teaching I've seen students get past that and take matters into their own hands to come out with a grade they truly deserve. Yes, it's true, if you have a poor teacher then you will spend most of your time becoming best friends with the subject textbooks. But let's be honest here, we don't live in a perfect world, hence we don't all have world class IB teachers.

With regards to the subject material, you should not have to worry too much if your teacher is clueless. But, when it comes to things such as external assessments and choosing options for examinations, you should ensure that they know what they are talking about. You don't want to sit a two-year program only to find that your teacher messed up the internal assessments you gave in and thus you lose almost 25% of your total mark.

By the time you begin your IB program, you will have heard all the rumours about who is a great IB teacher and who shouldn't even be teaching preschool. Don't completely ignore these. If you're the type of person who simply cannot take matters into their own hands and work independently for most of the year, then by all means look for the "best" and most engaging teachers that are available. If, on the other hand, you don't need to be spoon-fed information that is readily available for you yourself to read from the textbooks, then it shouldn't matter. In this case, you should choose subjects based on the other criteria I have outlined.

5. Subject Choice [Part II]

If you thought that those were the only factors to consider when choosing your courses, well you would be mistaken. The top students also consider some less obvious elements.

School records

If you are one of those students sitting the IB Diploma simply to obtain the highest score possible no matter which subjects then you would be wise to do a little bit of research. Find out how well your school has performed in different subjects over the years. If for the past ten years not a single person has gotten a 7 in Chemistry, then your best bet would probably be not to choose it if you are looking for a 7 in your Group 4 subject. If on the other hand, it has been decades since someone has gotten below a 5 in your school's History SL program, and you are the type of person that would be more than happy with a 5 or above then by all means go for it.

Don't limit this research to your school records alone. Go online and find out which subjects have the greatest fail rates, the greatest number of 7's, and what the median marks are. All of this information is readily available on the IBO website – under the section of 'Statistical Bulletins'. There is an abundance of information in these reports, so take the time to analyse them. I don't encourage making decisions completely based on statistics, but playing the numbers game will not prevent you from making better choices.

Difficulty

There is a myth in the IB world that claims that all IB kids do an equal amount of work, no matter what subjects they choose. Perhaps the phrasing is a bit unclear there. Yes, it can be that the actual amount of work (hours assigned) is the same from subject to subject. Don't be fooled into thinking that each candidate faces the same difficulty. This is especially true because of the IB's system of separating Higher Level and Standard Level subjects.

Take two random students with exactly the same subject choices, apart from the fact that student X takes Maths HL and Geography SL, whereas student Y takes Maths Studies (SL) and Geography HL. One would have an incredibly difficult time arguing that the gap in difficulty between Maths SL and HL is the same as the gap between Geography SL and HL. The gap in difficulty between Maths HL and SL is incomparable to the gap in Geography.

There is no point in kidding ourselves. If you want to challenge yourself, then by all means take HL: Economics, Mathematics, English, Physics, SL: History, Language B. If you want to lay back a bit and not be under too much stress and get a guaranteed pass, take HL: Theatre Arts, Geography, Environmental Systems, SL: English, Language (ab initio), and Business Management. Let's be honest here; it's no secret that Physics or Chemistry are academically more demanding than Environmental Systems.

All of this is not something to be ashamed of either. You may opt to take a less stressful route, with a lighter workload – and this is perfectly fine. The point I am trying to make is that you need to figure out what your ultimate aim is. Do you want to choose demanding courses that interest you and will challenge you? Or do you have little interest in what subjects you do as long as you get 35+ by the end of the two years? There is little wrong with either of the choices, but the important thing to remember is that the choice is real and the choice is yours.

Resources

As much as the IB tries to make their students more educated, inquisitive and imaginative, I am often shocked at how little students use the resources available at their disposal. The Internet is an invaluable weapon in your IB survival toolkit. Go online and find out if there are any great books available on your subjects of interest. Find out how long the course has been taught and whether it has been significantly modified in recent years.

Keep in mind that if the resources are scarce for your subject of interest, then it probably means that you will struggle to find help outside your classroom. More well-established subjects have an incredible surplus of information readily available to find on the internet and in books. The newer subjects, or the less popular choices, will undoubtedly have less helpful information.

On a final note, I fully appreciate that there are many students out there crying "my school just launched the IB Diploma program and I don't have a choice of what science to choose because they only offer Chemistry at HL!" Unfortunately, that is just a fact of life. Not a single school will offer all the IB subject choices that are available, so you need to make the best out of the situation. Don't waste your time protesting and making petitions asking your school to introduce a subject that would probably yield high demand from the students. It's much more complicated than that as there are monetary, time and faculty constraints that need to be taken into account.

In certain specific circumstances, however, there are ways in which you can 'create' a new subject for yourself – given your school allows this. You could potentially sit the two years in a HL class only to then undertake the SL exam. This may be frowned upon by your school, but try to see if this is possible. I initially started the IB program with the intention of doing four HL subjects (Economics, Mathematics, Geography and Physics) as opposed to the usual three. However, as the time came to make final exam choices, I realised that I would be better off dropping one of my HLs rather than risking getting a lower grade. Physics HL was unfortunately a bit too demanding for me, and I argued that it took away too much revision time from my other HL subjects in which I was trying to achieve 7s. I repeatedly asked the IB coordinator to be allowed to sit the SL Physics exam, and continue to sit the Physics HL class. Eventually all the details were sorted out and it worked out fine.

I'm not saying sit HL classes for all of your subjects, but this is certainly an overlooked tactic for the more ambitious students out there. If you are not challenged enough and would find it beneficial learning some HL material despite sitting the SL exam then try to make that possible by carefully discussing it with your IB coordinator. Note also that the HL teacher may be much 'better' than the SL one.

There is also the possibility of self-study or following online courses (check the Pamoja online education program). Again, you will need to check this with your school and IB coordinator. It is understandable why many schools are wary of external course providers. Also, there is a monetary burden to consider.

At the end of the day the choice of which subjects you will do will largely depend on how the schedule blocks in your school work and what subjects they actually have on offer. Don't make a huge fuss if you can't get exactly what you want. There are thousands of students out there in similar situations – if not worse. Work with what you have. Take my tips listed above, consult your parents, consult your teachers, consult your older school friends and hopefully this will help you reach a decision.

Do not choose a subject "because my friend is doing it as well." This is probably the dumbest thing you can do when it comes to making subject choices. Chances are you and your "friends" will see each other in other classes, and you'll have enough time to hang out outside of class.

Anticipated Subject

An 'Anticipated' subject is just the IB's fancy name for an accelerated subject. When you sign up to study an Anticipated subject, you have about one year to actually finish the entire subject. This means that you will have only 5 subjects to worry about in the last year of IB. But this also means a lot more stress during the first year of IB when you have to cram two years of content into just one year.

Most people's first reaction: What if I can't physically learn that much content in just one year!? Dispelling the anxiety: At my school, everyone (i.e., 150 of us) did one Anticipated subject. Some schools even allow people to take 2 Anticipated subjects. Achieving a grade 7 in Anticipated is also very feasible. So don't worry, the workload is doable.

You can only choose SL subjects to Anticipate. Most subjects are great to Anticipate, but I would personally stay away from the more notorious Anticipated subjects. History is already infamously difficult as a two-year course. I personally wouldn't select it as an Anticipated subject. English A Literature or Lang Lit – a very small number of 7s for the two-year course, so I wouldn't bet on getting a 7 in Anticipated. Mathematics – university admissions tend to require at least two years of senior Mathematics. However, Mathematics is one of those courses that works well with Anticipated. Maths is more about practice and I think you can pick up maths skills quickly. Second language subjects are fantastic to Anticipate if you are already somewhat proficient in the language.

I would advise most people to Anticipate a Group 3 Humanities subject (apart from History, of course!):

Psychology – a lot of people at my school did this. It worked great for me, but Psychology is a lot of rote learning and material. It's not an easy ride by any means, but it is probably more manageable than History.

Business and Management – even more people at my school anticipated B&M. Many people have the impression that it's an 'easy' subject, but I can't say anything on the topic because I've never done it. In the end, all subjects take time and commitment. Choosing the right anticipated subject is about knowing your strengths and considering the costs and benefits for you personally.

Doing an Anticipated subject is a good way to minimize stress and sleep deprivation in your second year of IB, with the trade-off being a slightly greater workload during your first year. You experience a real IB exam before you do all your other exams in final year. I found that the familiarity with the exam procedure really helped with nerves and pre-exam anxiety.

6. Do the Basics Right

The purpose of this chapter is to provide some basic guidelines and daily basis advice you should follow to survive in the world of IB. The degree to which you follow the advice in this chapter depends on what type of student you are. If organization, motivation and promptness are second nature to you then you will find most of the information in this chapter somewhat obvious.

Attendance

Although some of your classmates may beg to differ, missing school does not make you a modern-day Ferris Bueller. You must ensure that you are attending class as often as you can. Most of your classes are very demanding, and even one or two days missed could mean a lot in terms of catching up with the material. No matter how useless you think a certain class is, I would still recommend you show up because it is good work ethic and it will keep you busy.

In the rare case that you miss class because of an illness or any other valid reason, make sure that you talk to your teacher and get the correct material that you may have missed. Those of you who skip class regularly will find that sympathy is hard to come by when you have a genuine reason for your tardiness. This is yet another reason to avoid unnecessarily skipping class.

Free Periods

The term 'free period' has varying interpretations from student to student and school to school. To some of you this may mean an hour of playing solitaire on your laptop, to others it may mean an opportunity to finish last night's homework. Similarly, some schools are more stringent than others. At my school, most teachers treated 'free periods' as a quiet one-hour study session where students were free to do work independently. I want you to make the most out of the time available. Whether you do work, socialize, or catch up on sleep – make sure that it is not time wasted and that you are doing something that will benefit your grades in the long run.

Some schools allow students to arrive later (if the free periods are in the morning) or to depart before school is over (if the free periods are in the afternoon). Find out if you can do the same, and decide whether you would benefit from this. On occasion, I would try to miss any free period at the end of the day and get home to catch up on some sleep. You need to work out whether this is possible, and feasible.

Understandably, some schools simply do not allow students to have 'free periods'. Many of you studying in the US will find that any period not devoted to the IB will be packed with an alternative high school curriculum. Some schools prefer to devote more time to extra-curricular activities, or keep students busy with extra classes. If this is the case, then great. If you are being kept busy and productive, then you are on the right track.

Note Taking

Personally, I was never that great at taking notes in class. My handwriting was poor, and I found it difficult to take in everything that was being discussed and simultaneously jot down effective notes. I figured that if I can engage in the conversation and understand what the teacher is trying to say, then I could write down more effective notes after class. Unfortunately, too often I would forget.

Effective note taking is not something that can be mastered in a few months, let alone a few weeks. It took me nearly two years of university lectures to finally be able to write and process information fast enough to take very helpful notes.

I find that this habit differs in difficulty across students. If handwriting is your biggest concern, try to bring a laptop. A more drastic alternative (and one that should only be used during the most important and difficult sessions) would be to bring a voice recorder and make notes afterwards. Of course, this involves a great deal of dedication and motivation, however I do remember certain HL Mathematics classes where a voice recorder proved to be a life-saver.

There are two key things to remember when taking notes. One is to make sure that everything you write down isn't already explained in detail in your textbook and/or previous notes. This is very inefficient and you are better off simply listening and letting the information seep into your memory. The second thing to keep in mind is to only write down notes that make sense. If you find yourself writing words that are unfamiliar to you, then you are wasting your time. You need to raise your hand and ask the question.

You may find yourself lucky enough to have a friend or two who take outstanding notes. Although getting great notes from a fellow peer is better than having nothing at all, I would still be cautious before resorting to this option. No matter how good the notes are, they will never be as valuable to you as something you wrote down yourself.

In recent years with the rising popularity of Tumblr and Instagram, some students have begun to take great pride in their notes and photograph their hand-written works of art. They are called 'studyspo' or 'studygrams – and it is worth checking them out. It may inspire you to perhaps start taking clearer and better notes. Whether this will help you memorize the material better is an altogether different question.

7. Student-Teacher Relations

This chapter is not only important for your time in the IB program – but it is an essential skill to acquire if you want to be successful in life and get ahead. The skill I'm referring to here is, in the crudest sense, the skill of getting what you want from people in higher positions of power. You've probably already engaged in this in one form or other as a child manipulating your parents to get what you want, but as you get older the players in that game change, and your tactics adjust accordingly.

Now that being said, I would like to take a moment to remind you that being a teacher is one of the hardest and most underappreciated careers in the world. There is no glamor, and the pay isn't proportional to the amount of effort (most) teachers put in. Of all the people you will encounter in your short stay on this planet, your teachers are one of the few characters who genuinely want the best for you and care about your future and your well-being – and for that they deserve respect and gratitude. If you treat them well, you will get treated well in return.

Get used to it: teachers are your new best friends. Despite what teachers say, they do have favourite students and these lucky kids get preferential treatment (I was one of them). These students get this treatment as there is a greater level of trust and dialogue between them and the teacher, which makes the teacher more lenient. What does "lenient" entail, well…

1. Teachers will be more lenient when it comes to deadlines and will accept your work in late and still give feedback allowing you to submit better versions

of your work at later dates (this can be useful as time allows you to spot your own mistakes).
2. The feedback teachers give you will be more detailed and comprehensive as they believe their advice won't go to waste; hence, they don't mind the extra effort.
3. When time comes to grading both report cards and predicted grades the teachers will be optimistic. They believe that you are a good student and over time you will progress; hence if you are between grade boundaries you are likely to get marked up. Even better and more daring is the fact that you can discuss your grade. For example, if you know that it is important for you to get a 7 in physics (and you are getting high level 6s), you can discuss it with your teacher and ask them for that grade, justifying why you will be able to reach it. A few methods of justification would be as follow:
    a. Show them you planned revision, for example if you will be attending any summer courses or if you have bought anything that can help you improve at the subject. This proof should be tangible and significant.
    b. If you start the year with 5s in tests and are ending on 7s, your teacher might be tempted to give you a 6; however you can show him or her that you actually have shown progress and you "believe" you deserve a 7.
4. You can have detailed and private conversations on matters such as homework, IAs, exams, tests and things that you don't understand in your subject. Remember all the information you receive is useful if used properly.

Don't forget it, teachers are humans too, they have their faults and they are usually very fun people. Get to know them and you will understand how they think, and ultimately how they grade. But even more than that, you will have a great time in class learning and interacting with these interesting people. I can say as a matter of fact that I liked all my teachers both as academics and as people, we got along very well and even joked around.

IB coordinator

Although your interactions with this faculty member may be limited, they hold the key to your IB diploma – you do not want to piss this person off. Everything from choosing subjects to submitting crucial coursework on time, they will oversee. Understandably IB coordinators will vary in experience from school to school, but do your best to get on good terms and make sure they know how serious you are about achieving your diploma.

Remember that it's in this person's best interest to make sure the entire class does well on their IB. It will reflect poorly on them if students fail to get their diploma. For that reason, if there is something you feel will increase the scores of the students, you should share your thoughts with the coordinator. For example, if you feel like you need new textbooks or you feel like you desperately need to change class, they are the person to go and see.

In the following section I will go over a few key faculty members and try to explain the importance of fostering a healthy relationship. I am aware that not every school will be lucky enough to have a designated person for each role, but nonetheless the advice will be applicable.

CAS Coordinator

See Chapter 43: Conquering CAS

The Principal

The idea here is pretty simple – don't mess up and get into disciplinary trouble. Although they don't have an impact on your IB grades directly, they do have the power to kick you out of school if you are a jackass, so just don't be one.

Subject-Specific Teachers

Obviously, these faculty members are very important. From your IA work, to your predicted grades, to helping you revise for the subject – your daily teachers are instrumental to your IB success. You will see them almost every day, so you better make a great first impression. If you show them that you care about getting top marks, they will provide you with the necessary tools.

Will you click and get along with each one of them? No, probably not. Some will be more problematic than others, but learning the skill of getting past that is something that you will cherish for the rest of your life. You need to understand that part of the game here is just playing the part. Do what they want you to do and then it will be much easier to ask them to do you favours.

Make sure to pay close attention to the details of the assignments that your teacher gives (yes, the details). Basically, you need to know exactly what your teachers want. It might even be worth asking students who have had your teacher before what they want and what they like. Asking questions is also crucial to gaining your teacher's respect – basically don't be invisible, and don't let shyness get in the way of your learning.

If the teacher wants you to have a laptop and TI-84, have a laptop and TI-84. If they say you need a silver Mickey-Mouse balloon, have that. Don't skimp on required class supplies, even if inconvenient or expensive. It will handicap you. Again, you want to do everything you can to satisfy the teacher's expectations.

As covered in the chapter on subject choices – there will inevitably be teachers who you deem 'not good enough' to be teaching their subject. This happens, it's part of life. But that doesn't mean you have an excuse to just give up. You will need to take that subject much more seriously and do lots of independent study (great preparation for university). This is where our advice on revision and internal assessments will come in handy.

Keep in mind that the internal assessment means just that – *internal*. This means your teacher will be the one to give it a grade. Ultimately, a sample will be sent off to the IBO to be 'moderated' if marks are too high or too low, but this won't matter much if you've created such friction with your teacher that your IA marks are horrible. Teacher bias during IA marking is something that does occur, but you should be doing your best to mitigate this.

If there are some serious issues that can't be resolved with a certain teacher, you should seek to find a solution by approaching your IB coordinator. The hierarchy for resolving problems should be as such: teacher, then head of department (if there is one), then IB coordinator, then principle, then parents. Most problems can be overcome with simple dialogue. Finally, be polite to your teachers / professors and subtly let them know you wish to succeed in their class. Don't be a suck up, but don't be rude or lazy either. Grading practices are never completely objective, despite what you might hear - or how hard teachers might try to make it so.

University Counsellor

Another extremely important individual – both for US and UK bound students. Plan a trip to their office sometime early in the first year – maybe even over the summer. Discuss your options and get as many resources as possible (they might have some great university application books in their office). The university counsellor should help you with all things application related, but you would also be wise to do some research on your own.

Grade Predictions

Your subject teachers (and EE/TOK for that matter) will be required to submit grade predictions for your university applications. Here is where student-teacher relationships are crucial. Predicted grades are a tricky obstacle for any IB student. Nine times out of ten, students will feel that they are being under-predicted. Many schools refuse to disclose the predictions to students because they anticipate a large angry group of kids mobbing them with protests after school hours. Nonetheless, predicted grades are the golden ticket when it comes to university offers. If your predicted grades are below the usual entry standards, the chances of you receiving an offer from a UK university are slim to none.

Here is my simple advice when it comes to maximizing your chances of getting the best predicted grades: negotiation. The matter of the fact is that teachers often look at things like homework grades, test results and class participation as an indicator of how well you will do in the final IB examinations. Although some of those things may play a small role, the truth is that the best predictors of your final results are: internal assessments (coursework that counts towards your final grade), how well you take IB examinations, how well you prepared in the few months before examinations, and a small element of random luck. Luck and exam revision aside, the other two components are fairly easy to analyse.

If your teachers insist on looking at test scores and random homework assignments as a way to judge your future success in the final exams, you need to persuade them that your high-scoring coursework's (which account for 20-40% of final subject grades in most subjects) and your ability to study past-paper questions and handle mock exams are both a far better indicator of how well you will do. I understand that this is easier said than done, but I do remember spending a good week or so visiting various teachers after-hours to convince them that despite my so-so homework grades or sometimes uninspired class participation, I will score highly on my diploma because I know what counts and I know how to play the IB system. Those of you who have read my IB help book will know exactly what I am talking about.

Letter of Recommendation

It is imperative that the person who you choose to write your reference for university applications is not only highly literate, but more importantly can fill the reference full of praise and admiration. Obviously, the person writing your reference should be closely related to the subject you intend to study at university. There are minor exceptions to this. For example, when I was applying to study economics, my economics teacher at school did not necessarily dislike me, however I did feel that they would not put all their efforts into writing a stand-out reference and perhaps it would not be as elegantly written. Instead, I sought the help of my geography teacher (who happened to hold a PhD from LSE, and had previously taught economics and business at a high school level). The teacher in question clearly saw a lot of potential in me, so I asked for help and got a wonderfully written reference in return. Whomever you seek for this task, make sure they are not going to write a generic reference but instead something personal and something that will make you stand out.

The real objective of student-teacher relations in the IB is: 'why do work when you can get others to do it for you?'; some people call it 'leverage'. Unfortunately, getting your teachers to help doesn't mean you can just laze at home and do nothing. You need to make life easy for them - make plans, make time to see them, organize everything, be ready when they ask you questions. If you keep up a disciplined image, they will be lots more likely to take you seriously. For IAs...they can only mark one draft, but go see them in their office and make them read over-edited parts again and again. They want you to get a 7.

Yes, I understand that some teachers are quite unfriendly/unknowledgeable and so you don't want to see them. That's alright too. Just make sure you have everything under control and you haven't upset the wrong people.

8. Maximizing Productivity at School

If only I had an IB point for every time I heard someone mutter the words 'what, we had homework?' Keeping an agenda or a daily planner is a very simple solution to keeping track of what is due when. Make a habit of writing down important dates as soon as you hear about them. The IB does a pretty good job at reminding students about the big deadlines (Extended Essay, External Assessment, CAS portfolio) however any internal deadlines you may have are your responsibility to note.

There's no reason to go old-school when it comes to organisation. With the rise in popularity of iPhones, and personal laptops, it has become much easier for you to electronically set reminders. These items are also more likely to be consulted, and less likely to be lost than a simple paperback agenda.

Health

This is NOT a self-help book and nor do I ever intend to offer life advice to anyone. However, I do think it is worthwhile at least briefly mentioning the importance of things like eating right and exercising.

Research has shown time and time again that physical activity is crucial in maintaining mental well-being. IB students often report negative moods, irritability, and other stress-related problems. All of this can lead to more complicated emotional concerns. Exercise is a good combatant in your fight to a healthy physical and mental well-being.

Even just 20 minutes of exercise can lead to higher energy levels. You will find it easier to sit down and concentrate on your studies and may even feel more motivated. Also, you can easily combine exercise with socialising. Having someone to talk to while jogging or at the gym can be a great stress-reliever – just make sure the conversation steers clear of IB-related matters.

Just as important as regular exercise is keeping an eye on what you are eating. If you ever feel exhausted despite not really doing anything, or get easily distracted when you should be working, this could be down to your choice or lack of food.

Although our brain is only about 2% of our total body mass, it consumes roughly 20% of the energy you take in. when we concentrate the brain uses up to 200 kilocalories per hour – or 10% of your daily food intake. So next time you skip breakfast, or have a very late lunch keep in mind that your brain needs a steady supply of nutrients – many of which come from food.

For those more curious about how they can maximize brain function and energy levels with their diet, I strongly suggest you consider the 'ketogenic diet'. Many studies have reported that eating a diet high in fats and protein and low in carbohydrates (under 20g per day) results in 'brain clarity' and many individuals feel less lazy and more motivated – crucial attributes for academic success. I learned about ketosis and the ketogenic diet only when at university, however it has helped me greatly since then.

Homework

When it comes to homework, it is very difficult to prescribe specific advice because people have different preferences that work best for them. Personally, I found that doing homework in the late evening or at night was the most effective. This worked for me as there were little distractions and there was a sense of urgency which kept me motivated.

Besides timing, you also need to consider working effectively for concentrated amounts of times with no breaks. Ideally, working for 20 minutes non-stop with no outside interference and then rewarding yourself with a small break seems to be among the ideal strategies. Some of you may find that you work best with music in the background, or that your multitasking skills are so good that you can afford to flip your computer tabs from Facebook to iTunes to your lab report every few minutes. It's difficult to change this habit, and unless it is seriously damaging the quality of your work, I would not worry too much about it.

One tip that I found to work very nicely when doing homework was to save my favourite material for last. Getting all the difficult and less-favourable work out of the way early will not only lessen the chances of simply not doing it, but you will also have something to look forward to. Of course, one should be careful not to rush through the harder material just for the sake of 'getting it out the way' before moving onto the more enjoyable material.

Be heard

No matter how timid and shy you may be, there will be days when you simply need to make a formal comment or complaint about something that concerns you. In order to do this you need to build a constructive relationship with your IB Coordinator and any other influential teachers. This is much easier said than done.

Learn how to talk to authoritative figures. If you book a meeting with your IB Coordinator, then do not show up unprepared. If you show them that you care, they will care too. The same goes for most teachers. If you show an interest and a longing for help (perhaps by asking for a contact email or number to reach them at after-school hours) then they are more than likely to respond positively.

Helpful Apps and Software

Evernote – excellent note taking software, and free. Learn to use the software beforehand, there are lots of features that you may find come in handy.

Todoist – free and great to-do list app. Use it if you don't have a day planner/agenda. It also links up with google calendar/default Mac calendar.

OneNote – the following advice is paraphrased from one of my former students and is incredibly helpful. I strongly recommend you follow it for your note-taking if you use a laptop:

1. Create a Notebook for one of your subjects (the one with the smallest number of characters)
2. Create a "section group" called term 1 (or whatever measurement you use)
3. Create a "section" along the top called "week"

Then set it up like this

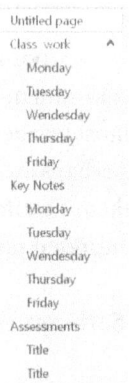

Class work

This is for stuff you do in class that you won't really need to look over when revising. Sometimes I just work in here for a class then take key elements out and put it into keynotes. But If I know what we are doing is just notes (like core concepts in maths or an English slideshow)

Keynotes

This is the stuff that you need from the class. The things that you would give a friend if they missed a class. Make sure that you type keywords, topics, connections (if you are doing a poem that mentions another poem if you put the name of the other poem). This is so that you can search for them later (maybe have a table that you put off to the side)

Assessment

This one is for longer projects like oral notes or things you do for more than one class

Make sure you either title them well or remember where they are

Setting up all the classes quickly

So this is where it gets a bit confusing. So you now have to find where your OneNote files are saved (default is "C:\Users[your name]\Documents\OneNote Notebooks". If not, then: Right click on one of your Notebooks, go to properties, click "change location", then open the same position in file explorer (or equivalent)

You should have a folder for whatever subject you choose in the "set up" . Open it and then open "term 1". Copy the file in there called "week"* Paste it And rename it week 2. Repeat for each week in the term.

After you have a file for each week "week 1" to "week 9" (or how many weeks you have in a term) Then go back to "term 1" Copy and paste it 3 times and rename it, "term 2" to "term 4". Then go back to the folder with your subject in. Copy and paste it for each subject. Rename them respectively. Put all of these into a folder called year 11 (or equivalent). Copy and paste this folder and rename it year 12. If you choose to implement any of the subject-specific things, add them at this stage.

Subject-Specific OneNote advice:

Psychology

Have a weekly subgroup for writing essays and study summaries (like Assessment but specifically for essays/studies). Maybe break this down into the levels of analysis (bio, cog, social, cultural and your 2 options).

Remember to use keywords and use the question exactly from the syllabus (so you can find it more easily). If you are smart with what studies you use, you can use some for many different questions.

English Literature

Similar to Psych, keep essays apart. Have a dedicated place for feedback from teachers (probably good for all subjects in fact) write notes for all your meeting

Maths Studies

You can do notes in OneNote by pressing "alt+ =" (the alt key and the equals key). There are lots of shortcuts within in this. If you have a touch screen/stylus it can be good write draw them straight into OneNote (there is an ink feature)

Language Ab

Have a place for words
Try to have the English (first language), your language, Example, any exceptions Useful phrases following similar structures as the words. As of the other subject, I haven't done them so pick the elements that relate to the parts (I know that might be hard) tricks

This advice is written for OneNote 2016, so some of these may not work on other versions. You can write maths in notation by pressing "alt+ =" (the alt key and the equals key). You can use it like a calculator such as " 3^4+(3/2)=" Then put a space afterwards and it should solve it if it doesn't work make sure there are no letters or non-mathematical things touching the equation.

You can write with a pen if you have a touch screen. It Autosaves but be careful to backup. If you want to really focus, try this View-> Always Pin on Top.

A OneNote page is infinitely large (this is both an advantage and a massive disadvantage). You can turn on grids which help (me) organise things on a page. You can make lots of different boxes which makes Selection (see Ctrl+A) and comparing things easier.

9. The Importance of IA

Internal Assessment (IA) is the easiest, most effective and fastest way to get top marks in almost all your subjects. You would have to be extremely ignorant to ignore that fact. Try doing some simple math. If we say that, on average, IA takes up roughly 25% of your grade for each subject then that means it takes up ¼ of the maximum grade 7 per subject – nearly two entire points. Now, this may not seem like much, but when you consider that you have 6 subjects plus the 3 bonus points from TOK/EE – this adds up to 15 points towards your IB diploma. Simply put: from maxing out on your Internal Assessment and EE/TOK you can get 15 marks even before you step into the examination room.

That's the beauty of it. You have no idea what a comforting feeling it is walking into the exam room knowing you already have 12 – 15 points in the bag. One must try to remain realistic. No matter how much you have studied, no matter how many past papers you have done, and no matter how well you have grasped the material, what happens on the exam day will to a certain extent be outside of your control. What if you break an arm, get a stomach ache or become ill during the exam? What if all three happen? What if your co-coordinator makes a mistake and forgets to give you a periodic table for your HL Chemistry exam (as has happened)? What if you just "go blank" when you open your exam and forget all that you have crammed the night before?

I have seen some of the best IB candidates underperform on exam day simply because of bad luck and misfortune. Another likely scenario is that you are simply not an exam person. I am usually very comfortable with the material, spend plenty of time studying, and usually can answer most questions when asked verbally in a non-exam situation. However, when the clock is ticking and the pressure is on, I tend to only perform at about 80% of my potential. I am not an "exam person". In fact, I hate examinations because so many factors are outside of your control. There are too many ways in which one can make careless mistakes and mess up.

As I was trying to point out, IA makes up roughly 25% of your grade for each subject. In subjects such as English it amounts to nearly 30% of the grade. So even before you sit your English exam, you are nearly 1/3rd done. This means that if you have done amazingly well on your IA, you already have 2 or 3 marks secured towards your English grade. It is a very comforting feeling to know that no matter how poorly you perform on your exam, you are almost definitely in the 4 to 7 range – in other words you are comfortably going to pass. This may not mean much to the more ambitious candidates reading this manual. If you are amongst the IB candidates who worry about failing the IB diploma, then this IA stuff can save you.

Now some of you may still need further convincing that Internal Assessment is extremely important. The words 'lab report', 'economic commentary' and 'World Literature paper' are so often used in the same breath as the word 'homework' that students forget to realise the importance of IA. The points add up, and before you know it, it might be too late to go back and capitalize on your IA marks.

Let's think about this logically. The assessment is usually given a week or even a few weeks in advance. For bigger assignments, such as the Extended Essay you have substantially more time to prepare. You are given weeks to complete something that will account for a generous fraction of your final grade. Now contrast this with the final examinations, which will usually take up the remaining 60% - 75% of your final grade. The exam duration per subject is rarely more than 6 or 7 hours. Those few hours will decide what you will get for the remaining portion of your grade. Would it not make sense then to work relentlessly on maximizing your mark for the IA simply because you are given so much more time and space? The final examination goes by in a blink of an eye whereas you are given an abundance of time to work on your IA. Once you realise this, you will make sure your IAs are as flawless as possible.

You are given weeks, if not months, to decide nearly a fourth of your grade, and then you are given two or three hours to decide the remaining three-fourths. It would be foolish to put in less effort for the IA then the actual examinations. They are practically handing you these marks. No matter how poorly you know the material, or how poorly you perform on examinations, nearly anyone can ace their Internal Assessment – especially given the advice provided further in this guide.

So, if you are one of those people who tend to underperform in examinations and simply can't bother studying, you absolutely need to take full advantage of the IA. It baffles me as to why so many students fail to see this loophole. Even the top IB candidates often focus so much on learning the material and doing well in the actual exams that they lose track of the fact that IA also counts towards the final grade.

With regards to the order of importance for IB-related daily matter, I would suggest the following rank: 1) Internal Assessment, 2) revision for tests, 3) homework. This means that if you have a lab report due in tomorrow and a test as well, you need to finish and polish the lab before you even start thinking about revising for the test. Tests will come and go, but you will have few opportunities to redo your Internal Assessments.

All the labs, coursework, portfolios and papers that make up your IA are of far greater importance than any test or homework assignment that you must do. Yes, your trimester grade may suffer. Yes, the teacher may get on your back for not doing the homework. Nonetheless, you need to keep a voice in the back of your head telling you that "at the end of the day, small tests and homework won't give me my 7's, the IB assessment will." Word of caution: if you have teachers who heavily rely on homework and tests as predicted grade markers, you will need to reconsider this advice.

Also, many students use IAs as an excuse to stop doing homework. This is a bad idea because homework is not 'skipped'. It only piles up and comes back to haunt you. We all know that there are two categories of homework...the necessary kind and the unnecessary kind. For example, necessary homework would be a Chemistry worksheet on Organic structures that is marked by your teacher as an assignment. Unnecessary homework would be a stack of 500 equation-balancing problems (you can do this slowly, especially if your teacher isn't collecting it).

The beauty behind Internal Assessment is that literally anyone, of any academic ability, can get top marks. This is great news for those of you who do not plan on studying much for the exams, or who are terrified of test-taking. All you need to do is spend an incredible amount of time constantly improving and upgrading your assignment. I have seen some pretty daft IB students ace their assignments simply because they spent day and night perfecting them. Although they may have not been academically gifted, at least they realised the potential impact that IA could have on their grades – and in that sense, they are geniuses.

It doesn't matter whether you are "smart". You simply need to be ruthless when it comes to completing your IA assignments. Follow the guidelines that I provide in this book for each subject on how to maximize your IA. If you do that, then regardless of how good or bad you think you are at a certain subject, you will be able to get a "handicap" of +2 on your final grade before you sit the exam.

You need to become the King (or Queen) of IA in your class. All the other students will be in awe as you get 19/20 back for your Math IA or near full marks for your Economics portfolio. They may say you are wasting your time aiming for the perfect IA assessment, but when you get your final grades back you will be laughing at them. You need to strive to have the best coursework possible.

I remember a few months before final examinations some teachers would announce whose work was getting sent off to be moderated. Now, I don't know how the system works inside out, but I have a feeling that for IA the IBO demands that a good distribution of student work is sent off. In other words: the top assignments, the average assignments and the assignments at the lower end of the grading scale. I would look around the class to see who else was having their work sent off, and immediately I could tell that my work was part of the "top assignments" (our teacher never told us whose work got selected). This took a lot of stress off the final examinations. It is an incredible feeling when you are revising to know that you are 25% closer to getting your 7s.

Getting top marks in your IA is not an easy task. Then again, neither is getting 7's in your examinations. The key difference is that whereas with the exams you are given a few hours to show your worth, the IA timeline is much more generous. You will need to work late nights, weekends, and holidays to get top marks for your IA. In fact, you would probably work just as hard (if not harder) a few weeks prior to your exams, so I don't see why this would be such a daunting task.

You need to develop a habit of wanting to strive for perfection in all your externally moderated IAs. Treat this as being just as important as the actual exam, or even more so. I want you to start feeling extremely disappointed if you are getting back labs/commentaries/portfolios that are below a grade 6. Not only should you be getting 7's, you should be getting high 7's. Keep in mind that what your teacher thinks you deserve is not the final grade. It will be moderated and probably hiked up or down a few notches. You should therefore make sure to leave a little room for change when you are told your predictions.

Given the fact that you are reading this book, I think I can safely assume that you are not the naturally gifted IB diploma student who is predicted to get a 45. You may struggle getting 6's or even 5's on your school tests. At the same time, you may be a student who is borderline failing the diploma program and is anticipating the worst when the final examinations come around. In either case, this advice about IA is of equal importance. IA can turn a failing IB diploma grade of 15 to a 30. Or a 30 to a 45. The important thing is that you take this advice and follow it through.

I firmly believe that if a student maxes out on his/her IA, then it is nearly impossible to fail the IB diploma. You will get somewhere around 15 marks for your assignments alone (given that you get all 3 bonus marks), which leaves just about 10 more marks from your actual examination. I have yet to meet a person that cannot scrape 10 marks on their actual examinations. If you maximize your IA marks, then you are entering a stress-free world of examinations. Instead of deciding where you will be on a scale of 0 to 45, you now can estimate your final grade on a scale of 15 to 45.

I know I am getting repetitive but you need to drill this into your head. You need to strive for perfection on your Internal Assessment. Do that and you are one step, one giant leap, closer to getting what you want from your IB diploma. Don't be ignorant, realise the power of IA marks and the effect that they can have on your final grade. You don't know how much you will hate yourself when you find out that the reason you missed out on getting your dream grade of 45 was due to a poorly done IA that dragged you down to a 44 overall. Or how about finding out that the only reason you failed IB was because you "forgot" to hand in an Economics commentary and this dragged you down below 24 marks. Be smart: milk the IA for all that it is worth.

It's a miracle that a notoriously "rigorous" program such as the IB diploma program would have nearly 25% of the final score decided on a non-exam basis. You are lucky that final grades aren't based entirely on your ability to perform well in exams as is the case in many other high school programs worldwide. This provides a great opportunity to those of you who are hard-working and intelligent, yet lack that cutting edge when it comes to examinations. Take full advantage of this – it won't be long before the IB starts to diminish the importance of Internal Assessment (they already have over the last decade) and add greater value to the actual examinations.

Students stress about final exams, but in this case you'll have got a whole bunch of grades before you even get to them. This has an extraordinary implication for you. Imagine an exam system in which they ask you whatever you want to study, let you decide how to study and even let you write some of the questions. This is basically the IB system: between 20% and 40% of your grades you can get from work that you can write, check, triple-check, get friends and families to advise you, change work, mark yourself, and work out certainly what mark the examiner will give.

IAs are the only aspect of IB that you have real 'control' over. You get to write your own questions and come up with your own answers. As mentioned, most IAs also make up at least 20% of your final grade and do make the difference between 6s and 7s. For example, if you got a low 5 on your Maths IA, you'd need to get 95+% on the final exam to get a 7; if you got a 7 already, you can make do with about 80%. That 15%, as we all know, is a huge difference. Don't treat IAs like projects in middle school. They are imperative and, as I believe, designed to help you gain marks before the final exams.

With regards to time management, I'm sure that nobody wants to hand in a crap IA. It's just that we are sometimes forced to that point by outside pressures, i.e. lack of time. What many students need to understand is that time is 'created', not 'found'. Nature does not give you any time, you need to squeeze it out by yourself. Confucius probably said something about time being like 'water in a sponge'. Unfortunately, time in the IB world is more like 'maple syrup in a sponge', and is hard to eke out. It is nevertheless possible to maintain high standards on your IAs.

General IA Advice

1) You need to choose the right question. This is where many candidates fail, as they are over-ambitious and bite off more than they can chew. Choose a question that you're interested in, but which also pertains to the course. Yes, IB is about learning, but also about passing. Also, get advice on your question ASAP. Even when the teacher has just announced the IA. Brainstorm as fast as possible, and ask for a quality check on your ideas. This saves you lots of time in the long run.

2) 'Why do work when you can get others to do it for you?' is an age-old technique; some people call it 'leverage'. Unfortunately, getting your teachers to help doesn't mean you can just laze at home and do nothing. You need to make life easy for them - make plans, make time to see them, organise everything, be ready when they ask you questions. If you keep up a disciplined image, they will be lots more likely to take you seriously. For IAs...they can only mark one draft, but go see them in their office and make them read over-edited parts again and again. They want you to get a 7.

3) Yes, I understand that some teachers are quite unfriendly/unknowledgeable and so you don't want to see them. That's alright too. You just need to replicate the 'teacher' process at home. You need to set goals for yourself. Don't say 'I need to get this done before July because it is the deadline'. You should tell yourself, "The first draft is due to myself/IB gods on 15 June." Get a friend to help you with accountability if needed - make sure to return the favour.

4) Squeezing out time is a special art. You need to look at your current life and do a 'time budget'. What are you spending time on? What can you cut out? It's like calorie counting but with minutes.

I know these measures sound quite 'hardcore' but...you will thank yourself when the final exams arrive and you know that you don't have to get an impossible score in order to reach your goal. This can actually give you a major confidence boost when it matters the most. Spread out your suffering. Piling up IAs are like cars. When you have an accident on the highway, they tend to pile up.

When faced with a developing or fully-developed pile, the first thing you need to do is be honest with yourself. Take a survey of the situation and write down all that you must do. Then do these by priority. Many students confuse 'priority' with 'preference'. Yes, doing your History IA is more fun than making graphs for your Math IA. But if your Math IA is due next week and the History IA is due next month, don't even think about doing History first. If you're having too much fun with a pileup on your plate, chances are...you're not prioritising.

You can also try a 'war of attrition' against your work, but this is more of a pre-emptive measure. Basically, do a bit of work at every available opportunity. Social lives are important but...if you need that extra 20 minutes, man up, skip recess, and do your chemistry assignment. That 20 minutes can then be saved at home for EE writing purposes. Basically every second counts.

With regards to sleep, you don't need to stay up till 3am or pull an all-nighter. Most people go to school from 8am to 3pm or similar hours. What are you doing from 4pm to 10pm? That's a full 6 hours for you to get some stuff done. You have months to do your IAs. The rest of your time can be used for study, recreation, and much-needed sleep. You don't feel it, especially if you're hopped up on caffeine, but your work quality is going to be lower after a whole day of school and not sleeping.

One final pro-tip: get your hands on the subject reports. These are reports where the examiners explain what exactly was good or bad in last year's IAs (and exams) and give a whole section of advice to teachers and students on how to do better. Your teacher should have them, and you should seek these out.

10. Managing Stress

There is no hiding from the fact that the IB Diploma program can be very stressful. There will be certain weeks or days where you will feel like you are juggling six plates with the weight of the academic world on your shoulders and a ball and chain with the words 'EE' and TOK' around your legs. Nonetheless, I will now introduce a few tips to help you deal with the strain and anxiety.

Nutrition

Ah, food. Food is good. So, eat something. Don't stuff your face with crap all the time. Be reasonably healthy and save all the beautiful fried chicken for the weekend. Eating properly has a great effect on your energy levels. Don't starve yourself either. Working on an empty rumbling stomach is like listening to a baby cry. They can both be stopped with some warm milk and cookies.

The stereotype of the IB student as someone surviving on caffeine, Pot Noodles, and energy drinks is, in many cases, not a complete exaggeration. If you are up late at night busy working then you are more likely to consume foods and drinks that require little time to prepare and give a good energy boost. Although I have already reminded you about the benefits of eating right during your two years in the IB program, the exam period itself will pose its own challenges. Even if you are frantically revising all day and all night, try to still get your three meals a day and eat plenty of vitamin rich foods.

I found myself chewing a lot of gum during the late nights and the revision stages. Personally, I found that this helped me focus more and kept me awake. Those of you that smoke will probably find that you are smoking a lot more than normal. If you are a big coffee fan, then be careful not to overdo it.

Sleep

I'll be the first to admit that the amount of sleep you will get during the two year IB program will probably be less than any other two year period of your life. On any given day, I could spot several of my fellow students drifting off during class, or having serious bags under their eyes from the lack of sleep.

Making sure that you get enough sleep is once again due to good time management skills. I found that I would come home from school too tired to be productive so I would make it a habit to get a couple hours sleep in the evening. Usually this would just be on the couch, but it was nonetheless enough for me to get up and feel reenergized. Studies have shown that even a 15 minute nap can be enough to make you feel revitalized.

You need to find out when you are at your most productive state. I slowly discovered throughout highschool that I worked best at night or at least the very late evening. Going to bed at 2 am was not uncommon during school nights, but this was fine for me because I would make up the hours by napping once I came home. Although it was hard to adjust to such a schedule I eventually made it routine. I enjoyed working at night because there was an added element of urgency and there was little room to procrastinate. Working under pressure is not for everyone, so you need to figure out what works best for you.

As an IB student you also need to learn to get sleep wherever and whenever you can. My bus ride to school took around an hour. I made sure that unless I had a test to study for or an assignment to complete I would try to sleep for most of that hour. Other classmates of mine would politely ask to nap during 'free periods' and sometimes this was permitted by the teacher. Those who pulled all-nighters would even try to nap during lunchtime after having something to eat.

Sleep is essential to being productive and motivated. A lack of sleep can result in careless errors in assignments and missing essential information in class. For the 16-18 year old age group, the recommended amount of sleep is usually quoted as 6-8 hours. If you are getting less than 5 hours on a regular basis then there might be cause for alarm. Remember that although this is only a two-year program, you could potentially be doing more long-term damage to your health by missing out on sleep.

Second-hand Stress

It is often said that being surrounded by negative people can be contagious. The same is true for stress. If you surround yourself with students that constantly complain about the workload and the pressure then you are more likely to succumb to their state. Make sure you have plenty of people to talk to that are on top of their work – this will also incentivize you to work harder and be more efficient.

Although you may think that by surrounding yourself with students who are behind on their work and always worrying will somehow make you feel better about your own situation, this is usually not the case. These people will make you worry more. You need to avoid this second-hand stress at all costs.

The Goal

Also, motivate yourself towards your goals. If you find no interest in working, the fact is you will not work. Just think about how good you'll feel once the exams are done.

Every crappy score you're getting right now is giving you a better chance at acing your finals. It means you've made lots of mistakes that you're never going to make again, because now you can learn from them. Don't let them get you down - focus on the feedback rather than the grade, and take it as a guide of how you can do better. If you're getting 6s now, there's room to improve. Doing past papers will make a huge difference.

Make time for yourself to just chill out, sleep, and be with friends. My friends and I tried to hang out regularly during senior year, even though it meant just sitting together in a library, each doing our own work. Give yourself a 5 minute break every 30 minutes. Walk around, stretch, do some push-ups. Exercise has been scientifically proven to be healthy. So you should do it. Preferably everyday if you can. It's a great way to release stress and make you feel good.

Stress at school is mainly caused by lack of organisation. So sorting that out could half or even eliminate your 'I want to rip the hair out of my head' feeling. Invest in a folder if you write notes with a notebook and use folder separators to make things easier. This makes losing notes a lot less likely because they are in a named folder.

If you're feeling that things are getting to you, just step back for a little bit and think. You don't need to be getting overly stressed because that hinders your work and can result in tears, this isn't helpful to your development because it lowers your confidence. Try drinking some water, taking a short break from revision or going for a walk. Clear your mind.

These are some brief thoughts about how to manage stress throughout the IB exam period and in general. I welcome anyone and everyone to share the techniques they use to manage stress.

Firstly, if you want to effectively reduce the amount of stress you feel with your workload, managing your time properly will help cut down on the level of stress you feel when working.

I'm not going to put any of these techniques in order because some people prefer different things. I should also mention that these techniques will only work if you actually use them. Don't just read them, ignore them, then come back after the exams and exclaim that your hair is turning grey because of stress.

It seems like when students think of studying they think of it as an extremely painful process which requires a lot of stress in order to be useful. 'You need to live in the library to get good results', 'studying is just student and dying put together' that sort of thing. None of that is true. You don't need to strain yourself while working in order to do well. You learn much better when you're relaxed.

Meditation

Meditation is a great way to prepare yourself for a school day in the morning as well as wind down before you sleep. Thanks to its calming effect on your sympathetic nervous system, meditating can help you cope with academic stress and make you a master at handling high-pressure situations. This, of course, includes things like meeting a looming deadline or writing an IB exam.

How do I meditate?

There are many techniques you can use to meditate even as a beginner. One the most used among students is called 'box breathing'. This simple method requires you to inhale, hold your breath, exhale and hold your breath again all in 4-second intervals. While you're doing this, try to focus on the sensations that arise in your body. This includes the air rushing in through your nose, your chest expanding and contracting and your lungs periodically filling up with air. As you do this, you will start to feel your stress and anxiety dissipate. This method can be used as a quick de-stressor whenever you feel anxious, even at school. Unsurprisingly, I saw a group of classmates do a collective box breathing exercise before their first official IB exam.

If you're looking for something more intensive, there are also heaps of guided meditation videos available to you online. A short search for 'guided meditation' on YouTube or Spotify will provide you with hundreds of videos in which you're given a step-by-step walkthrough through a meditation session. Each video will have a different length, so if you're a person who has trouble focusing, perhaps try a 5-minute session first before gradually moving on to 10 or 15 minutes. As you meditate more and more, you'll notice it slowly becomes easier to enter and stay in zen mode.

How do you get started?

Sit down (or lie down if you have back problems), and spend 5 to 10 minutes just focusing on your breathing. Don't try to alter your breath patterns. You'll probably find that it's quite difficult to just focus on your breath because thoughts will pop into your head but that's normal. Just gently return your focus to your breath. I'd recommend meditating at the start of the day then again at the end of the day if you want to.

Schedule time off

Don't cram your schedule with work and actually let yourself have a prolonged break. If you feel up to it, schedule a whole day off every week and do whatever you want absolutely guilt free. It will help you approach the next week with a bit more energy and you won't be in a continuous battle with your work if you completely separate yourself from it for a while.

Have regular breaks

While trying to complete a huge task, it can be easy to lose track of where the time is going. Then you end up working for months without having a break. This can make you feel extremely frustrated when you're not making progress on something. However, you should wait until you feel like it. The point is to work with as little stress as possible. I'd recommend breaks as frequent as one every 25 to 30 minutes.

Plan your work

If you don't have any clear idea about what you're trying to accomplish then you'll always be in an uphill battle. Take some time to make a detailed plan about what you want to do and when.

Also, assume you've underestimated the amount of time you'll need to complete something. If you've set aside 2 hours to think about an essay or make notes on a topic, give yourself 3 or 4. It'll stop you from getting stressed about not being on schedule (that wasn't realistic in the first place) and give you spare time at the end of the day.

Clean yourself

Ok, admittedly that sounds like a dumb statement to make. But I have a point. I promise. There's very little point in being in an environment that either makes you feel like you're boiling or freezing or generally uncomfortable. So if your room feels stuffy, open your window a bit (and the curtains. I don't know why some people enjoy darkness so much. It makes no sense to me).

Groom yourself in the morning instead of groggily getting out of your bed and working away in pyjamas. Be comfortable but shower or something. If not for yourself, do it for everyone that'll come into your presence that day. You'll hopefully feel a bit more energized before you start your day.

Manage expectations

It's important to manage the expectations you have of yourself and the expectations other people have of you. We're often extremely self critical because we either just want the best for ourselves or there are visible pressures from other people. This isn't an admirable trait. Yes, we should try to find ways to improve our work but not at the expense of harmful negative talk and self-hatred. It isn't useful and won't help you progress at all.

If you don't complete all the tasks you wanted to complete that day, check if you've been too unrealistic, make the appropriate changes then forgive yourself. It won't change much in the long run especially if you've made changes which could improve how the next day goes.

If you find yourself talking negatively, ask whether you'd talk to a close friend the same way. If you wouldn't, you're probably being too harsh. Trust me; you do not deserve the negative self-talk you might put yourself through.

Have fun with friends

It might be odd to be reminded to talk to your friends but you should. You don't need to be in complete seclusion in order to be efficient. You can study alone but you don't need to be alone for the whole week. And enjoy time with them without feeling guilty! If you always feel guilty, you won't enjoy the company or get any work done. You'll just be in a weird purgatory that doesn't let you do anything.

11. Procrastination in the IB

So, you now know how to maximize productivity and you're thinking that planning and getting on top of all your work seems like a pretty swell idea, but you have one major problem left: procrastination. It is one thing to plan and be organised, but it is another thing to follow that plan and get things done because they aren't going to get done by themselves.

Here are 5 easy steps to beat procrastination:
1. **Just 5 minutes** – start the task just for 5 minutes. Just do 5 minutes. Chances are, you'll be able to start, if not try any of the following.
2. **Break it down** – putting on your planner "Do EE" is a large and unreasonable task. Break it down into smaller chunks and work with one chunk at a time; e.g. gather research for EE. And then just do that (and tick it off). Each day, do a little more until it gets going. If the task is too hard for you, see what you can do first, then seek help after.
3. **Get away from your laptop/phone/internet** – put it in a different room, or turn it off. Honestly, I know how distracting Facebook is when you are in the mood to procrastinate. You'll find you will get going as soon as you can't get to it. If you need your laptop, use an app like Self Control to block your "procrastination sites".
4. **Plan a reward** – "After I do this, I can do whatever I want for the rest of the evening." Or, promise yourself that if you do everything you planned to during the week, you can take the weekend off – now that's a good deal!

5. **Keep busy** – don't leave yourself a ridiculous amount of time to do minuscule homework tasks that you'll put off anyway. Get involved! Go and play sports, hang out with friends, volunteer, then see how well you work afterwards. Don't give yourself the time to procrastinate.

Procrastination is horrible. I hate it loads and I have a half decent way of sorting it out. Just know that you cannot get rid of it completely otherwise you'll probably end up not enjoying life. No one can seize every single opportunity they must work. It's just not realistic.

The reason why procrastination happens is because there are two parts of your brain. One part sees the short-term benefit of everything, like going on Facebook or staring into the sky. This part is much bigger than the part that sees the long-term benefit of working now. Plus, the long-term benefit part (the determined one) gets tired quickly. Ok, now imagine yourself as two people: 'present' you, and 'future' you.

What you need to remember is that it isn't now that you will be feeling the consequences of your procrastination, it will be in future you. You need to look to future you and think that you want to have less work so you'll do it now. Procrastination isn't because you're lazy, it's because you're weak in the sight of distractions (that sounds mean but everyone gets distracted for the reason I stated above). Some overall advice:

- Keep your work neat.
    - You don't want to be revising and realise that you cannot read half of anything that you've written. Some care will go a long way.

- - You don't need to write full sentences when making notes, just something that can remind you what was taking place in class.
- Try organising your work daily.
  - This further reduces the chances of losing sheets and notes, hole punch it and keep it safe. You'd be surprised how much they can help .
- Lessen the distractions!
- Disable Facebook or move the Facebook app from the homepage of your phone.
- Mute your computer so you aren't hearing all sorts of notifications. Same goes for putting your phone off. Not on silent or vibrate – OFF.
- Clear the cookies from your computer so you must enter your password in every time you want to log into something. This makes logging into stuff an added effort so you're more inclined to just not bother and start your work. This process is automated if you use 'incognito mode' on your browser.
- Give yourself motivation
- Put pictures up of what you want to achieve (e.g. a 45 point diploma?)
- Plan a little treat you can have only if you've completed a certain amount of work, not if you've done something for a specific time. It's too easy to say 'I've read for half an hour, time to chill'.

Also, there is such a thing as 'helpful' procrastination. So when you feel lazy instead of refreshing the Facebook homepage, read an article from the news or a page from a book relating to your subjects. Or read a few more chapters from this book! In addition, don't mistake procrastination for having a break, breaks are good. They keep your sanity intact.

There is a fundamental cognitive difference between procrastinators and normal people. Everyone gets overwhelmed by work sometimes. Even the busiest or most efficient people might feel overwhelmed when there's too much work and not enough time. But the procrastinator is different. The procrastinator might have plenty of time, however he puts off work until there isn't enough time and then feels scared, stressed and overwhelmed. This means the procrastinator makes his own life much worse – does that sound like anyone you know?

This sort of behaviour has a massive effect on our IB scores, both in exams and especially because of coursework. By putting things off and avoiding work we leave ourselves no time to work well. There's no time to complete tasks to our satisfaction and we end up with worse scores and worse universities than we could have reached.

So why do we keep procrastinating? When we keep making poor decisions which are illogical, the reason is almost always an emotional one. The three most common causes of chronic procrastination are fear, anxiety and shame. This could be fear that the work won't be good enough, that it won't score high enough, that peers will be better etc. Whatever the reason, it is emotional and causes real problems. Fortunately, the problem tells us the solution.

Let's say you have a big project to do – maybe an Extended Essay, maybe revision for the IB exams. Whatever it is, you might find yourself procrastinating. If you're honest with yourself this is probably because you're worried that it won't be good enough. This is because the procrastinator only sees giant goals – so he sees 'The IB' as one goal, or Extended Essay as a goal. Of course these are impossibly big goals to take action on. But the non-procrastinator sees things differently. Non-procrastinators realise big goals are just groups of small tasks. While doing the EE might seem impossible, googling the markscheme, emailing your teacher for guidance and looking at the textbook are all easy tasks. And this is the secret: seemingly impossible tasks are just made of lots of very possible smaller tasks!

To change from a procrastination mindset to a non-procrastination one is not really that hard. The next time you start to feel nervous about a task grab a piece of paper and start to list all the things necessary to complete that task. Maybe to do an essay you would have to: do background research, find appropriate books, make a mind map, make a plan, write, edit and submit. Now focus on the first thing: for example, the research. What small tasks does the first thing include? Google the question, look at Wikipedia articles, look at the textbook. Now do that first small task, like checking the Wikipedia article on a certain topic.

That's it! You're working! Keep doing that over and over again and the essay will finish itself. It is possible to rewire your procrastinator brain. Now that you know how, test it out. Even at this moment you have things to do…yep! You just thought of one right? Probably one you really don't want to do. So grab some paper right now, I'll wait… Good! Now write the task name at the top and just start listing all things you have to do in that task. Ok, now write all the subtasks. If it looks too hard, just keep doing this. When you think you can do the first task, get going! And good luck!

12. IB Friendships

Friends are here to help you get through the IB and vice versa; it is therefore crucial that you surround yourself with the correct people. Throughout our 2 years of IB if it were not for certain friends we would not have been able to get the grades that we got. They reviewed our work, corrected mistakes they saw, helped us learn and explained things that we didn't understand. But most importantly, as cheesy as this may sound, your good friends will always be there for you.

I remember after the mock exams when a good friend of mine got a whopping 28% on his HL Math Paper 1. He was feeling horrible. I mean he had always been a great student: 7s in math during the MYP were no problem. But as you may know, HL Math is a totally different kind of beast. So, being one of his best friends, I really had to comfort him and help him recover. No, we didn't passionately cuddle or feed each other chocolate ice-cream, but instead I gave him my honest opinion about his results and how he wasn't working hard enough. I told him that he was going out too much, and that doing well in HL Math wasn't possible with minimal studying. Fast forward six months, and he came out with a solid 6 at the end of the IB Exams.

The beauty of having good friends is invaluable. They make you smile, laugh, and love. The quote that goes 'Friendship is like peeing on yourself: everyone can see it, but only you get the warm feeling that it brings!' (Robert Bloch) is so true. Don't seek quantity. One really good friend is better than three or four average ones. Spend time with people that you connect with, want to learn off, and genuinely enjoy conversing with.

No, don't do it for the popularity aspect or seek people to validate your ego. You are better than that and you know it.

Your Squad

You will almost certainly develop a core group of friends within your IB classes. Try to be friends with students who have similar goals and aspirations as you, stay away from the trouble-makers and keep in mind that it's not 'cool' to be a total failing slacker. It's good to have a group with different genders, cultures, and nationalities. Being at an IB school means you are likely exposed to a myriad of cultures – make the most of this so you can enrich yourself with other perspectives.

With your closest group of IB friends, I suggest you guys keep a WhatsApp group or a Skype chat open together. Surprisingly, this makes it easier to motivate and help each other. There are no better comforting words to an IB student than 'I haven't started it either'. Studying with your close IB squad over digital mediums is also an invaluable practice if done correctly.

Competition

The most important thing I can say about your in-class friendships is this: remember that the IB is not a competition amongst you. As in, marks are not standardized, certainly not in your classes. If you all deserve a grade 7, all of you will get a grade 7. Just because you get a very good mark on an assignment, does not mean that others cannot also get good marks. This means that there is a great incentive to help each other out and not withhold anything from each other.

I'm not saying copy and share your work; I am merely suggesting that you get the idea of 'competition amongst my peers' out of your head because there is no such thing. You should see your entire IB friend-group as one team, and you want everyone on that team to do well because you are not competing against each other.

So effectively that means you should study together. You should lend them your spare calculator if they forgot theirs. You should double-check the spelling and grammar in their IA if they ask you kindly. Within limits, you should have a very productive and co-operative friendship with your close IB friends.

Online Community

Undoubtedly, building strong IB friendships in your class will not be possible for everyone. Some of you may have fewer IB students at your school than there are fingers on your hands. Some of you may just find it hard making friends. Some of you may have some anxiety issues and would prefer to keep to yourself. This is where I am grateful that we live in the digital age and that there exist online communities to cater to anyone with an interest in anything.

Reddit IBO/ IBsurvival / Discord / Telegraph app

These are all alternative digital avenues for finding IB students around the world. The Reddit IBO subreddit is actually really helpful and insightful:
(www.reddit.com/r/IBO).

Discord is the name of a chat program, and you can find the official IB channel via the Reddit page.

IBsurvival.com was once the only place to go and meet new IB students online. I used it quite a bit back in 2007 when it had less than a few thousand users. Recently it has undergone some less than ideal changes with regards to its moderators and changes to its files policy, but it is still worth checking out sometimes.

Whether online or in real-life, the friendships you develop during your IB years will be friendships you remember for a long time. There is a certain 'comradery' in knowing that you are all in this together, and the amount of support you get will be very comforting. It's kind of like you are all jumping into an abyss with friends from all around the world and you are all coming out together as a whole community. The IB and the exams will make you feel oddly closer to those already close to you. Don't take them for granted.

13. Time Management

You probably have heard stories about how IB students have no life. I disagree; this is my life. Like many of you, I find myself juggling schoolwork, extra-curricular activities, friends, and unsatisfied parents. It came to a point when I just had to say "No" to certain activities that I absolutely love and "Yes" to the mountain of homework piling up on my desk, or in my MacBook, to be exact. So how do we determine when to say "Yes" and "No"?

Schoolwork is important, but so is the upcoming basketball game. Can you excel in both? Yes. But can you also fit in student council, Model United Nations (MUN), robotics, service projects, photography, chess, youth group, table tennis, and SAT classes? Probably not. The key word is to prioritize. Say "Yes" to activities that you are passionate about, challenge yourself to something new, and wholeheartedly to it. Say "No" to activities that are not meaningful to you, and do not blindly join boring activities just because your friends will be there. Although you may develop a new hobby once you join a club, if you know you will waste your whole afternoon in the martial arts club painfully wishing you were somewhere else, or will stay up until 2 am doing homework because you have three after school activities in a day, say no.

I kept my main activities every year throughout middle and high school: volleyball, basketball, student council, piano, and church. I also attended various other activities such as the school musicals, badminton, and service projects. Unfortunately, I had to sacrifice soccer, dance, and MUN. I still feel a hint of regret at not being able to do these things. I love group activities because I can meet other enthusiastic people and become more motivated to achieve certain goals. Sports games and other events brought excitement into my life, and gave me an overwhelming sense of accomplishment when they went well. As an emotional human being, I noticed that when I was in a good mood, I was more likely to be energetic and ready to tackle difficult assignments, especially those dreadful analytical essays.

How many activities should you join? Aim for at least three big projects, and participate in as many activities as possible when you still have the time and energy. Depending on your personality, you can lean towards group or individual activities, if you have a mix of both. Group activities are great for socializing while individual activities such as reading and playing the violin can be very refreshing. Fill out all your CAS (Creativity, Action, Service) forms and reflections as the activity is going on, because your life will be in chaos by senior year.

From endless lectures, you already know that time management is crucial and procrastination is deadly. It is especially evident as IB diploma students attempt to accomplish internal assessments, extended essays, language orals, Theory of Knowledge essays, exams, and the required CAS hours. What worked very well for me was to take a 15-minute snack break after I get home from after school activities, and then start on my homework right away. My concentration level would be very high and I could actually get a lot done before dinnertime. Once my brain switched to relaxation mode after dinner, it was much more difficult to focus again. Give it a try for a few days and see if it works for you. Instead of daydreaming on the bus, mentally list out your homework and the order you will do it in. This saves time and gives you a goal. All-nighters may work once in a while, but sleep deprivation will just lead to lower concentration levels and more all-nighters. Just remember, if you do not feel like doing work now, you will not feel like doing it later either.

The perfect balance between activities and IB varies among individuals, but there are a few universal tips. Remember, say "Yes" to studying during study period, doing productive work instead of chatting to people on Facebook, and sleeping before midnight. Say "No" to messy desks, over-commitment, and any type of distraction that will cause procrastination. Life should never be extremely boring or painful. Just learn to say "Yes" and "No".

Parkinson's Law states that: "work expands so as to fill the time available for its completion"; this means that sometimes it is better to leave work for the last minute. My TOK presentation can serve as the perfect example. I was great at understanding TOK when we spoke about it in class, but when it came to creating the presentation I struggled. I worked on it for two months but most of the useful work was done the day before the exam in Luton airport, on napkins using my phone and airport internet. Now, how well did I perform? I got a 9/10 which allowed me to get a B in TOK and 3 bonus points. Don't get me wrong, most work left to the last minute won't get you a good grade and you should always try to get things done in advance, but it won't be possible with everything.

I had done research and asked for a lot of advice from my TOK teacher beforehand and each time I was told to re-plan and remake my Knowledge Issue. This allowed me to gain pertinent knowledge in my area of study and the way the TOK presentation works. This allowed me to finish my presentation in 4 hours once I had an approved Knowledge issue. Being good under pressure can help too, and you will be using that skill a lot in the IB, but you need to know when to use it and when to work in advance. The earlier you start working on something the better it will be. However, people and IB students have the tendency to go off topic and attempt to dazzle their examiners with bullshit (IB therefore I BS). Remember, as Parkinson stated, the more time you have the more work you will make for yourself. So be sure you know what you need to do (look at the grading scheme and ask your teachers) and only include what's necessary and occasionally a little extra.

Get this done fast, hand it in before it's due, get feedback and improve. This is the best way to maximise your time and improve your grade. The extended essay must simply be done. There's no time to think and ponder. Once you have finally chosen your subject and area of interest, put aside one week to develop your guiding question and create a plan. Review this with your mentor and improve on the structure during that week (this may include several meetings). Then put aside a second week (preferably during holidays) to work on the essay and its content. This should be an intensive week of data collection, processing and synthesising by the end of which your essay should be 70% done.

Starting from that week, meet weekly with your mentor and get through specific points in your essay. With about three hours of work a week on your essay and consistent modifications it should take you a month to finish your work. I was originally planning to write my essay on mathematics and computer algorithms, but at the end of the first year of IB I changed my subject and mentor, selecting computer sciences.

The problem was that I didn't take IB computer sciences. I started freaking out as I thought I was honestly screwed. I spent the summer holidays reading some books on computer sciences (the theory) and reviewed the course guides and grading schemes from the IB. Once back to school I met with my new supervisor and we quickly developed a question. I was later able to do most of the writing during October break and any changes after that were mainly re-edits. Despite starting late, I was able to still get an A in my Extended Essay.

This was possible because I had a strong plan and solid, well defined guiding question, a passion for my subject, and finally because I wrote the essay in a short well defined period of time and spent even more time improving it.

14. IB Efficiency and Self-Improvement

The Pareto Principle, when applied to studying at school, states that roughly 80% of your results (achievements, good grades) come from 20% of your studying habits. This means that the biggest reasons behind you doing well on an exam or assignment will come from a limited time of studying. This is often an extremely difficult concept to grasp, because ever since you've entered high school your teachers and parents have told you to work long hours and slog it out.

The problem with this mentality is that you often end up spending 4-5 hours on topics that you already understand really well, and thus waste your time. Still, you go to bed that night thinking that since you spent 4 hours on something, you must have accomplished the task. This is simply not the case. The longer you work on a topic is not proportional to how well you know that topic. Instead, the smarter you work on studying a topic ensures your proficiency in it. What do I mean by smarter? I mean doing things like active studying, moving on when you're stuck, and talking closely with your teachers.

Here's a really good example of the Pareto Principle in action: to prepare for my SL Math Exams, I used to go through very long past papers, doing every single question and looking at the markschemes very closely. Now before the exams, this is something that you're going to have to do. It builds stamina, helps you understand the questions better, and builds comfort.

However, I had a problem with probability questions; I simply couldn't do them. After looking over my mock exams, my problem sets that my teacher had assigned, and my own workbook, I realized that there were a particular set of probability questions that I wasn't getting; those that had to do with expected value.

So, what did I do to get better? Well, I still continued doing full length past papers once a week to build stamina and get practice, but to really strengthen my weakness of probability, I firstly made custom problem sets for myself using the question bank filled with only probability questions. Then, I even narrowed those problem sets down to questions with only the topic of Expected Value. This allowed for smart, focused, weakness-based revision. I soon noticed an improvement in my results, and this was all down to working more efficiently and applying Pareto's Principle.

Don't Try to Do Everything at Once

I think that overexerting yourself is relevant to a lot of students because when you're surrounded by high-achieving individuals that are of the same age, you feel compelled to do stuff – and most of the time this is okay. You work hard, try new activities, and engage in healthy competition. But I feel as if it can be really harmful too.

Just yesterday, I heard some girl almost 'bragging' about how little sleep she got the other night. She was saying something like 'I had 5 hours of band practice, then I had to attend my MUN meeting, then I had a tutor for 2 hours, and then I had to do all my homework. Oh I slept at like 4am, I work so hard!!!'

I mean, don't get me wrong: doing stuff is good. But there's a limit, you know?

If we try to do everything, if we try to make everyone happy, and if we try to say yes to everything, we're missing out on some valuable time. We're missing out on time and energy that should be spent on ourselves.

How often do you spend time on self-reflection? How often do you analyse your strengths and weaknesses?

A common theme that I've noticed in so many successful people is the amount of time they spend taking care of themselves. This can be through meditation, running, reading, whatever; the point is that if you're not setting aside time to work on yourself, you're massively limiting your potential to grow.

In the IB, I think it's the same way. You must prioritize. You must find a way to maximize your output & productivity but at the same time you can't survive on four hours of sleep every night.

I know that when you're taking the IB this all sounds very abstract and meaningless, but please do take some time to self-reflect. In the long run, are you better off spending some time with your little sister who you're not going to see next year or should you attend a club meeting just so that you can put it on your CV.

99% of people will carry on their lives keeping themselves busy and doing meaningless activities. The 1% that succeed will be self-critical (and accountable), pursue activities that they are genuinely interested in, and aim to maximize happiness (and not wealth or status). You have the potential to do anything in this world if and only if you don't try to do everything.

That will surely lead to unhappiness and regret.

Self-Improvement

If you have plateaued at increasing your efficiency and feel like you are not improving, try going through this checklist quickly, which covers some of the aspects discussed in the previous chapters:

1. You Don't Want It Badly Enough

You say that you want to get better grades and that you're willing to sacrifice certain aspects of your life, but when it really starts to matter you don't walk the talk. This is the most common reason: people spend hours reading motivational articles and watching videos, but their inability to ever take action, or rather to only sustain action for the short-term, leads them to keep repeating the same mistakes.

How to fix this: Try to keep some system of accountability, by either telling someone that you're about to do something meaningful (and keeping them updated on your progress by sending them weekly emails), or another way would be to have a calendar filled with crosses when you achieve your goals for the day. This is surprisingly helpful, as you don't want to 'break' the crosses streak that is building up on your calendar.

2. You're Surrounded By Toxic People

They say that you are the average of the five people that you hangout the most with. Either way, if you're hanging around with slackers that keep claiming they 'have the potential' to do amazing but simply don't try, then you're doing it wrong. Or, maybe, that's the type of people you want to associate with. On the other hand, if you want to do well in school and are ambitious about your future, surround yourself with the right people. By this I don't necessarily mean the smartest; I mean people that bring positive energy to your life, people that help you out in times of need, and people that themselves are amazingly motivated to do great things with their education.

How to fix this: All up to you. Don't be afraid to completely disconnect with people that bring you down. Easier said than done.

3. You Are Being Stubborn

I realize that throughout all of middle school, studying at the back of the bus with your textbook open in one hand, a bag of Cheetos lazily scrawled over your lap, and one Apple earphone plugged in might have gotten the job done, but it won't do for HL Math. You need to try new techniques that you may have previously totally dismissed. Take it from me: I was horrifically repulsed by the idea of meditating. I mean, what the hell is meditation? Now in college, I can't survive without it, and it's done wonders to my memory that has benefitted me enormously in my studies.

How to fix this: Venture out of your comfort zone, try new study techniques, and consult people that you look highly up-to and ask for their advice. If you don't try anything right now, you might regret it later.

4. You're Scared To Ask Questions

This is a really important one. People love to protect their big old ego; they're scared that if they ask a stupid question everyone will think they're not so smart or that they're inferior.

It's all about status, after all, isn't it? Society has constantly drilled into us that our self-worth is based on how smart or good-looking we are relative to our peers. And it's all complete nonsense. People that actively seek out feedback, who ask questions because they genuinely want to better themselves and not for the sake of looking smart, do much better in the long run than their counterparts. Be vulnerable; don't be afraid to put your intelligence on the line. You're here to learn, and the best way to do that is to question absolutely everything.

How to fix this: I already addressed this above but something else that I'd recommend is to read the book 'Mindset' by Carol Dweck; it's an amazing read and it'll change the way you look at progress, especially in terms of your academic life.

5. You Are Too Comfortable

If you're really serious about improving yourself, whether that is academically or in any other aspect of your life, you should always strive to seek new uncomfortable situations. This is because when you're comfortable, you get stuck in a routine that, although may be getting you good grades and make you feel happy, is not ideal at all for bettering yourself. And trust me, there is no better feeling in the world than looking back and seeing how far you've come after genuinely having put yourself in new, vulnerable situations to learn something new.

How to fix this: Say yes to opportunities that are outside your comfort zone; aim to better yourself a little everyday by doing something that you're not used to at all.

6) You Need to Actively Change

This literally applies to anything you do in life. If you're not happy with the way things are going, find a solution. Don't just sit there and hope that things will get better. If you don't understand a term in your Physics class, and you're magically hoping that your teacher will omit it from that exam, you're screwed. Be active about learning; as I've mentioned above, ask questions, try something new, and don't be afraid to fail.

7) You're Not Taking Care of Yourself

You might be actively learning, trying out new things, pushing out of your comfort zone, asking tons of questions, but if you don't get enough sleep, keep yourself happy, exercise, and maintain your social wellbeing, nothing will get better. You only get one body: take care of it! If you're sleep deprived, nothing you learn will actually stick. This is especially true during exam season; it is absolutely vital that you keep yourself mentally refreshed! So many people just focus on studying 24/7, and that's just plain stupid. To do well academically, it is imperative that you keep yourself healthy.

How to fix this: exercise regularly, eat right, spend time with friends (before you start shouting at me that all of this can't be done- yes, it can, I did it myself) and make sure to remember that at the end of the day your mental health comes first.

15. Improving Memory

Upon graduating from the IB, many current students at my previous school had countless requests for notes. This surprised me, truly it did. Why would someone ask for my notes, surely they would find them useless?

Think about it, what are notes? It's a summary of some textbook, often riddled with spelling mistakes and abbreviations that make it almost impossible to read. So why would someone go through the trouble of deciphering my hand writing and reading bullet points of much better textbooks?

I have always viewed notes as a retention tool, something that helps you remember things in the long run. But you don't remember better by reading over them, you remember by writing them. 80% (I may or may not be making that statistic up – hey, I am an IB student okay) of the benefits of creating notes comes from actually creating them: putting the pen to paper will help your retention of the information.

I know it's an unpopular opinion but I do suggest you create a large chunk of your notes by hand and not on a PC. Firstly you will be writing your exams on paper (unless you have the permission to use a word processor) hence you will be able to recall the information better during the exam. Secondly, it's much easier to draw diagrams and little graphics by hand than on a computer, and having graphs and pictures in your notes will help.

So why do notes help you remember better? It's a combination of different things. For example, if you were to read a textbook, you might not be actively thinking about the information presented to you, but rather skimming over it and taking in the "words" rather than the concepts. If you are making notes, abbreviating into your own words, you are forced to process the information you are reading. This extra level of processing that happens in your brain creates more and stronger memories, ones that will last longer. Additionally, writing brings another dimension to learning. You are no longer simply thinking or reading, you are also creating and moving in the physical realm. The more senses you can associate with the learning process the easier it will be able to remember things.

Now in the future if you still have your notes, and you are reading over them you might notice that you remember things much faster then if you were to read the textbook. This is because your mind has created a particular association with the notes you created, much like little "checkpoints" in your brain that are triggered causing old memories to come back.

Some of you might have been blessed with the best memory in the world: you learned something once and you will never forget it. Unfortunately most of us aren't so lucky. So if you are like me and constantly forget things, you should listen to this advice. I'll talk about a few techniques I've learned over the years on how to remember things better.

Don't simply read, actively read. That extra word "actively" makes the difference. Reading actively means that you are highlighting, writing into your book and really thinking about what you are reading. This last point might sound rather obvious; however trust me when I tell you it's far too easy to read but not actually take in the information. So be sure to stop every few paragraphs and reflect aloud on what you have read.

Discuss with yourself the points you have gone over, even go online and do some further research on the subject.

The second point is to take notes, as mentioned in the previous chapter. I have gone over this before, however I want to emphasize it yet again: NOTES HELP. Make notes, even if you aren't going to read over them later. Having to process the information into your own words makes it more likely that you will remember said information. The combination of actually writing things down (do it by hand as your exams will be most likely handwritten) and converting other people's words into your own helps with information retention.

Reviewing your material is yet another key way to improve your memory. When I talk about review, I don't simply mean doing a few hours of revision before the exams. Proper review entails that you take 15 min per subject every day to review your day's notes and class work. You should also put in addition to your homework, half an hour at the end of each week per subject to review the week's lessons.

This is the most interesting and exotic part of memory retention in my opinion. I have over time tested two techniques that have helped me with improving my memory; I don't know if this has been due to a placebo effect or that they actually helped, anyways here they come.

16. Writing IB Essays

You may think you know what an essay is. You may *think* you do.

IB essays test whether you can give a precise answer to a very precise question. IB essays also test whether you can use evidence and logic to support that precise answer. Keep that in your head because it seems simple, and is some ways it is, but it's too easy to drift away from that concept. Your teachers will give you a method for writing essays. Almost any method can work – just hang onto the idea mentioned above: a precise answer to a precise question – with evidence and logic.

It can be very useful to think of the process backwards, to think about where you want to end up, and then how to get there. It's probably how you tackle the job of writing the essay. Therefore, this is something like what you do when told to write an essay:

Someone asks you a question – your overall answer is going to be the last paragraph or conclusion of the essay. You will have to support or prove that answer/conclusion, giving your evidence and your reasons – that will be the body of your essay, which leads up to that final paragraph. You'll have to start by discussing a few ideas and definitions to explain yourself – that will be the introduction which clears the way for the body of the essay.

So, the process should be: I) think of what your answer is to the question ii) think of the reasons/evidence/proof for that answer iii) plan the sequence of the ideas, check that they answer the question iv) write the essay.

In your school the teachers will hopefully teach you a method of writing essays. They will tell you it's the only or the best way to do it, and will demand you do it, and maybe even mark you down for not doing it their way. This is entirely reasonable, but only part of the truth. It's the International Baccalaureate – in other words, IBO needs to accept lots of different conventions and methods for doing work in many different countries. If there is a single correct method for doing anything, then the IBO must explicitly say that – in the case of essays, they don't.

The Introduction

This is really important – in fact this is probably the most important aspect of the essay. Examiners will tell you that they basically have a very good idea what your final mark will be after they have just read the first paragraph. For example, in Language A, if somebody asks, 'Do you think love is an important theme in the texts you have studied', you're going to say which kinds of love you're going to focus on – love of country, parents, animals, sports, etc. You will want to define what you mean by 'important'.

Always re-check your first paragraph. You should absolutely never misspell the name of an important text/person/character/country – the examiner will have a hard time believing that you are not an idiot. Under no circumstance do you want to give them that benefit of the doubt because that will then be on their mind the rest of the time.

So, in the introduction, be sure to define any central key terms you will be using throughout your essay. Mention what texts/areas/periods/ you will be focusing on. Outline and signal the points you will be discussing. It really is that simple.

The Body

The body of the essay is where you discuss the points you are trying to prove, which lead to an answer to the question. In general, in literature and social sciences, there are usually no 'right answers' that the examiner will be waiting for you to produce – although there are certainly 'wrong answers'. The examiner probably doesn't care much for your opinion – they are only concerned with the criteria that has been given to them.

As long as you are good at arguing your point across, it doesn't really matter which side of the argument you choose. What matters is whether you can explain your ideas, and whether you can find evidence to support them. Three good points is usually a good amount – for an essay or a presentation or commentary. Two points may look like you don't have enough ideas, and four solid points may mean you don't have enough time to go into enough detail.

Thus, the body needs to i) say what the point is ii) explain it iii) give support and evidence and iv) show how it helps answer the actual question.

Conclusion

If you have done the previous work right, then this becomes very simple – it's just your overall answer to the question in the final paragraph. It's where you essentially say 'having looked at these three points, it becomes evident that the answer to the question is…' So you end up with a complex answer, but the examiner understands how you got there, and they see your reasons. They also understand you have chosen what to say out of many possibilities you were aware of.

So, in the conclusion: i) make sure you've got an explicit answer to the question ii) explain/show how that answer is supported by the three points you discussed and iii) check for mistakes – you don't want to leave a bad impression with carelessness.

17. Mastering the IB Presentation

There will be plenty of times when you will be required to do an IB presentation – in Language A, Language B, TOK, Group 4 projects etc. Presenting is a set of skills that you must learn – organising ideas, and finding vivid ways to show them. In this section, we will try to go over some preliminary bits of advice that should help you maximize your marks on general IB presentations.

First, find a topic that actually interests you – this way you are more likely to do better research and you will be more lively talking about it. Obviously there will be limits to this depending on what subject you are presenting for, but most of the time you will have some degree of flexibility on what you wish to talk about.

Just as with the perfect IB essay, the perfect IB presentation also has a beginning, middle and an end. The beginning should have some kind of captivating hook to get the audience engaged: like a puzzle. You should also make an effort to inform your audience *exactly* what you are going to talk about. So, you should say, 'I'm going to argue x, y, z…'. If your audience knows what you are going to focus on, they will follow much better. Also, if possible, try to make the presentation relevant to your audience from the start – give them a reason as to why they should listen.

The middle of the presentation will be the points which are the heart of what you're about and what you want your audience to think about. When you're preparing, try to put each point in a very clear single sentence. Look at your ideas from different points of view. What are the problems with or arguments against what you are saying? Make sure to show the transition between each point. If using multiple speakers, this might be a good point to choose a different speaker to address that point. Make sure to vary your method of presenting for each point as students tend to drift off after 2-3 minutes.

The end of your presentation is arguably the most important part. It's what is in the teacher's mind when they give you the mark. You need to make sure to wrap it all up. Ensure that the audience got the points you were making and give them a conclusion – so they see what the purpose of the presentation was and why it mattered. You should also open up your presentation to your audience and if allowed, give them a chance to express their opinion or arguments. At the very end, you will need to give them the answer to whatever the hook of the presentation topic was.

How to Present

It's important to think of the presentation as not just talking. It needs to really engage the audience. Think of it as a series of images, pictures, diagrams, maps, film clips and interactive materials. What you and your group might do is talk about them, comment, and then explain connections and implications. Using visuals also stops the audience looking at you – which makes it more interesting for them (no offence) and less panic-inducing for you.

Use the Criteria

This is probably the most important take-away from this chapter on IB presentations. For the love of god, please consult the grading criteria upon which you will be assessed for that specific presentation. Remember, the criteria is all that any examiner has, including your teacher. Even if you have an 'excellent' presentation (in the sense that it was exciting and interesting and everyone enjoyed it), you could still score poorly if you didn't tick the boxes on the assessment criteria. I see this happen time and time again with students.

For example, if the TOK criteria says 'identify a knowledge question relevant to a real life scenario' then you better damn well do those two things to get the full 5 marks. You need to i) explicitly identify a 'knowledge question' and ii) explicitly identify a real life scenario. Failure to do either will prevent you from getting top marks.

You have specific assessment criteria for TOK, Language A, Language B, Group 4 and so on. They are not the same, and in fact the differences are very important. Get your hands on the relevant criteria and turn them into a bullet point list or checklist. You may even want to hand in a copy of this to your teacher so they can see that you know what you had to do.

18. IB Exam Revision [Part 1]

Preparing for the final exams can be a daunting task. Once the examination timetable is published your first exam date will remain cemented in your mind. Although there are hundreds of ways to revise for the examinations, many are largely ineffective and far too time consuming. In this chapter I will give you some general guidelines for how to best revise for your final exams.

Time Management

Having me preach to you about the importance of time management is perhaps hypocrisy at its best. For me it was not until I got into university that I really started to understand how effective time management can be. If you are one of the few who has mastered the skill at an early age then consider yourself lucky. This is an invaluable ability that you will use regularly throughout your life.

One of the great rewards of undertaking the IB challenge is that you will have the opportunity to learn amazing time-management skills. The key to good time management is not just writing up a good schedule, but also imposing consequences when you fail to adhere to that schedule. For example if you promised to revise biology for 45 minutes a day every weekday and then you only manage to do 15 minutes on one of days, you must make sure you catch up on the remaining half an hour the day after.

When Do I Start?

I had a teacher who once told the class (with 4 months remaining until final exams), "I hope your revision is going well... and if there are still some of you that haven't started revising, well you are already behind." Hearing those words I got uncomfortably nervous and stressed. Not only had I not begun revising, I didn't even know where to start. Several weeks passed as I procrastinated even more and eventually "mock exams" came around. I didn't study much, except for glancing over a few past papers from the previous year. Luckily, it turned out that some of the "mock exams" were in fact last year's actual examinations. Nonetheless, I didn't have a good feeling about the whole thing and my grades reflected this – I got a 36 overall with a 4 in HL Mathematics. This was a real wake up call as my university offer was given on the condition that I get a minimum of 40 points overall and a 7 in HL Mathematics and Economics. I feared the worst.

With less than a month to revise and no quick solution in sight, I was probably justified in my distress. Some of my friends had been "revising" since the beginning of winter break. I was too busy partying and procrastinating. With less than a month to go until exams I knew that this month would make or break me. I quickly made a demanding exam schedule and started it the following day. For a whole month I practically lived in a cave, having deactivated Facebook and deleted Skype. I read, breathed and lived revision. The only thing that kept me going was a voice in the back of my head telling me "you did nothing for two years, the least you can do is work mercilessly for one month, and then it will be all over."

The whole point of that little story is not to suggest that you should only leave a month for revision. It was simply to demonstrate to you what you will have to go through if you do leave revision so late. I was never one to miss a party – there was no way I could give up weekends, and sports, and all my hobbies just so that I could start revision many months in advance. I left revision too late, but I paid the price. Whatever choice you make, you need to realise that you will have to bear the consequences when your actual exam preparation comes around.

There is no ideal time to start revising. That being said, you should never leave less than a month, and you would probably be wasting your time starting revision any sooner than 3 months before exams. Some of you may seem confused as to why I am suggesting that you don't study too much, but that's not what I am saying. There have been studies done that show how students can reach the "peak" of their revision too early, and have a "meltdown" before actual exams. This usually happens to students that start revising nearly a year in advance. By revising too much in advance you may run the risk of failing to recall the earliest information and start to panic.

Perhaps the golden rule to IB exam revision can be worked out logically. If you still have assignments to finish that will be graded by the IB, it's probably safe to say that you should not even think about starting revising. Your Internal Assessment is far more important than early revision so make sure you get that out the way first. Once all your work has been sent off you can drop everything else and just focus on revising for your exams. Always remember your priorities: first get all the IA out of the way, and then you can centre all your attention on revision.

The IB is too demanding for you to be starting revision early. With all the tests, assignments, sports meetings, CAS reports and homework that you will have on your hands, you will not be able to begin preparing too much in advance. Don't forget however that all the tests and coursework that you are doing is a form of revision. It's not the best, but at least you are doing something to reinforce your knowledge of the subject. So don't think you are doomed if you haven't been revising out of a textbook with a month to go before exams. You have been revising "indirectly". At least that's what I told myself to be able to sleep at night.

Mock Examinations

Most schools will administer "mock" examinations several weeks or months prior to the actual exams. This is not really a test of your knowledge and how well you will perform on the actual exam. It's more to get you familiar with examination conduct and protocol. You will need to get used to arriving punctually, having the right materials, and following exam rules and regulations.

Nonetheless, I suggest you make full use of your mock exams and treat them almost as if they were the real deal. You will be able to see what you would achieve if you had sat the real exam and not done any revision. Thus, it is kind of a test of how focused you were in class throughout the year. For most of you this experience will be a wake-up call.

Once your mock exam results come out don't just glance at the grade and move forward. Find out where you went wrong and where you could have done better. Although these exams are graded by your teachers, it doesn't mean the marking will be much different when done by examiners elsewhere. Look for places where you lost marks due to silly mistakes and try to work on these mistakes before your real examination.

One final note on mock examinations. It is no hidden secret that most schools use last year's real paper as the current year's mock paper. Don't think that you are a genius for figuring this out. This has been a tradition in most schools, however some now started to come up with new material. Nonetheless, if your mock exam paper happens to be a past paper that you have already worked on yourself then don't feel guilty or feel like you didn't deserve the grade you got. If you did well that just shows that your work with past papers has been worthwhile. You were able to apply the material again, meaning you probably learnt something along the way. If you still did poorly despite having seen the paper and the markscheme beforehand then you have reason to worry.

19. IB Exam Revision [Part 2]

What do I revise?

You should by now realise that you will not be devoting an equal share of revision time to each subject. Some subjects you may not even bother with until perhaps a few weeks before the final exam. Other subjects you may like to start revising several months in advance. This will all depend on what your strengths are, as well as what your aims are.

For example; my IB results needed to coincide with my university offer from Oxford – I didn't really care about much else. This meant that I needed a 40 overall, 7's in HL Mathematics and HL Economics, as well as 6's in all of my remaining subjects. As soon as I learnt of this offer, I immediately outlined my problem areas. I knew that getting a 7 in HL Mathematics was by far my greatest weakness. I had never gotten a 7 in any test, and was probably averaging out a 5 overall. I felt uncomfortable with a large portion of the material. I also knew that getting a minimum of 6 in HL Geography and SL English should not be too big of a problem. I felt very comfortable with the Geography material, and my IA for English seemed good enough. Having gone over all of this in my head, I began to formulate how I will go about revising. I ended up spending more than 50% of my revision on Mathematics (doing a past paper almost every other night), then 30% on Economics (because I couldn't take any risks as I had to get a 7) and the rest of time I divided equally amongst the remaining subjects.

This may come as a shock to a lot of you. How can one spend more than half of their revision time on just one subject?

Instinctively, you would want to divide your time equally amongst the six subjects giving you an equal chance of doing well in all of them. This is not the correct way to think. You need to identify your weaknesses and base your revision around this. If you are borderline failing Chemistry and sailing through Business Management, then focus all your attention on getting through the Chemistry material. You may not enjoy it as much as BM but it's by far more important to you and your overall grade.

Figure out what your problem areas are by looking at your predicted grades and talking to your teachers to check where you stand in terms of their predictions. More importantly, you should know by now what your aims and objectives are. Do you need a minimum of a 6 in this subject for university or university credits? Do you need a 7 in this in order to fulfil the requirements? Once you work out what you are aiming for then make sure to focus your energy on this specifically. If you don't have any set aims and you are just trying to get the greatest points total then your task may be slightly easier. Find out where your Achilles heel lies and focus on this and this alone.

How Do I Revise?

Although there are a multitude of methods to revise for the actual exams, you need to be careful and avoid doing redundant tasks. Out of all the possible methods that are out there, I highly recommend you try to focus your revision around past papers. For a full detailed explanation of this method please refer to the specified chapter on Past Papers.

I know that this method may not work for everyone. Perhaps you made great notes throughout the year or you enjoy learning from the syllabus and the textbook. Nonetheless, more often than not the most successful IB candidates will tell you that they revised primarily with the help of past papers and markschemes.

If you still insist on studying from textbooks and notes, I recommend you cover some basic study tips. For example, some subjects such as biology may require more 'visual learner' skills – using your eyes and memory to recall the information. I know some students get very creative with this process and create highly effective 'mind maps' and 'word association' memory tools. I guess the theme here is sticking to the revision method that you know works for you the best. If you don't think you have one, I highly suggest you get cracking on past papers.

No matter what method you choose, I highly recommend that your revision remains active. By this I mean you are constantly writing, making notes, and writing again. Although lying in the grass with a book to cover your face from the sun sounds like a good plan, you are wasting your time. Sit at a desk, grab some plain white paper, and make good use of your pen and pencil. You are twice as likely to remember what you are revising if you are constantly writing and not just reading.

Some of you may find that study groups work well for particular subjects. I myself found it extremely useful to work together on a maths paper with another person, or to discuss economics material in a group. Choose your groups wisely though. Avoid students who are far more advanced than you and avoid friends that seem like they attend revision sessions more for the social aspect rather than actual studying. The point is that if you find revising or working through past papers with a group of equally motivated peers useful then by all means proceed with that.

You will probably have a good week or two of no school before your examinations begin so make full use of that period. Make sure each day is productive and that you set yourself mental tasks to complete every day. Don't be alarmed but you should probably be aiming to get at least 7 hours of pure revision done every day that week. This isn't really asking that much given that you probably haven't been doing much revision all year.

Don't panic if you come across something during your revision that you have never seen before. Chances are it probably isn't in the syllabus anymore or maybe you just missed it out in class. Ask your friends or your teacher for advice. You shouldn't spend hours and hours stuck on one section or problem – remember this should be revision and not first-time learning.

Another common mistake made during the revision period is setting yourself goals that are simply beyond your reach. No one expects you to revise for twelve hours a day straight, sleep for eight and leave four hours for washing/pooping /eating. It shouldn't have to come to that. You should be studying hard but also leaving a little time to relax and recover. Remember that there is a huge number of resources available for you to aid in your revision.

20. IB Exam Revision [Part 3]

Let's be real here, if you haven't been paying much attention during class like many of my old classmates, there's a good chance you won't have much clue on the topics covered in your subjects, let alone how to do any questions related to those topics. If this describes your current self, please don't start doing any past year papers. You will feel frustrated looking at foreign words you don't understand every time you see a new question. You will probably spend more time figuring out what the question is even asking in the first place, instead of actually figuring out the question.

That is why it's pretty important to have a decent foundation of your contents before attempting past year papers. Besides that, as mentioned in the previous chapter, topical revision goes hand-in-hand with past year paper revision. If you notice the mistakes that you have been making belong from the same topic, it's probably a good sign for you to do some topical revision before continuing your past paper revision.

With that said, the thick textbooks that you have to go through every time you want to do some topical revision doesn't make it easier. Thus, I will be sharing some tips in this chapter to make your topical revision more efficient and effective.

Syllabus Guide

Whether its extra explanations on certain topics or entirely new topics that are not even tested, a lot of IB textbooks contain extra information that make the book longer than it should be.

Sure, having some extra explanations and supplementary materials might be useful in making what you learn more interesting. But if you're currently intensely revising for exams, you can get confused on what to actually revise for the IB exams. This can lead you to waste hours upon hours trying to master and understand a topic that is not even tested and even worse, make you not focus on the topics that you should be revising on the first place.

I had a friend who spent hours studying how a certain stomach medicine works, only to find out it was not part of the Standard Level syllabus. This is just an example of how not knowing what you need to study can detriment you.

Luckily, you have the IB syllabus guide to guide you. In the previous chapter, I mentioned how the IB syllabus guide can help you filter out which past year papers are relevant or not. Likewise, in this case can help you know what concepts to understand and at what depth to understand in.

For example, the economics syllabus guide clearly states out the topics and concepts you need to learn in bullet points. It labels each of this point with "AO1" or "AO2" or "AO3" or "AO4". This labelling tells you at what depth you need to understand a concept. AO2 usually means that you need to be able to explain such concept in an essay. While AO3 means that you need to be able to explain such concept while using real-world examples. This labelling is really useful to know at what depth you need to be studying something. For example, this made me know that I did not need to find any real-world examples to illustrate the poverty cycle and that I just need to know how to explain it in an essay format.

So, this just shows how much more you can be efficient when you revise using your subject's syllabus guide. Save yourself some time and look up those syllabus guides online.

Note Making

I know that making notes seem like a very tedious thing to do. During my IB journey, I also thought the same thing. But being faced with thick textbooks that don't display the information you need in a concise way, I finally budged in and made my own notes.

You don't need to make some fancy handwritten notes with different coloured highlights and beautifully drawn diagrams. Sure if this is what you like to do, then go ahead. But for many of us who dislike handwriting and spending hours making your own notes, you just need to make some notes that help you can access the content you need in a quick manner.

My notes were nowhere near fancy, in fact, it was filled with a lot of screenshots of definitions, diagrams or even certain paragraphs from my textbook. I only included what was relevant from the textbook and removed everything else. This way, whenever I wanted to revise something I forgot about, I didn't have to open hundreds of pages in my book and read through paragraphs of fluff content before finding what I want. Instead, I just have to quickly read my notes and be done with it.

If you make notes how I did, it won't take much time, a full day of screenshotting your textbook is probably enough to summarise everything you need to learn. Trust me, this goes a long way in saving time from flipping your textbooks.

I also found making notes a good way to do my first round of revision, as I was forced do determine what I wanted to put into my notes, I naturally was exposed to some concepts when I made my notes. I think this helped me a lot during my topical revision as sometimes you have some topics that you understand better only after you have seen the bigger picture. Thus, these notes helped me revise faster and better.

So please. Don't be lazy and make some notes. Also, don't forget to use the syllabus guide to make your notes. If not this whole thing would be redundant.

Topical Questions

I had a lot of friends who simply read the content from their notes or textbook and called it a day for topical revision. Sometimes you may think you understand a concept after reading its explanations thoroughly, only to find yourself utterly confused when faced with questions related to such topic. This usually happens more often within the Sciences or the Maths subjects.

I personally experienced this when revising for Physics, I thought I understood projectile motion pretty well until I was faced with some intermediate-level questions. Doing topical questions exposes you to the thinking processes that you need to have. For my case, doing projectile-motion questions taught me that often times you have to solve one dimension of movement to solve the other dimension of movement. You won't really be exposed to this type of thinking if you simply just understand the concept. So please just do some questions after revising each topic to not only test your understanding but to also make sure that you will be able to translate your content understanding into actual problem solving skills later in the exams.

Beyond that, doing practice questions is actually a form of 'active recall'. It's a well-researched study method where you actively try to recall what you have learned prior. Doing this helps whatever you have learned sticks much better in the brain. I hope this further convinces you to do some topical questions while doing revision.

Skipping Content

My last bit of advice, especially for those of you who want to safely score a good seven in your exams is to not skip any content.

This may sound like a no brainer, but during revision: me and some of my friends tend to focus on common questions or topics that often appeared on past year papers and brushed over topics that were less uncommon, despite knowing it was inside the syllabus guide.

This is probably the biggest weakness of over-relying on past year papers for your revision. You can sometimes develop a mindset of "no way they're going to test that, it has never appeared in a past paper before". This makes you ignore more obscure concepts and limits the scope of necessary things you need to study.

I was actually a victim of this myself for maths. I did not study on the "linear transformation of a single random variable" formula as I never saw it come up in my mock exams or in any past year papers that I did. This led me to ignore this formula, despite it clearly being in the data booklet. Thus, I was very shocked to see a weird question come up during the paper of 2 my HL Maths AA exam. Seeing this question caught me off guard and made me spend too much time on what was supposed to be a 2 minute question. This made me and a lot of my friends lost some easy marks during exams.

So let my story be a lesson to you. Don't be some wise guy who thinks they know what the IB can or cannot test, just trust the syllabus guide and don't skip obscure topics. In fact, not understanding an obscure concept should give you more motivation to revise on it; and most of the time these obscure questions aren't very large and don't actually take too much time to cover. So don't be an idiot like me and put yourself at risk of losing easy marks.

Hopefully you learned of some tips and tricks that help make your topical revision more effective. But remember this does not mean you can slack off on your past year paper revision. Topical revision builds a good foundation of your understanding, but doing past year papers is what's going to safely secure your seven. So take my advice and have a balance of topical revision and doing past year papers.

Cramming: The Night Before

No words of advice or comfort can really help ease your pre-exam stress and make you relax the night before your first examination. You will remember that date for a long time. For most of you, this is probably the first official externally graded examination that you take (unless you've done GCSEs or SATs). This can be a scary notion but you just need to realise that in a matter of a few weeks all of this will be over and you will embark on the longest holiday of your teenage life.

Now, what should you be doing the night before an exam? Well, as a golden rule, you should restrict your revising only on material for which you will be examined the following day. This means if you have a math exam tomorrow, you should be doing just math today – not biology which you have in a weeks' time or something like that. You need to keep the subject fresh and familiar in your mind – focus all your energy on it the night before and hopefully you will wake up with most of it still in your head.

Now, what about cramming? There is a heated debate as to whether cramming even works. Some say that having late night cram sessions is not only ineffective, but that it can put you in unnecessary stress and increase your chances of "going blank" the following day. Others will tell you that cramming is the best form of revision, and everything you stuff into your brain the night before just spills on your exam paper the next morning. Then there are also those who will tell you that cramming works – but you should not do it because you are not learning long-term, you are merely memorizing stuff in the short-term which you will probably forget in a weeks' time. Those people are missing the point.

From a personal viewpoint, cramming the night before an IB examination was helpful, but only to a certain extent (and only for certain subjects). For example, I found that cramming popular mathematical proofs was extremely helpful, however cramming an English novel was not. Use your common sense a little when it comes to cramming. More importantly, don't overdo it. Your sleep and nutrition can play a large role in your examinations, so make sure you are getting a minimum of six hours of sleep most of the days. Exceptions can be made when you have an exam the following day, and then after that you have a day or two break from exams for recovery – in that scenario I have seen some students even pull off near all-nighters.

Disappointment: The Morning After

However well your exam went, you are more than likely to come out feeling rather disappointed. This is natural. If you come out of the exam room very cheery and happy that usually means that either you have been very lucky and really aced it, or you really messed up a question or two because you misunderstood what was being asked. Either way, the most important thing to remember after every examination is to move on. Don't hang around outside the exam halls asking all your friends what they answered or what they thought of a certain question. The exam is over. Whatever you say or do after is not going to change what you wrote on that paper or the outcome of the exam. You need to revise for your other papers.

This is one of the biggest mistakes I see students make when it comes to revision. Instead of studying for the next paper, they waste time talking to their friends and trying to figure out how they got this or that answer, or what they wrote about in their essay. You are likely to get even more disappointed and discouraged if you waste time asking your friends what they wrote down only to find out that your answer was totally different. After you have just sat an examination, just go home as fast as you can and focus on the next one.

Moreover, if you have finished the last paper for a certain subject, then make sure you get that subject totally out of your head. Clear all the notes and papers for that subject out of the way and pretend that you don't even know what it is. Instead of doing six subjects, you are now only doing five. It is of vital importance that you make the transition from one subject to the next as smooth as you can as the exam schedules can be very hectic.

Method of Elimination: A Technique

One factor that separates the more successful exam candidates from the others is that they have picked up certain examination techniques along the way. One of these is a revision technique by which you use a process of elimination to make an educated guess as to what might show up on the next paper. Let me give you an example: when I sat my HL Economics exam, Paper 1 had a big question on monopolies, but neither Paper 1 nor 2 had anything on negative externalities. I made an educated guess that there would be a big question on negative externalities on the Paper 3, with little emphasis on monopolies. This was indeed the case that year.

You can do this for almost any paper. Each subject has its key syllabus areas on which students should be examined. This is perhaps more true for Group 3, 4 and 5 subjects than the others. You can use the process of elimination to make a clever guess as to what could potentially show up on the next paper having already sat the first one. Discuss this with your friends as they probably have a similar inkling. This technique, combined with cramming, can practically make you an overnight expert on an area with which you were previously not that comfortable.

Last Minute Revision

You need to make full use of the last few moments before you enter the examination room. Find a nice quiet place to quickly run through key points and get any last-minute cramming done. Avoid large groups of people as you will probably not be able to concentrate that well. You should probably even revise in the car/bus ride to the examination place. Just don't waste any valuable time that you have on useless distractions.

21. The Power of Past Papers

I'm sorry to disappoint you but if you have come here looking for free past papers and markschemes you are out of luck. At the same time, I wish to congratulate you because that kind of "I-need-past-papers" mentality is exactly what you need. If you have flipped through to this chapter in hopes of finding out where to get past papers and how to use them, then you can pat yourself on the back because you are now one step closer to getting 7's in your subjects.

If you have been reading this guide carefully then you should know just how much I have stressed the importance of past papers. Let me put it to you this way. If Internal Assessment takes around 25% of final IB grade, then your experience and practice with past papers could determine around half of what your final IB grade will be. The remaining 25% is down to a mixture of determination, natural academic ability and luck. Past papers are everything when it comes to acing your examinations.

Once again, to truly understand the power of past papers, we need to think logically. The syllabuses for most subjects have been written many years ago. The IB examinations are written to test your knowledge and grasp of the syllabus material. Thus there is only so much that they can possibly ask. If you look through past papers over and over again you are bound to see major similarities. Once again, the degree of similarity will vary across subjects, but nonetheless it is a fair generalisation. Think of it this way: there is a set amount of information you need to learn and the IBO wants to test your knowledge with respect to this information. Every year they will ask questions to test this knowledge. Surely there are only so many different ways they can test you. Eventually they start to run out of original questions.

Luckily for you, this has already happened. Look at the grade above you; they arguably were worse off. Similarly, the grade below you is better off. Why? Because yet another year of modern IB examinations has gone by. That means another set of past paper questions and markschemes has been made available. Consider yourself lucky that you have so much access to past papers and markschemes because ten years ago this was certainly not the case.

At the top major UK universities (including Oxford and Cambridge) you will find it impossible to get your hands on any markschemes. Past examinations are usually available (and even that can be a hassle), but markschemes are non-existent. The reasoning for this is quite simple to understand. The universities don't want students to simply digest the markschemes without learning the material properly. It levels out the playing field and makes the competition for top marks fiercer. Luckily for you the IB does not have this policy. Past papers and markschemes are recommended by the IBO and made available – albeit at a monetary cost.

Where do I get them?

The simple answer to this is anywhere you can. If you are amongst the lucky few then it can be the case that your school has an abundance of money and resources and will readily supply you with past papers and markschemes because they know how valuable they are. On the other hand, you may be at a school that lacks the financial muscle to buy these for students and is honest enough to not photocopy any. Nonetheless the first place you need to go to is your school.

Your teachers, the library, your IB coordinator – basically anyone that might be able to help you. At some schools, students have access to nearly all available past examinations; however, the teachers may restrict what they give out because they may use them as future mock examinations. Even if the papers are covered in cobwebs and in a dusty old closet, make sure to get them out and look for more.

If that route fails, your next best option would probably be to go to the one place that has the answers to almost everything; the Internet. Be aware that there are several problems with this approach. First of all the IB strictly forbids any independent persons to host past papers and markschemes on the Internet and they regularly hunt down and threaten anyone who doesn't follow these rules. If you are lucky enough to find a website that does host past papers then it's unlikely to be there in a few weeks' time.

The last option you have is the most hassle-free: buying past papers and markschemes directly from the IBO website. Now don't get me wrong. I am against spending any more money on what is already a very expensive program. Nor do I understand why the IB would charge students more for additional "information."

What I strongly recommend you do is round up ten or so classmates that are interested in getting past papers and markschemes for a particular subject. If you each chip in, then together you can buy a copy from the official IBO past paper provider (the Follett IB store). Once you have all the papers you need you can share the papers between each other because they will be made available in a downloadable pdf format. Additionally, once you're done with your exams you can sell the papers off to the grade below.

All in all, you should never be spending more money on past papers than you would on a textbook – and past papers are technically far more valuable than any textbook (in my honest opinion). You need to get your hands on these papers, one way or another.

How many?

Although I usually urge you to do more past papers in rough rather than one or two thoroughly, this approach also has its limitations. A good general approximation that I recommend is doing at least five years worth of examinations (both May and November papers). This adds up to ten separate examinations – which is a considerable amount of practice. Of course this will vary from subject to subject. For example for Group 1 topics, there is very little point in looking at more than 3 years worth of exams whereas for HL Mathematics you wouldn't do yourself any harm working through ten years of examinations if you really want that 7. A good rule to follow is to make sure you do enough past papers so that you start seeing repeat questions. Only then will you become comfortable and familiar with what the questions ask you to do.

Avoid going too far back into the database if you know there has been a serious change in syllabus/exam structure. For example, the HL Economics Paper 1 exam used to be multiple choice questions a decade ago. There is little point in looking at too many of those multiple-choice papers because you no longer have to sit such a paper. That being said, just because there has been a slight change in method of examination doesn't mean you should ignore the papers totally.

There are few feelings worse than having just sat an exam where one of the questions was incredibly similar to a past paper that you decided not to do. I highly doubt you can feel overly confident going into an examination if you haven't taken your chance to do all the past papers you could get your hands on (or at least glance over them properly). Make sure you don't have this regret – do enough past papers.

Past Papers vs. Markschemes

Some of you may be asking what's more important, the past paper or the markscheme? They are both of equal importance and you can't really have one without the other. There is no point in running through paper after paper if you have no way to check if your answers are even remotely correct. Similarly, you cannot just flick through random answers in the markschemes if you have no idea what the question was asking (unless, that is, the markscheme has the questions included).

Ultimately, you need to have both the past paper and the markscheme for every examination that you are interested in. You will undoubtedly spend more time with the markscheme than you will with the past paper because you will want to see exactly what examiners are looking for. Nonetheless, get the past papers as well in case you want to do a practice examination or want to get a "feel" for the structure of the exam.

How do I "do" the past paper?

Contrary to what your teachers may have told you, it is not a crime to have the markscheme with you whilst you are answering questions from a past paper (sometimes!). This is one of the best forms of revision and is a method that is severely underused by students.

Ideally, you would want to complete each paper properly in the time set and only then get out the markscheme to see what mistakes you made. But we don't live in an ideal world. You don't have the time to sit 3-hour mock examinations for tens of papers in 6 different subjects and then go through each one with the markscheme. Your revision doesn't even really start until all the assessment is sent off so you will at best have a month or two of pure revision.

So what's the best thing to do once you have obtained the papers and the markschemes? Well, it will largely depend on you and what works for you individually. Personally, I found that for subjects such as Economics and Geography, I needed the markscheme near me as I was answering the questions from the past papers. I would have a scrap piece of paper next to me as well, glance at the question, jot down a rough answer, and then check with the markscheme what I missed out.

For Mathematics and Physics however, I found that by looking at the answers before I fully finished the question I was cheating myself. As a result I usually kept the markscheme away until I was totally stumped or found some sort of answer. The key thing to keep in mind is that you need to be constantly writing. Don't fool yourself into thinking you can go and lie down on your couch, past paper in one hand, markscheme in the other. Your revision needs to be active.

From my experience, I found that writing bullet-point scrap answers for past paper questions helped me learn the material much more than simply pondering over the answer and glancing at the markscheme. Remember what you are ultimately aiming for: to understand the material and be able to answer the question to the examiner's expectations. Your work with past papers and markschemes should make you feel more confident. If you pick up a past paper and are in total fear of what they ask, then clearly you are not yet prepared.

Don't underestimate the power of this technique. Markschemes are everything when it comes to scoring 7's in your subjects. Not only do they provide model answers but there is also a clear breakdown for the examiners for when to award marks. You have at your disposal everything that makes for a perfect examination. The closer you get to this perfection, the closer you will get to that grade 7. You will learn what it takes to make your paper worthy of a high mark. Learn to speak the examiner's lingo. Look for keywords and phrases, memorize certain model definitions, and learn to give them what they are looking for.

By the time I was midway through my exams I had past papers and markschemes all over the place along with the model answers I wrote myself. The coffee table, the bedroom, the bathroom, the kitchen – everything and everywhere was covered with past papers. When you surround yourself with this information, you are less likely to forget it. By constantly consulting the past papers and markschemes you ensure that you will not be surprised by anything that could come up in the real examination.

SL/HL

Some of you may wonder whether there is any sense in going through past papers at a level which you do not necessarily do. This is at times fine if you are a Higher Level student looking to get a greater grasp of the questions and the syllabus, but I would not recommend that you go through Higher Level papers if you are a Standard Level student. You will not be "challenging yourself". You will probably just get confused and frightened because you won't be able to answer most of the questions. For example, I avoided looking at HL Physics papers because I found the SL ones challenging and adequate enough. That being said, I got too familiar with most of the HL Geography papers available so I started to go over a few SL papers (which was ok because the gap between SL and HL was not that great). Use your common sense and don't waste your time doing papers that are of no use to you.

IB Past Papers Petition

Granting students access to the past papers has been a mission of mine for the past decade. So much so that I started a petition that asks the IBO to release all the materials for all students. I believe this is the only fair thing to do and I explain why in this change.org petition, which I have linked here:

www.change.org/p/international-baccclaureate-organization-make-past-papers-and-markschemes-freely-available-smartib

You can also find it by searching chang.org for the 'IB past papers petition'. Please if you could read the petition and sign it, it would be one step closer to getting all future students access to these essential materials.

The point of this chapter was to make you appreciate the potential that past papers and markschemes offer. The most successful IB candidates nowadays heavily rely on past examination questions simply because it is an unbeatable strategy. Your teachers will probably disagree that learning from past papers and markschemes is a more effective study technique than learning from textbooks/notes but they have not done the exams themselves. Trust me on this one. Unless you have done absolutely as many past papers as you possibly can you will not be ready to sit the examinations and get that grade 7. I cannot stress this enough but I trust you have enough good judgement to see the logic behind this.

22. The Power of Past Papers [Part II]

As established in the previous chapter, doing past year papers is almost crucial in excelling your IB exams and achieving a high overall grade. Nonetheless, it is also undeniably true that this process can feel excruciatingly repetitive and tiresome. With two to three papers per subject, one set of papers can consume four to five hours excluding the extra time required to check it. With six subjects and multiple sets of papers to do, this process can easily take hundreds of hours. I personally found this process to be boring and daunting during my IB days. Fortunately, along my revision journey I acquired some handy tips from my fellow peers to make this process much more efficient and manageable. I will be sharing those tips within this chapter to help you reap maximum benefits from doing past year papers and save some time as well.

Making Spreadsheets

Navigating through past papers can really get messy. With so many papers to complete and mark, it is common for one to lose track of which papers have been attempted, how did one do in such paper, etc. I recounted many instances where I started a paper only to realise halfway through that it was a paper I had already done before. This is one of the many ways being disorganized can waste time and hinder your past paper revision process.

Seeing how disorganised I was, a good friend of mine took 10 minutes of his time to make a simple spreadsheet for me. The spreadsheet contained a page for each subject, a column for the paper name (number, year, month, and time zone), a column to fill in the grade and a column to fill in extra remarks. Despite this solution's simplicity, it had significantly made my revision progress much easier. It spared me the mental effort of figuring out whether I had done a paper yet, this also meant that I would never do the same paper twice. The 10 minutes spent in making these spreadsheets will easily save you hours of time.

Beyond the time saving benefits, these spreadsheets can also help you keep track of your revision progress as now you can view all your paper scores at one place. This information can give some insightful implications that will make your revision process more effective.

Let's say you have been doing Physics papers. Through your spreadsheets, you will be able to see your performance on each paper. For example, if Bob consistently scores around 80% to 90% in Paper 1 and 3, but only scores around 60% to 70% for paper 2. Bob can do more Paper 2s as he is performing well enough for his Paper 1s & 3s. This is just an example on how making spreadsheets can make your past paper revision more focused and targeted. Not only do these spreadsheets save you a massive amount of time, but it also helps you take notice of and address your weak points.

The same thing can be said across different subjects. If you observe that you have been consistently scoring in the safe grade 7 range for your past papers in a subject, this can be a signal that tells you can work on your weaker subjects instead as there is not much practical use in scoring a really high 7 if your other subjects are still lacking. Therefore, do yourself a Favor and spend 10 minutes setting up these spreadsheets before you start your past paper revision. It will do you wonders.

Checking the Syllabus

As mentioned in the previous chapter, it is recommended that you do at least 5 years' worth of papers. However, every seven years, IB changes its curriculum for a subject. It is therefore beneficial to check the IBO website regarding the latest curriculum change. Sometimes these curriculum changes can be minor but often they are quite drastic. A different curriculum might include different topics, different questions, or even an entirely new paper. Therefore, doing past papers from the most updated curriculum is much more effective. So, for those of you who want to save a bit more time, you can do papers from the latest curriculum instead of doing 5 years' worth of papers.

I had a friend sitting for the November 2023 examination session who was determined to do 12 years of papers for Mathematics, starting from 2010. He did about 7 years' worth of papers progressively up to 2017, performed quite well for those papers, and decided to stop there and not do the more recent papers. During the official IB examinations, he told me that he was shocked to see the style of questions change drastically. As a result, he didn't do so well and did not get the grade he wanted. Therefore, a lesson to learn from this incident is that there shouldn't be any situation where you are doing the old curriculum's papers if you haven't done the newest set of papers yet. As doing well on older papers might not mean that you are prepared to tackle the newest curriculum.

However, if you have done all papers from the latest curriculum update feel free to do more papers for the practice, but don't feel too scared when you see a completely alien question, as it is likely that such question is no longer in the new syllabus.

Reflection

A common mistake that many people make when doing past papers is that they simply do past papers, mark their papers, and then move on to the next paper without any reflection. This causes students to spend hours upon hours doing past papers, while repeating the same mistakes and experiencing minimal improvements since the first paper they did. It is definitely recommended to do past paper revision with a good dose of reflection and content revision.

What I mean by this is let's say you're doing a Paper 2 for Chemistry. After marking your paper, take some time to analyse your mistakes. Did you make the mistake because you were careless? Was it a conceptual error? Or was it because you misunderstood the command terms? Subsequently, act upon your analysis and do necessary content revision. This could involve re-reading the entire Organic Chemistry chapter, or it could be something small like remembering how to calculate the formal charge of an atom. This way revision also becomes less boring as you take a break from doing questions to do your content revision.

Usually, a mix between doing past papers coupled with content revision results in a much more effective revision process. If you do this, you should see the average score of your past papers to increase. This is much more effective than passively doing your past papers without any reflection.

Record Your Mistakes

Everyone hates that feeling when they are unable to do a question that they have gotten wrong in the past. There's an easy way to prevent this from happening during your actual IBO exams. When you're doing past papers, compile every mistake (and its correction) that you made in one document. This especially applies to the mistakes that you made that were very silly, specific, or niche, e.g. Colour of a gas or what is an aprotic or protic solvent. This consolidated list will prove to be extremely valuable. A quick look at this list will allow you to remember all the silly mistakes you made on previous past papers and ensure you steer clear of repeating the same mistake on exam day.

Replicate Exam Conditions

I know in the previous chapter it was mentioned that you can do past papers in various settings, such as doing it with the mark scheme next to you, it is still recommended that you do one or two past papers for each subject in strict exam conditions. This means no mark scheme, no phones, no breaks, time yourself as you would in an actual exam. Use a physical data booklet if you can as well and don't even stop the timer for toilet breaks. Replicate the exam conditions as closely as possible, as this can really help you prepare for what otherwise would be unforeseen problems.

I made the mistake of not familiarising myself with my data booklet during my IB Chemistry exams. This led me to copy down the wrong bond energy value for the C – C bond as I did not know there were different bond values which costed me quite a few marks. Luckily, I still got my grade 7, but I know many others who lost their grade 7 due to easily avoidable mistakes that could have been prevented had they familiarised themselves with the data booklet. This is one of the ways replicating exam conditions can help you see unforeseen circumstances that only you would know once you are in such a condition.

This chapter aims to provide further insights on how you can maximise your past paper revision. By using some of the tips in this chapter, you are sure to save ample amounts of time and also reap more benefits from past paper revision.

23. Examination Technique [Part I]

Although you should keep in mind that you need specific revision techniques for each individual subject, there remains much to be said about examination technique in general. Your success in the exams will not only rely on how well prepared you are in terms of the material, but also how well you perform under pressure. To deal with this you will need to master a few exam techniques. Most of them are simple, but nonetheless are often forgotten or severely underestimated.

Time Management

You need to be able to allocate your time proportionally across the entire duration of the exam. This includes taking off a few minutes from the beginning for reading and the end for proofreading. Whatever time you devote to actual writing and working out should be spaced out across the whole exam. Luckily, the IB have made your task even simpler as they now indicate how many points each question and sub-question is worth. For most papers this is the same year in year out however pay close attention to this as it will decide how many minutes you will need to spend on the question. If it takes you less time to answer than you had anticipated, then move on to the next question as you may need that extra time.

You absolutely must, and under no exceptions, finish your exam from beginning to end. If you have not answered all the questions that were required of you then you can consider your grade 7 a missed opportunity. Once the examiner sees that you have left questions at the end blank, this immediately sends out a signal that you have mismanaged your time. This mistake is made every year by countless bright students and the only reason for it is poor organization and time use – something that is not expected from the best candidates.

There is absolutely no reason why you should not have enough time to finish the exam. I hear this excuse all the time but the truth is you did have enough time, you just didn't use it wisely. It's one thing to leave a question blank because you just had no idea how to answer it – which is something I also highly discourage. But it's a totally different matter if you didn't answer the last few questions because you messed up your timing.

Command Terms

These 'command terms' are specific words and phrases that the IB like to use in their exam questions. The IB examiners are not just trying to grade you on your knowledge of the subject, but they want to test your ability to answer the question that they have set out for you.

This is not something that is unique to the IB examinations. At university, and also in some job applications, you will be tested on your ability to really understand what is being asked. There is no point in answering *how* something happened if the question asked *why* it happened. Get used to reading questions carefully and answering accordingly because this is a skill that you will reuse often.

Again, your success at identifying and answering these command terms will largely depend on your practice with past papers. That being said, no amount of preparation can spare you from being careless. For this reason make sure to double-check what is being asked. If time is available then I even recommend you highlight or underline the command term so that you don't forget what it is you need to answer. There's nothing worse than writing an answer explaining something when you were simply asked to define it.

A full list and explanation of command terms can be found in the syllabus/subject guide for the subject in question. These can be found online, or by asking your teacher. The terms differ from subject to subject. Please make sure you understand the command terms well before you go into the exams.

Extra Materials

Along with your lucky charms and favourite pen I strongly advise that you bring in a well-functioning clock in order to be able to manage your time properly. This varies amongst personal taste but I know that some like to have wrist watches, while some bring digital clocks, and I have even seen some bring countdown timers that were preset to countdown the exam duration. You need to keep in mind that although there may already be a clock in the exam room you could be assigned a seat all the way in the back. Perhaps your eyesight isn't as great as you thought it was and as a result you struggle to see the time. Don't take any of these chances. Bring some sort of time device with you.

I always have a little bit of paranoia when it comes to calculators malfunctioning in exams so I strongly recommend that you bring a spare calculator (not necessarily the graphing one) or at least a spare set of batteries for the calculator-based exams. It goes without saying that you need a spare pen or two just in case the one you have runs out. Also, try to bring a set of highlighters because you can use these to remind yourself of the key terms in a question as discussed before in this chapter.

Answer the Whole Question and Nothing but the Question

This is self-explanatory. When answering any question on the IB exams you must make sure you address the exact phrasing in the question and give the examiner exactly what he/she is looking for. For all my examinations, I brought along a highlighter or two so that I could highlight key words in the question sentence. For example, if a math question stated "give the answer in cm^3" I would highlight the cm^3 part. I know that this might sound a little pointless and a waste of time but you would be surprised to see how many candidates "forget" certain parts of the question. One common example is when a question asks you to "explain why" and you write an excellent essay on "how". By highlighting the "explain why" part you will significantly reduce the chances of this kind of slip up.

There is usually absolutely no reason to write more than what is required. If the question is worth two marks this means the examiner is probably looking for two key points – no more, no less. You don't have time to be writing everything you know. You need to pick the most valuable bits of information and keep to your own time limit. There are no "bonus" points and you will not get extra credit for writing what is not required. Remember, the key is to write efficiently and aim for maximum marks with minimum nonsense.

Less is More – Usually

There are a few exceptions to the above paragraphs. If, in the unlikely scenario that you stumble upon a question you don't know how to fully answer, then sometimes (very rarely!) writing something that you do know on the topic might give you a few marks. This technique is very beneficial if used wisely, but it can also be very risky and damaging to your time if you abuse it. I can give you a good example. Suppose you get a "define" question worth two marks. This usually means you need to give two concrete points in order to get full marks. Let's suppose that you could only remember one. Whereas normally I would suggest that you not waste your time and just move on to the next question, there will be times when a little bit more 'filler' might get you that other mark. Either expand on your first point or throw in some other information that could, maybe, give you the remaining mark (like adding an example).

Remember that directly you will not get marked down for writing more. Indirectly, you always run the risk of losing valuable time. There is a general belief that examiners will only read the first few points you make and ignore the rest if you haven't hit the nail on the head yet. Personally, I find that this notion is too general to apply to every examiner in every subject. Your best bet is to keep writing "educated guesses" until you think you have good odds at getting most of the marks. You won't lose marks, but you might not gain any either. Remember that you are facing a balancing act – writing more BS versus having more time to answer later questions.

24. Examination Technique [Part II]

Give Yourself Space

One of the first things you should do when you sit at your desk is carefully lay out all your materials. You don't want to be doing a three-hour examination curled up uncomfortably in a tiny working space. Place the examination paper on one side and the fill-in answer booklet next to it. Arrange your pencil case and all of your materials somewhere neatly in the corner. Make sure that your workspace is not one giant mess or else this could reflect negatively on your answers.

Start With What You Know

If the exam is parts-based, then I highly advise you to start with the parts where you are more comfortable and ones that you find more enjoyable. Not only will this ensure that you do not waste time attempting trickier questions but you will also feel more confident and optimistic knowing that you have already answered many questions correctly. There is no strict rule governing where you need to start and finish your section-based exam so don't treat it in a strictly chronological order. Do what you feel happier doing first and leave the trickier bits for later.

Handwriting

Do you have handwriting that needs its own Rosetta Stone? If so, you need to make at least some effort to improve it or else you risk having your paper deciphered angrily and possibly downgraded. I highly suggest that when you are doing past papers in your revision, you start to focus also on the neatness of your handwriting. I personally haven't heard of any cases where a student's paper was simply illegible, but I am sure that they exist. If you find that your writing speed is significantly slower, then you might be better off not bothering with drastically improving your handwriting. If your teachers need to constantly remind you to write neater then please do pay attention. Nothing is more frustrating to an examiner than to decode your cluttered calligraphy.

Leaving Early

There are very few things in the world that frustrate and anger me more than seeing candidates get up and leave examinations with plenty of time to spare. You are given the time limit for a reason – use it! You must be incredibly careless to give up and just leave the exam with an hour to spare. There is absolutely no reason – none whatsoever – for you to leave before the time is up. Don't think you can just cross your arms on your desk and put your head down for a nap either. That would be equally retarded. I don't care whether you think you have answered all the questions and proofread enough. Unless you are 100% confident that you got 100% don't even consider leaving early. And no, you're not "cool" or "rebellious" for leaving with time to spare.

Proofreading

You absolutely must make sure you leave a few minutes at the end of your examination for proofreading. This is more important in non-essay based exams such as Mathematics and the Group 4 topics. Even in examinations for Economics, going back and making sure your diagrams are properly labelled could score you a few extra points. I'm not suggesting you make sure that you crossed all your T's and dotted all of your I's but at least make sure the majority of the exam is legible and that you avoided any silly mistakes. The few marks that you pick up when proofreading could prove vital if you're on the edge between two distinct marks. You will lose and gain most of your marks in the beginning and at the end of your examination – so make sure you make a positive start and always go back and proofread at the end.

Ignoring Distractions

Although the exams are supposed to happen in complete silence there may be times when distractions are simply inevitable. For example the kid sitting next to you who has never heard of cough medicine and is having non-stop bronchitis-like coughing. Or the student who accidentally drops his pencil only for it to roll all the way across the room. I remember for one of my first Mathematics exams the weather in the morning was terrible. It was hailing, raining and thundering all at once. The fact that our examination centre had a semi-glass ceiling provided a very surreal Dolby-Digital surround sound. It was probably the most frustrating thing to encounter when you are trying to focus on a HL Mathematics paper.

You need to teach yourself how to work around distractions. Don't become frustrated and punch the desk. Nor should you start to complain and lash out on your examination coordinator for having so many distractions. Just sit your exam and focus on what's in front of you. Do whatever you need to do to clear your head and relax. Perhaps invest and get used to wearing earplugs to drown out the noise?

Last Minute Exam Checklist

Have you done the following before entering your exam:

- Did you bring two pencils and two pens?
- Are they sharpened / refilled?
- Is your calculator charged?
- Do you have at least 1L of water for every 2 hours the exam goes for?

It may seem obvious, but last year when I did the exams I forgot some of these due to stress, and thus did not score as highly as I could have scored. Trust me, you'll want to have water when you're staring down a 20 mark multi-part physics question. The point is spare yourself the misery and just make sure you've prepared your stationary and water beforehand. However, don't drink so much water that you have to take a bathroom break and waste valuable exam time – this is a mistake that too many students also make.

You will do fine.

Good luck with the exams!

25. Acing the Literature (Group 1) Exam

The following sections of the book will attempt to cover in greater detail the specifics behind each IB group and subject.

We begin with group 1: studies in language and literature.

Paper 1

This will be a short snippet on the best way to practice English and prepare for the exams, but first a short back story on my love hate relationship with the subject at hand. I was never particularly good at English. Despite trying very hard I always found it difficult to perform as well as other students, most of all I found it difficult to break that 6-7 barrier (which I did during the exams, but not with my external assessments). Had I known what I know now I would have been able to achieve a solid 7 without any problems. My class work averaged out to a 6, however to my astonishment I received solid 7s in both the exams (19/20 and 20/25). I was 3% off a 7, so had I put in that little extra effort to get my IA grade from a 13/20 to a 16/20 I would have been able to cross that grade boundary.

Now, the first step towards being good at English is of course listening and participating in class discussions, in addition to reading the books and texts that are assigned and doing your work on time. In addition to these tips a few things I found to be very useful were:

1) To read around the subject, this entails learning about the authors, their style, their motivation and other authors that resemble them. By doing so you will be able to explore and reflect on very advanced concepts in your essays. You will be

able to justify the author's choices in theme, rhetorical devices and why they even explored the subject matter at hand. Put effort into this and you will be able to hit those top scores in the essays.

2) Practice, practice, practice. Don't worry if your essays aren't perfect, as the exams approach, you should time yourself doing essays (past papers), get feedback from your teachers and improve using that feedback. The point is to improve one aspect of your writing each time, (these may include things such as organisation, inclusion of rhetoric devices, tone and so on). I was able to move from scoring 13/20 to a 19/20 in two months. You should aim to do at least five practice essays for each paper.

In English A L&L, Paper 1 is a textual analysis of either one (if you're SL) or two (if you're HL) unseen texts. If you're SL, you typically get a choice between a literary and multimodal text, while HL students must write about both. This section provides various ideas to develop the necessary skills for Paper 1. I have also provided a short list of tips, which should help you prepare for the exam in a more focused way.

The Band Descriptors

The first piece of crucial advice is something that you should do for all of your subjects really – get your hands on the official subject guide and read the band descriptors for the Paper 1. I'm not going to replicate them for fear of copyright infringement, but you know where to find this document. It will give you a sense of what the examiner is looking for and merely writing one relevant sentence which 'answers' one of the descriptors could easily get you an easy mark or two.

The Basics

As was mentioned, the externally-assessed Paper 1 consists of two unseen texts, one literary and one multimodal. Possible literary text types include a brochure, a travel guide or an opinion column while possible multimodal text types include a comic strip, an advertisement or infographic. Both texts are accompanied by one guiding question for which you must construct an essay response within the allotted time, which is 80 minutes for SL and 140 minutes for HL including 5 minutes of reading time during which no writing is allowed.

Firstly, whoever you are, wherever you live, whatever subjects you're taking, and whatever your favourite food might be, I want to let you know that you are capable of acing this.

You're capable of acing this because you're brave enough to be doing the hardest possible high school curriculum offered in the world. The technique that I'm about to outline was shown to me by my High School English teacher (she is awesome). It helped my peers and me a lot and I hope that it'll help you as well.

The P.E.A.L Method

I'm going to keep things short and simple because I know you're super busy. So, what is PEAL?

P = Point

E = Evidence

A = Analysis

L = Link

It's really simple and straightforward. Essentially, what we're trying to do here is to break down a seemingly complex and wordy text into a manner that we can best understand it and then effectively communicate it in our essay. Let me give you an example:

Imagine that you want to analyse the following paragraph:

'In LA, you can't do anything unless you drive. Now I can't do anything unless I drink. And the drink-drive combination, it really isn't possible out there.

If you so much as loosen your seatbelt or drop your ashes or pick your nose, then it's an Alcatraz autopsy with the questions asked later. Any indiscipline, you feel, any variation, and there's a bullhorn, a set of scope sights, and a coppered pig drawing a bead on your rug.

So what can a poor boy do? You come out of the hotel, the Vraimont. Over boiling Watts the downtown sky line carries a smear of God's green snot. You walk left, you walk right, you are a bank rat on a busy river. This restaurant serves no drink, this one serves no meat, this one serves no heterosexuals. You can get your chimp shampooed, you can get your dick tattooed, twenty-four hours, but can you get lunch?

- Excerpt from Money by Martin Amis

It doesn't really matter where this comes from: in fact it'll be better if we don't know context here as you'll truly be able to see this technique put to good use. So, let's start.

(1) The point that I want to make here is that Amis (the author) utilizes hyperbole to effectively mirror the personality of the narrator (a man with a big ego called John Money) with the way the text is written.

(2) The Evidence that I'm going to use is:

'If you so much as loosen your seatbelt or drop you ashes or pick your nose, then it's an Alcatraz autopsy with the questions asked later.' to describe the danger of driving in LA.

and

'This restaurant serves no drink, this one serves no meat, this one serves no heterosexuals' to describe the varied and distinct tastes of the city.

(3) My Analysis is the following (in super rough terms, don't worry we're going to clean this all up when we put it all together):

Amis hints at his character's grandiose and outspoken personality by making him mention that seemingly small, inconsequential actions (picking one's nose, dropping a cig) can lead to huge car accidents, outlined in a humorous, entertaining way (Alcatraz autopsy with the questions asked later).

This use of hyperbole can also be seen when referring to LA's normally distinct and niche restaurants: Amis juxtaposes in a comical fashion the pickiness of these restaurants (this one serves no....etc) and can effectively communicate his character's distaste whilst simultaneously keeping in sync with his personality.

(4) Finally, you Link everything back to your thesis. I kind of already did this in my last paragraph by stating 'whilst simultaneously keeping in sync with his personality'. What you're trying to do here is to make sure that this micro-argument of yours is doing something to advance your thesis statement and makes cohesive, structural sense to your whole essay. As in this case we don't really have a thesis (I obviously can't write you a whole essay right now, but you get the point).

It can also be seen that (1) Amis utilizes hyperbole to effectively mirror the personality of his narrator (John Money) with the way in which the text is written. Indeed, (2) when describing the danger of driving in LA, Money states that 'If you so much as loosen your seatbelt or drop your ashes or pick your nose, then it's an Alcatraz autopsy with the questions asked later.' (3) Amis hints to his character's grandiose and outspoken personality by making him mention that seemingly small, inconsequential actions (picking one's nose, dropping a cig) can lead to huge car accidents, outlined in a humorous, entertaining way (Alcatraz autopsy with the questions asked later). This use of hyperbole can also be seen when referring to LA's normally distinct and niche restaurants: Amis juxtaposes in a comical fashion the pickiness of these restaurants (this one serves no) and is able to effectively communicate his character's distaste whilst simultaneously keeping in sync with his personality. (4) Insert Link Back to Thesis, something like: this all steers us towards the main idea that Amis is utilizing a wide variety of literary techniques to emphasize certain aspects of John Money's character to the reader.

This may seem like an extremely mechanical way of writing, but the transitions can get much more fluid, and you can intertwine your quotations in a nicer way than I just did to show you. This is just a basic, rudimentary way of writing: sometimes I hear my friends telling me that they get too lost reading the texts and can't structure their writing, and I advise this method to overcome that problem.

Literary or multimodal text? (For SL students)

In the exam, many students prefer the multimodal text as it doesn't require hefty amounts of reading and may appear easier to interpret. However, it is definitely worth it to at least skim through the literary text during the 5-minute reading time, as it may actually end up being the easier option. This is because multimodal texts, especially if they are satirical or humorous in nature like a comic strip, often aim to convey deeper messages that may go over your head in the heat of the moment. If these messages and critiques are left unmentioned in your analysis, your ambitions of getting a 7 are pretty much out the window. Because of this, it is definitely worth it to consider both texts and think seriously about which one you'll write about.

How do I plan?

When it comes to planning, the 5-minute reading time is your best friend. During this time, you should already start brainstorming and planning in your head. Write your thoughts down right after the 5 minutes are up. After that, I'd recommend spending a maximum of 20 minutes on annotating your texts and further planning.

When planning, make sure you ask yourself the following questions:

1. What is my main argument/thesis? Your thesis should be a direct answer to the guiding question. No matter what you write in the essay, all of it must link back to the thesis one way or another, so make sure you're frequently referring back to it even in the planning stage.

2.	How will I split my body paragraphs? Say the question is "How does the author convey a sense of urgency?" Of course, you could go the classic route and divide your body paragraphs by technique i.e. he conveys urgency through short sentence structures, by using emotive language etc. You could also, though, divide them based on effects on the reader i.e. he conveys urgency by making the reader panic, by reminding the reader of a time when he himself was in need etc. You can also split paragraphs based on, for example, target audience. When you're planning, make sure you choose the option you feel most comfortable with given the provided texts.

3.	What are my best points of analysis? If you look at the mark bands for Paper 1, you'll see level 7 analysis must be 'insightful'. This means that, when you're planning, you need to make sure your points are strong and worth at least a few lines of analysis. Also, if you can manage to connect features of the text to real-world contexts, this is great, as that is where your analysis truly starts to become 'insightful'.

Additional Tips

- Remember the big 5 (structure, stylistic devices, tone/mood, content/theme, audience/purpose)! Write about each of those and you're golden. Also remember to breathe and take a break when the time is halfway. Just relax for a minute and set your mind straight.
- Annotate what jumps off the page - recurrent ideas, devices, links in sentence structures or themes, punctuation... anything that holds a purpose. However, be sure to push these ideas further in your annotation than just noting them down - develop links, themes or motifs discussed by the author, negations in the text, tentative assumptions/conclusions and so on. This is by far the most important step and will save you time, brain space and stress once you begin writing.

The conclusion really brings home the analytical findings of your essay, hopefully in such a way so as to contribute to a nuanced discussion of the text. I would include sentences briefly (and I mean briefly!) recounting the findings of each paragraph, and then I would have a final closing sentence which summarized what I believe to be the author's/poet's main argument within the text. The conclusion often takes me 20+ minutes. I think strong control over language definitely helps here the most with a nice final clinching paragraph. Writing a conclusion is not something you just do after you've written your paragraphs with no planning in advance. Your paragraphs should all slightly hint towards it, and the conclusion should tie all the paragraphs together to strongly support your thesis statement.

Finally, try getting help from your teacher, or someone who you think could most closely emulate an examiner. Write an essay based on a practice prompt, either look at it yourself impartially or ask whenever you've found to look at it for you and point out its weaknesses. (While doing practice essays, I suggest limiting yourself to around 10-15 minutes less than exam time.)

Do that twice or thrice. Find out what mistakes are minor issues you can remember to handle, and what mistakes are major things you need to learn to do better.

Paper 2

In the English A L&L Paper 2, you will be given four essay questions which you will have to answer with reference to two of the books you studied. Therefore, it is a test of understanding literature in context. Although the questions will vary from exam to exam, they will always focus on the connection between style, form, author, purpose and audience as well as central themes like identity, environment or setting.

These pages offer an overview of the requirements, the criteria and tips on Paper 2 essay writing. Besides familiarizing yourself with these pages, you will want to study previous exam questions, practice writing under exam conditions and research your literary texts carefully.

Although it seems as if a quarter of your IB grade is determined in one brief sitting, in fact you can do a lot to prepare for this exam so that it is not so nerve-racking. Careful planning and a clear strategy are half the battle. What one writes is only the tip of a very large iceberg.

The Basics

Answer 1 of 4 unseen essay questions. SL and HL students receive exactly the same 4 questions.

Essay must answer one question in relation to two books studied. You CANNOT write about the book you used for your Individual Oral.

Proposed Paper 2 Essay Structure:

A. Introduction
a)   Hook (one or two sentences addressing the guiding question or statement in relation to broader real-world contexts)
b)   Background summary (brief background to the texts and authors)

c) Thesis (what are you trying to prove?)

d) Focus (how will you prove your thesis? This is where you state your arguments)

B. Body (aim for three or four 'PEACE ACT' paragraphs following this structure)

a) Point (topic sentence for first work)

b) Evidence (direct quotation or description from first work)

c) Analysis (specific focus on literary techniques and their effects on the reader in first work)

d) Connect (connect first book analysis to second book analysis using transitions like 'Similarly...', 'On the contrary...')

e) Evidence (direct quotation or description from second work)

f) Analysis (specific focus on literary techniques and their effects on the reader in second work)

g) Compare (compare similarities and differences between the two works in relation to the guiding question)

h) Thesis link (link all analysis back to thesis with one or two sentences to keep focus)

C. Conclusion

a) State Thesis (using different words/phrases)

b) Summary of main arguments (do not include new information)

c) Clincher (final sentence: should leave examiner satisfied you have covered all areas, but should also attempt to provoke further inquiry, or new dimension of looking at question)

So, this is the structure you want to follow. A common query that students have is in regard to how they should mention their quotes whilst writing their essays. What I like to do is integrate them fluidly within my paragraphs; this takes practice, but here are a few examples from my writing:

Natsume identifies intricacies and details in British culture that seem entirely foreign to him coming from Japan; he notes the impeccable fashion sense that surrounds him: '*herds of women walk around like horned lionesses with nets on their faces*' and notices a distinct height difference '*but when we rush past one another I see he is about two inches taller than me*'(Natsume in Phillips, R161). Natsume's experience as an outsider in Britain, according to Caryl Philips, '*helped him to become the fully mature and outstandingly gifted writer that he subsequently became*'(Phillips, R161).

I hope you can see what I'm trying to do; note that each quote naturally complements the flow of the paragraph. You never need to explicitly state that you are about to use a quote; rather, just insert it within your body as nicely as you can.

The thesis statement of your essay is also extremely important; many English teachers have told me that often to gauge a writer's quality they examine his thesis statement. The more clear and compelling it is, the more credibility you gain as a writer in their eyes. Remember that you should be aiming to provide an argument; otherwise, your whole essay won't really have any meaning or substance (every single word you write should in some way back that thesis up).

BAD THESIS:

In this novel, Kanye West argues that we cannot justify the usage of drones and that their increased prevalence is harmful to members of society.

GOOD THESIS:

Though there may be considerable advantages to the usage of drones, West attempts to demonstrate that the worrying possibilities of mass surveillance and civilian losses, specifically in regards to the recent incidents in Orange County, are ultimately too precarious a path to follow.

I'm going to be honest: you should try to use flowery language to spice up your essays. It's just the truth. Before you go sit that exam, go on www.thesaurus.com and try to replace some common words you'd use with some nice, juicy ones.

In terms of transitioning between paragraphs aim to be clear and simple. 'It is possible to see the idea of..' or 'One argument put forward is…' are pretty good.

Now, listen up: I'm about to share a very valuable piece of advice with all of you:

Get your whole class to create a shared Google Doc with the following table:

Themes	Book A	Book B
	Quotes + Analysis	Quotes + Analysis

Then, together with your class, start filling the table.

It should get to a point where you have about twenty themes and plenty of quotes and analysis to back it up. Sharing is caring, and in this case, sharing will get you good grades.

Memorizing the quotes may seem daunting but it doesn't have to be that hard: what I recommend is that you paste about ten quotes you may use around your house. Literally post them outside your shower, perhaps, so that each time you bathe your beautiful body you also remember those quotes. Or put them up somewhere near your bed so that you go to sleep thinking about English.

How to Score in IB English Paper 1 (advice by a 45 pointer who scored 19/20)

Hello IB Students!

Struggling with **IB English Paper 1**? Not to worry, here are some free and proven strategies I personally used to not only score a 19/20 for my Paper 1 but also 45 points for my IB!

The 2 Road Block Students Face:

There are two reasons students struggle with IB English Paper 1

(1) The challenge in effectively analysing and discussing the unseen texts. Many students feel overwhelmed by the need to quickly comprehend, interpret, and write about a text they've never seen before. It can be daunting to dissect the nuanced meanings and language, all under exam and timed conditions

(2) Missing out on the Purpose. While the Paper 1 largely tests you on your understanding of literary devices and techniques, many students forget to link these to the primary PURPOSE of the text. This is single-handedly the difference between scoring a 5 and 6, instead of a 7!

Effective Strategies to Overcome This:

1. **Practice Regularly**: Start early and make it a habit to analyse a variety of texts. This includes prose, poetry, and visual texts. The more you practice, the easier it becomes to **identify** devices and you train yourself to understand more and more nuanced texts!

2. **Develop a Strong Thesis**: Your thesis is the backbone of your essay, without one you would have nothing to link your claims to! Make it clear, argumentative, and directly related to the question. A strong thesis will guide your analysis and ensure your essay remains focused rather than explaining devices for no reason.

3. **Analyse, Don't Summarise**: Focus on how and also WHY the author uses specific literary techniques to convey issues or opinions, and be aware when you might be retelling the text!

4. **Personal Voice and Insight**: Finally, while it's important to use evidence from the text, also include your own interpretation and insight which are relevant BEYOND the scope of the text. This makes you stand out among examiners, showing that your claims are relevant even outside of the text and making them even stronger.

TLDR:

Remember, to score high in IB English Paper 1 it is not enough to simply show your understanding of the text. Rather, how effectively you can analyse and evaluate the authorial choices with relevance to the PURPOSE, and doing so all under exam conditions. With consistent practice and a strategic approach, I'm confident you can overcome the challenges and excel in your IB English exams.

26. IO Tips and Tricks

The Individual Oral is for many students one of the most daunting tasks during the IB English A L&L course. It involves a 10-minute commentary on a chosen literary extract as well as a studied body of work both in relation to one global issue. This is followed by an approximately 5-minute student-teacher discussion during which the teacher asks the student additional questions about their analysis. This may all sound quite complicated, so how do you do well?

Oral Commentary Tips

Listen in class when analysing the texts and bodies of work (BoWs). If you take detailed notes on them in class and ask questions to the teacher if there are any sections you do not understand or have neglected, this will make the final stages of your IO preparation a lot easier.

It helps if you get a clean printed copy of each extract and BoW with enough space between the lines and in the margins. This will enable you to make annotations using a range of sources such as your class notes, your own interpretations, and the Internet. From these annotations, you can begin constructing the 10 bullet points of analysis that you're allowed to take with you into the examination room.

The Text Discussion

Make sure to read the text extract very carefully – and more than once. Reading the text extract at least twice will allow you to pick up on some of the intricacies that you miss in the first reading when you are focusing on literary devices and broader themes.

Also, you need to make sure to have a good set of notes. On average, you can have up to 20-30 handwritten pages of notes for the lengthier texts. Things such as plot analysis, structure, context, character analysis, thematic/symbol analysis should all be covered. This will give you a holistic and diverse understanding of the texts, and also give you the option to link to all aspects of the text during the actual discussion.

Make sure to revise well from these notes. There is absolutely no point in spending many hours creating amazing notes if you don't understand them and remember them. You will need to make a conscious effort to revise both the body of work and the literary extract at least five times before the final IO. This way you will have a thorough understanding of the main conventions of the text, and will be able to recite certain quotes to support your answers.

It is also a good idea to practice an IO discussion with a friend. Preferably you should run some trial IOs in the week leading up to the real deal. You can do this in person or even on the phone. If you have a list of questions ready, this will be great practice. The questions don't have to be perfect – just enough to let your partner practice responding to oral prompts and displaying their knowledge of the text. You should benefit from this practise on both sides of the table. Doing it yourself will obviously show you your own flaws and let you know where you need improvement, but acting as the examiner can help you get in the mind of the examiner for when you do the real thing, so you're better able to know what sorts of things you should cover in your initial commentary, and how to respond to questions. It's all about practice.

General Tips

1) You must know the author's background, important themes/motifs, poetic concerns, and the general context behind the work in question. Typically, these will all contribute to form a coherent, roughly one-minute-long introduction into which you can fit some of this knowledge to prove you have a broad understanding of each work.

2) If you are studying prose or plays, I suggest you literally re-read the book several times. I went to the extent of annotating each page of the novel and making important notes of motifs, dialogues, and important plot points for each chapter. Of course, this helps when the work is divided into chapters or sections, but if it isn't, you could always devise your own organization and structure to the work in question. If anything, this should only strengthen your understanding of the work. I suggest you first become very familiar with the text.

3) Throughout your analysis, it is also quite important to embed both the larger effects of the features you are discussing. For instance, you could say: "the racist remarks and scathing diction are utilized to portray a shift in John's character". You could go about developing it and say this instead: "the racist remarks and scathing diction utilized by John aim to not only portray John being desensitized towards racism, but also the prevalence of Apartheid during the 1950s." Not the best

example, but it extends the analysis and indicates that you are knowledgeable about the work's theme and implications.

4) In your conclusion, make sure to make some lasting impression. Don't be that person who says "In conclusion, author X utilizes various literary devices such as Y and Z to develop her thesis". That's garbage. Rather, try to synthesize your analysis into a whole and give it a larger meaning. What does it all mean? What was Sylvia Plath's purpose in writing this essay? What other works of Plath does this work relate to? As a reader, what can we get away from it? Always remember that literature is a powerful tool. With just pen and paper, one person can evoke an emotional response from an entire population or spur change. Consider the larger implications of each work, even when you think there really isn't much -- I can assure you that it can be found.

5) A couple days before your exam, practice your presentation over and over with a stopwatch showing you how long you've been speaking for. Chances are the first draft of your IO structure will not fit within the 10 minutes you're allotted, so it's imperative that you shorten/elongate your analysis so it fits neatly into that timeframe. Also consider whether or not you speak faster or slower in high-pressure scenarios, as this may also impact the final commentary's length and thus your marks (especially in the 'Focus and Organisation' criterion).

6) Familiarise yourself with the author's style. An excellent way to prepare for your IO is to familiarise yourself with the sorts of literary features and themes most common within a text. So, a good idea for your preparation is to flick through and look very closely at the author's styles for various things and make sure you're aware of a few key instances where the style is used. As an example (because I realise that's not the greatest explanation), Jane Austen always introduces characters with a

few key descriptive words which cause the reader to form a view of a character usually before hearing them speak or seeing them do anything. So, knowing that this is one aspect of her style and that it's possible an introduction or description of a character might pop up in my IO, I would make sure I was aware of at least one key instance of this happening so I could knowingly refer to it in my IO.

Be sure to look at all aspects of writing style so you literally know enough about the general way the author writes that you can say something about almost any page in the book/body of work etc. when you're asked about it in the follow-up discussion! You always want to show good knowledge of the work as a whole.

7) Imagine it is on paper and structure it. Literally imagine that your essay is being written by you rather than spoken by you. What do you need in every essay? Introduction, main body, conclusion. Don't forget to include an introduction (including that all-important putting the extracts in context chronologically, briefly mentioning the authors, dates of publication etc.) and also a conclusion. The beginning and ending of presentations are both extremely important for the overall impact. You can do a great job but have a terrible ending and it's the lame ending which sticks in people's minds.

8) Don't fail to show outside knowledge! Reading through the extract and finding yourself remembering a related fact/incident as you read? Say it! It's really important that you make the context (and your excellent knowledge of it) very clear, so if you remember something related, pop it in.

Think that something a character does is reflective of something they do later, earlier, or their general behaviour? Mention the other event as well. Don't waste loads of time on it, keep all these outside points reasonably succinct, but whatever you do don't overlook them or fail to mention them.

9) Set yourself up to achieve fluency via knowing how you work. You want to appear extremely competent and fluent. Generally, when in a state of panic, the only way to achieve this (besides obviously making sure you know what you're talking about!) is to make excellent use of the 10 bullet points so when panic strikes, you can stay on track. If, when you're practicing with a stopwatch, the notes you've made aren't enough to stop you blanking, re-consider the way in which you make notes.

10) Final tip. Know EVERY literary device by heart. Not just the generic ones like metaphor, simile, allusion, etc. Know the obscure ones like asyndeton, synecdoche, antithesis, etc, PARTICULARLY the ones that pertain to your BoWs and extracts. Don't forget that syntactical analysis is also important, especially for prose. It helps when you know grammar too (infinitive verbs, cataloguing, etc.).

27. Blasting Through Language B

Language B is a great opportunity to score a 6 or 7 easily for most students. For convenience and consistency, this section is written from the point of view of someone taking French as their Language B subject, however almost all the advice can be applied to other languages as well.

How is the Language B examination structured?

As of 2022, every Language B examination consists of four parts: a writing paper, a reading comprehension paper, a listening comprehension paper and the individual oral (IO) which, like in Language A, acts as the course's IA.

For Paper 1 (writing), you are given three prompts from which you select one. This can be a little tricky, as not only do you have to understand each prompt and choose the one you can write about best, but you are also responsible for selecting the most suitable text type for that prompt. If you select the wrong text type from the three options you are given, you are at risk of losing a whole bunch of marks.

Paper 2 is split into two parts: reading and listening. For reading, you can expect a booklet containing three texts that increase in difficulty as you go along. Each text is followed by a series of questions that will ask you to find synonyms for words from the text, determine who or what pronouns in the text refer to, answer general questions about the text and so on. For listening, you are likewise played three audios that gradually get more difficult to understand, each of them followed by their own set of questions as well. Each audio is played two times.

What are the differences between SL/HL Language B?

One of the biggest differences between taking a language B at SL and HL is the structure of the often-dreaded individual oral. Throughout the two years, HL students study two works (usually plays, novels or short stories) written in their target language. During the IO, they must then give a roughly 4-minute-long presentation about an unseen extract selected from one of the two works. This is followed by a question-and-answer discussion between the teacher and the student about the extracts and works as a whole.

In this initial portion of the IO, an SL student, instead of being given a choice of two unseen literary extracts, is given a choice of two unseen pictures/photographs that somehow relate to the main themes of the Language B syllabus i.e. identities, experiences, human ingenuity, social organization and sharing the planet. Like an HL student, the SL student must give a short presentation about the picture, after which he is asked additional questions about the picture's theme by the teacher. The last portion of the IO is yet another (it seems like a lot, I know) discussion in which both SL and HL students answer more questions about another one of the five prescribed themes. In total, the duration of the IO will vary from student to student, but you can expect it to last 12-15 minutes.

Other than the IO, the SL and HL exams are similar, the only other 'structural' difference being that for Paper 1 SL students are expected to write 250-400 words while HL students must write 450-600. Of course, though, the salient difference across all exams is that the HL reading and listening exams are more challenging in terms of grammar and vocabulary, which HL

students are also expected to use more accurately and fluently when actively using the language in the IO and Paper 1.
So, how do I succeed?

The key to doing well in IB Language B is to be open minded and willing to do the work set by the teacher. This subject can be an easy 6 or 7 if you put in the effort and do all the assignments set. This is how I was able to attain a 7 in French, by not skipping on homework. Furthermore, it is important to use what you learn in class in real life. To accomplish this, it may be in your interest to get a language tutor or, if you live in a francophone country, take a step outside and join some sports clubs in order to meet and socialise with locals. If you are a shy person this may be very difficult to do, so having a French tutor is the best option. By having one hour of extra French practice will help you to develop your vocabulary.

In addition to practice and doing homework, maximizing your grades on the IO will put you on the right path to a 6 or 7. Even if you don't live in a francophone country and getting a tutor isn't an option, you can always go to your teacher to get advice on how to improve your speaking skills. Sometimes, just adding a few filler words (like 'alors' or 'en fait' for French) will make you sound native without actually having to learn anything new, which is something your teacher will advise you on. Also, if you don't live in a francophone country, you can try to find French-speaking friends and environments online. You can, for example, watch French live-streams or follow French influencers on TikTok and Instagram, where you're sure to get both listening and reading practice just by watching and reading the comments.

Getting a 7 in IB French SL isn't as impossible as it might seem. Admittedly, French B (even at SL) in the IB can be a challenging and daunting course if you are not 1) fluent/native or 2) been on a long enough exchange that you are comfortable with your French (even if just speaking) or 3. a language wiz that is just naturally good at languages. However, it is still possible to get a 7 in this subject if you are none of the above (me). It does require quite a bit of effort, but the work pays off if you stick to it.

Read, read, read, read, read. Yes, read. Find articles online relating to the five prescribed themes you are studying in class and draw out all the specific vocab and phrases that could be useful in writing tasks or that may pop up in Paper 2. From this, you can compile vocabulary lists for each theme. Notes are literally just a ton of phrases bullet pointed in a word document, under subheadings to sort out the "subtopics" of each topic. A very easy way to "study" for French, especially as it is quite brainless – all you must do is type up and memorise all the phrases that you like/have highlighted!

Learn your grammar structures. A good Paper 1 does not need to be overly-complicated, it just must be accurate. For French, 'sophisticated' language structures could just be the subjunctive used correctly and in the right place, or the correct use of a direct object pronoun. Especially at SL, they are more concerned with your accuracy.

Learn your text types. It's five easy marks that you should always be getting. Practice a wide variety of text types so that you are free to choose whatever question no matter the text type in the final exam. Be comfortable with your question form for interviews, and with imperatives in brochures. Know how to structure a formal and informal letter, an article and a diary entry. You'll always have a favourite, but you still need to practice – what if your favourite text type is paired with your least favourite question in the final exam?

Practice good exam technique for the reading part. For example, if a verb is being used in the question, there should be a verb somewhere in your answer (if the question is asking for a phrase that is synonymous with "concerne chacun" then your response should have "verb —"). Learn how to manage your time and get used to the amount of time (roughly) you should be spending on each text so you finish in time to do a good check. Paper 2 can be very challenging at first when you haven't learned your grammar structures and vocabulary, but once you start reading more, writing more and just doing more French, Paper 2 is a source of easy marks that can boost your grades.

Practice speaking French often. Participate in class, find a friend you can do French debates with once a week, get a speaking tutor. There are so many ways to get yourself more exposed to the language and more confident speaking it. This will help your IOs massively! If you're SL, practice describing photos related to the option topic you are studying at home by yourself and then practice linking it back to the topic to complete your presentation. If you're HL, identify the pivotal moments in your studied works and do the same for those. It is useful to learn phrases that will help you describe features of the photo/extract and linking phrases you can use to round out your presentation. Subject specific phrases are great for when your teacher asks you questions on the topic, so learn them, and also know very clearly what your opinion is on that topic, because the IB loves it when you have an opinion.

Acing the Oral

The French Individual Oral can be scary. For me, it came 2nd on my list of scariest IAs. But never fear, because even if you have never been on a language exchange trip, do not like your language B and just do not have a knack for languages, you can still do well in this internal assessment, I promise. Nonetheless, you still have to work hard for it. Here are my 7 tips on effective preparation and study for the oral:

1. Have your notes compiled.
2. Memorise the key phrases relevant to the topic that you are studying. We call this subject specific vocabulary. The more you have of this, the better. All of this will help you immensely in your discussion.
3. Transition words and phrases are essential. You need to be able to effectively link between the photo/extract and the topic to show the examiner your knowledge of the issue at hand. Descriptive phrases. Obvious now you think about it, right?
4. Grammar! Nothing worse than making a load of grammar errors in the oral – sure-fire way to lose marks. Make sure you have revised your grammar, and that you understand and can execute the structures accurately. Simple things like masculine and feminine nouns (especially the ones that come up over and over) must be perfect!!
5. Practice, practice, practice describing photos/extracts and linking them back to the topic. Find photos on the web/extracts from your works and practice them and record yourself. You can request practice runs with your teacher, or just practice with friends or your tutor. There really isn't anything more useful than this..
6. Participate in class. Sounds irrelevant, but when you begin to get involved in class discussion you'll find it is a lot easier to answer the questions in the discussion. Also very useful to have those discussions with friends and classmates.

7. Stay calm and relaxed. Try not to think too much about it, and if need be, don't talk about it with friends. While you are waiting outside the room the most important thing is to stay calm and perhaps go over some of the key phrases in your head. Speak clearly, and if you need to fill gaps try "euh" instead of "um" for French (it really breaks the flow).

Anticipated Subject

We covered anticipated subjects in the first few chapters of this guide. Language B is an excellent choice for finishing an IB subject in your first year, I have seen plenty of students do so and do so successfully. You should really inquire with your IB coordinator and language teachers if this is a possibility. It will save you the hassle of studying for 6 subjects in your final exam stretch, and you could already possibly have a grade 7 in the bag.

28. The Group 3 Struggle

The Social Sciences can be some of the hardest subjects to study for as they require one to retain lots of information, whilst at the same time necessitating critical evaluation. With Economics for example, to get the top mark, you need to know your diagrams by heart, as well as all the definitions. No way around that.

However, what separates the students that get 6s from those that get 7s is the evaluation. Examiners want to see an opinion; they want to see that you can weigh the pros and cons of an issue, and then decide, based on evidence and case studies, what the 'right' option is. This not only applies to Economics, but all the other social sciences as well. Here, we've examined a few students that each got 7s in their respective Group 3 subjects, and how they did it.

Economics

This can't be stressed enough: do actual exam questions. If you can get in the habit of answering essay long questions at least once every week in your group 3 subject, you will have a huge advantage over individuals that do not do this. This improves your evaluation skills, allows you to distinguish between different keywords in questions (for example: evaluate, describe, analyse, compare), and ensures that come exam time, you won't be fazed by something unusual.

I would also recommend reading the news on a daily basis. Real-life examples are like gold dust when writing for 15 mark evaluative essays. Besides, reading the news will ensure that you have a grip on what's going on in the real world, outside of the IB. Out of all the group 3s that you could choose to take in the IB, I would have to say that Economics is one of the easiest. Getting a 7 in this subject is not hard at all, just follow 3 simple rules:

Practice Essay writing – dig out past papers and write those essays/data responses under timed conditions, and then give it to your teacher to mark. Slowly, you will find your pitfalls are in the same places (for me, it was forgetting to define!) and eventually these mistakes can be easily fixed.

Understand your content – so much in Economics doesn't necessarily need to be rote learned, but you do need a solid understanding of each topic and how it relates to the other topics to write those essays well.

Write syllabus notes – write yourself a set of notes under the syllabus bullet points. Try to summarise as much as you can so it's easier to learn, and in doing so, you will find that you understand the content a lot better! You can also draw mind maps to help sort out all the connections between the different topics. Try to write your notes as you go along, the IB Economics syllabus is lengthy and you will have a hard time trying to finish them all right before the exams.

For complete information on how to ace your economics IAs, we strongly suggest getting our book devoted to just that: *The IB Economics Commentary: Examples and Advice* by Alexander Zouev (available on Amazon).

Geography

For Geography, Paper 1 is very easy if you have studied. Thus, it's important to maximize your marks on this paper. Apart from memorizing a few case studies and knowing your definitions (which is a given, at this stage), there are only graphs and diagrams to analyse.

For this, I recommend the 'OSO' Easy technique. Essentially, you say something that is Obvious about the graph, something that is Specific (quote a numerical data-point), and something that is Odd. This will almost guarantee you all the marks for that question.

I also advise studying hard for Paper 3, the part of the course that encompasses Global Interactions. This is a section of the course that a lot of students are often intimidated by. If you can learn all the definitions and engage actively in class with your teacher, this paper essentially looks at your ability to recall information.

Paper 2 is more of a lottery. Some options are easy, some are really tough. I personally found the Tourism option to be very easy, and actually self-studied it two days before the exam (this is by no means a recommendation for your approach however). I got a solid 6, and thus for my limited studying time, was happy. With it you can maximize your Paper 1 and Paper 3 in Geography, Paper 2 shouldn't be too much of an issue.

The IA is something that you just must work hard on. Don't leave it to the last minute, as examiners will see that you've put in minimal effort. Instead, gain feedback from your teacher and ask them how you can improve. Ask your peers, and help each other. To be completely honest, the Geography IA is normally not a big concern for IB students, and thus as long as you are well-planned and don't panic, you'll be just fine.

Try "profiling" countries that you use for case studies. For example, I profiled China because China is often a country that many of my case studies overlap (One Child Policy, globalisation, disposal of wastes, etc.) and made several statistics on it like population, GNI, migration, etc. I'm doing this for all my countries that are very relevant. It can be helpful in getting a clear idea if anything comes up. Also helps with memorizing (for me, you may be different).

Memorize case studies, know them off the top of your head. Know how to spell them right, for example the Kissimmee River. Be sure that you can write a good paragraph about each of them, and for higher marks memorize specific numbers: dates, statistics, places, etc.

Another tip is that Paper 1 essay question essentially covers three of the four core topics. You could essentially study essay topics for two of the four topics and 1 question that you studied should come up in the Paper 1. I've been doing this method for IB1 & IB2 mock exams and it all worked out fine. But if you're a "better safe then sorry" you can always learn three topic essays and omit the topic you hate the most.

Try to learn flexible diagrams to draw for essay questions. For example, population pyramids are good go-to for many of the core points like Development or Populations in Transition, and even migration (for example, you could draw the Philippines and have a huge gap and label that as "OFW (Oversea Family Worker)" which can link to P3 Globalisation too!). Diagrams really add to the last criterion of the markscheme.

Prepare your hand for a lot of writing. Practice writing essays under a time limit. Remember Paper 2 and 3 are on the same day normally, that's pretty much four essays in a row. Set your timer, take out a pencil, and get lots of practice beforehand working against the clock.

History

Essay structure in history matters just as much as actual knowledge. You can know absolutely everything but if you can't communicate it in a way that is cogent and clear, you won't get high marks. For Paper 1, you should become a sort of 'wizard' at analysing all kinds of sources. To do this, you should study a lot of past papers and improve your information collecting skills.

For Paper 2, outlining your essay is just as important as writing it. Thus, I recommend spending about 5 minutes before you start writing your essays on making a clear outline of what you're actually going to write. Don't forget that history isn't just about memorizing a whole lot of events in a particular order. You have to learn to think critically, and analyse all the aspects of an event; its causes, implications, consequences, motives etc.

For complete information on how to get a grade 7 for your IB History, we strongly recommend getting our book *How to Write an IB History Essay: The Safe Hands Approach* by Joe Thomas (available on Amazon)

Business and Management

It's a known fact that only 4% of all IB BM students worldwide achieve a grade 7. This is one of the hardest courses to earn a 7 – but if you get there, you will breeze past any first year university-level business program. That being said, ask your teacher for a command term sheet and the rubric/marking criteria for answers. Failing that, ibbusinessandmanagement.com has a great command sheet that breaks down all of IB's favourite command terms (comment, identify, analyse, to what extent, evaluate, etc.) what each term expects, and the general order of marks allocated to each command term.

Get as much material as you can from your teacher and ask to see the syllabus guide. There is also a very complete Internal Assessment guide that breaks down the criteria and how to structure it. Get your hands on that too. The more information you have at your disposal, the higher your chances of a good grade. Also, you have to think outside of what you learn in class for a 7, so read up on business articles and get used to using 'business language'/terminology.

Solving past papers will be good as far as practicing how you structure your answers according to the marking criteria. It's an opportunity to get used to IB answer structure, and your ability to form arguments and back them up. But do it sparingly, it may not be the best use of your time in Year 1, as you'll have to focus primarily on understanding the main content and concepts.

You can grade your own work, which will be handy for the IA as well. Read your paper and compare it to the mark scheme, look at what you've missed out. For example, is it too focused on explanation of facts/figures and not enough on analysis or recommendation? Same applies for past papers and sheet-work that your teacher gives you. It's also worth buddying up with your classmates and taking a free period to check each other's class work to see what went wrong and what went right.

29. Engineering A 7 In HL Economics

What do I Need to Memorize for the Exam?

The exam is broken down into FOUR assessments (THREE for SL) - here is a breakdown of what you'll need to know and what to expect from each section:

Paper 1 of the Economics HL exam is like a thrilling race against time! You've got 1 hour and 15 minutes to showcase your economic wizardry. Get ready to dive into a world of extended responses, where your mission is to dissect all the units from the syllabus. This paper is all about demonstrating your deep understanding of economics by applying theories, models, and concepts to real-world scenarios. Think of it as your chance to shine by connecting classroom learning to the complex, buzzing world of economics out there! Remember, it's a test of your knowledge, skills, and your ability to think like a true economist. So, gear up, get your economic thinking cap on, and get ready to ace Paper 1!

Ready to tackle Paper 1 of Economics HL? Here are some handy tips! First, practice makes perfect: do lots of past papers to get familiar with the question style and time pressure. Time management is key – allocate your time wisely between questions. Understand the syllabus inside out, focusing on key concepts and theories. When answering, clarity is your best friend; make your points clear and concise. Use real-world examples to illustrate your points, and don't forget to explain economic terms. Lastly, review your answers if time permits, ensuring they're well-structured and address the question directly.

Paper 2 in Economics HL is your chance to dive deep into economic issues with your data response skills! You'll have 1 hour and 45 minutes to show off your analytical prowess. This paper is all about interpreting and evaluating economic data based on the entire syllabus. It's like being an economic detective, where you get to unravel the mysteries behind numbers and graphs. Your task is to connect theoretical economic models to real-world data, making sense of complex economic scenarios. So, sharpen your analytical tools, and get ready to explore the exciting world of economic data in Paper 2!

Ready for Paper 2 in Economics HL? Here's how to ace it! First, get comfy with graphs and data - they're your best buds here. Practice interpreting different types of economic data. Be clear and direct in your answers, connecting data to economic theories. Time management is super important, so plan your responses wisely. Use real-world examples to strengthen your arguments, and explain how they link to economic concepts. Finally, keep your answers focused and relevant to the questions asked.

The portfolio part of the Economics HL course is all about showcasing your economic insight through a series of commentaries. You'll create a portfolio of three commentaries, each focusing on different units of the syllabus (except the introductory unit). These commentaries should be based on published news media extracts and analysed using various key economic concepts. It's your time to shine by blending theory with real-world events, demonstrating your understanding of economics in action. Think of it as your personal economic journal, where you get to be the analyst and commentator!

For the portfolio section in Economics HL, start by choosing intriguing, recent news articles related to economics. Then, analyse them using economic theories and concepts from your course. Make sure each commentary focuses on a different area of the syllabus. Balance theory with practical application, and don't forget to cite your sources. Write clearly, concisely, and critically. This is your chance to demonstrate not just what you know, but how you apply it to real-world scenarios. And remember, quality over quantity!

Paper 3 for Economics HL is all about policy paper questions, covering the entire syllabus. In this 1 hour and 45 minutes exam, you'll need to demonstrate your understanding of economic policies and their implications. This is your opportunity to shine by applying economic theories and concepts to policy issues. Think of it as your moment to play the role of an economic advisor, using your knowledge to suggest practical solutions to economic problems. Get ready to put your economic thinking cap on and delve into the world of policymaking!

For Paper 3 in Economics HL, first, familiarize yourself thoroughly with economic policies and their impacts. Practice applying theories to real-world policy issues. In the exam, carefully read each question and plan your answers, focusing on clarity and relevance. Use specific examples and economic terminology accurately. Also, manage your time well to answer all questions thoroughly. Lastly, review your answers for precision and directness in addressing the policy issues. Good luck!

How should I study for the IB Economics Exam?

For Paper 1, focus on understanding and applying economic theories to real-world scenarios. Read past Paper 1 questions and try working them out. Additionally, work on your writing skills and make sure that you can consistently write clear concise essays with a clear beginning, middle and end, along with transitions between each paragraph.

For Paper 2, get comfortable with interpreting economic data and graphs, linking them to economic concepts. Look up past economic graphs and see how well you can pick apart the data and interpret the graphs. That is a huge part of Paper 2!

Paper 3 is all about policies, so study various economic policies and their impacts thoroughly. Make sure to use legitimate sources!

For your portfolio, regularly read news articles and practice applying economic theories to current events. Make sure to go over the IB Economics exam review and your IB Economics online IB notes to ensure success. Remember, practice past papers, stay organized, and keep your study sessions interactive and engaging!

5 Tips to Score 7s in Your Econ IA

The IA's make up 20% of your final grade in IB Economics, so you cannot underestimate their importance! If you find yourself struggling with anything from finding a topic to writing your evaluation, here are the answers to 5 of the most frequently asked questions about the econ IA's, answered by expert IB graduates.

1. How do I choose my topic?

As IB Economists we're expected to write 3 separate commentaries based on three areas of the syllabus: one in microeconomics, one in macroeconomics, and one in either international trade or development economics.

The best topics tend to be those that have a clear economic theory, but have scope for relevant and detailed evaluation. Taxes and subsidies, for instance, are perfect topics for discussion as they both have clear diagrams in the syllabus and are also closely related to externalities and elasticities. Don't make it unnecessarily hard for yourselves – you won't get bonus points for writing about an obscure economic theory. The following is a list of topics we think give you the foundation for an amazing assignment:

Microeconomics Topics:
Taxes, Subsidies
Price Controls
Externalities
Monopoly Power

International:
Tariffs, Subsidies. Quotas
Exchange Rates
Macroeconomic Topics:
Interest Rates
Fiscal Policy
Unemployment

Development:
Trade Strategies
Market-Based Strategies
Interventionist Strategies

2. How do I choose my article?

Too many candidates limit their chances at nailing their IA by choosing a bad article. Here are three pointers to avoid that mistake:

Make sure that the article comes from a reputable news source. Well-known news agencies like BBC News, CNN, or The Guardian should be your go-to sites. As a rule of thumb, if you've never heard of the news source before, don't use it! Be wary of economics-focused sources like 'The Economist' or 'The Wall Street Journal'. Since these kinds of sources generally already contain economic analysis, there isn't much scope for you to explore new ideas, limiting your potential for a high score.

When you google search 'name of topic, name of reputable news source' (cigarette tax, CNN) to find your perfect article, make sure to use google tools to set the publishing date to be in the last year. You can't use an article that was published more than 12 months ago!

Choose an article that explores the imposition (or proposed imposition) of a policy. Writing an IA based on an article that outlines 'Country X is set to increase fiscal spending as it is facing a recession' is much easier than with another article that simply says 'Country Y is facing a recession'. The ability to analyse and evaluate the potential consequences of a policy that could be implemented to prevent a recession, as opposed to simply commenting on the demerits of facing one, leads to both more interesting content but also more marks!

If you can find an article published in the last year from a reputable news source, which mentions the imposition of a specific policy without going into excessive economic analysis, you're on the right track to smash that IA!

3. How do I structure my IA?

On top of making sure the content of your IA is top-notch, structuring it effectively can make a large difference to your final mark. Most high-scoring Economics IA can be broken down into 5 sections:

Introduction (75 words) – outlines and summarizes the article in 2 or 3 brief sentences. In this introduction, define a few key terms that will be used going forward through the essay. Make sure that this doesn't just become a list of definitions, though! Only define a key term if relevant, and if you've already used it in a sentence.

What was the underlying problem? (100 words)– let's say the government is considering imposing a soda tax. In this case, the underlying problem may be the market failure caused by sugary drinks. You may want to draw a diagram and give a clear explanation on how sugary drinks cause market failure through negative externalities, and how that may be a detriment to society.

What is the proposed policy (and what is its intended effect)? (200-250 words) – the bulk of your analysis will fall under this section. This is where you explain and show how, for example, an excise soda tax is intended to shift the supply curve in order to curb consumption/production of that demerit good and thus reduce the market failure.

What are some unintended effects of the policy? (250-300 words) – this is where your evaluation comes in. Don't underestimate the importance of in-depth evaluation for your IA. Tip #5 in this article does a deep dive into all the essentials of the perfect evaluation

Conclusion (75 words) – concludes your main ideas in 2-3 sentences. Recap the reason behind the policy implementation, the intended effect of the policy, and summarize your evaluation of the situation. Don't bring up any new thoughts/ideas in this section as you won't be able to thoroughly explain them!

4. Do the diagrams really matter?

We all know diagrams are at the heart of IB Economics. For the IA, this is no different. When we insert diagrams, we need them to be large, labelled, clear and correct. Beyond this, however, we also need to make sure that our diagrams aren't left 'hanging'. What do we mean by that? Even if your diagrams are clean and accurate, if you don't explain them, you might as well not have drawn them as it doesn't show that you understand what the diagrams are showing! The rubric clearly outlines that all diagrams need 'a full explanation'. Don't undo your hard work by failing to connect your analysis to your academic artwork!

Top Tip: To boost your score even more, see if you can add some figures from your article onto your diagrams.

5. What do I include in my evaluation?

If you take a peek at the IA rubric, you'll see that the evaluation section is weighted the highest! It's all well and good explaining the economic theory that an article refers to, but unless we can examine that material in light of the information found within it we're limiting our score.

But what does evaluation actually mean? And how can we do it effectively?

The acronym CLASPP is your guide to evaluation inspiration:

Conclusion (see above in tip #3)

Long-Term vs. Short-Term – will the effectiveness of the policy change over time?

Assumptions – what does economic theory suggest that is undermined or neglected by the content of the article? How does this affect the proposal?

Stakeholders – how are those parties addressed in the article affected differently (consumers, producers, government)? Even within these groups, who wins and who loses?

Priorities – in the economic context, what should be the priority of policymakers and is the content of the article in line with that?

Pros & Cons – what are the advantages of the policy in the article? What are the disadvantages?

To score highly under the evaluation header, we need to choose a few of these subsections to analyse how the policy or its proposal might support, undermine, or develop existing economic theory.

30. Hacking History

To achieve a grade 7 in IB History, you should concentrate on mastering the exam format, which includes Papers 1 and 2, the Internal Assessment (IA), and Paper 3 for Higher Level (HL) students. It is crucial to develop a thorough understanding of historical events, themes, and historiography. Success depends on producing well-structured, evidence-supported essays and conducting comprehensive research for the IA. Engaging in critical analysis by comparing and contrasting different viewpoints is important. Regular revision, using feedback, and practising past papers are key. Having strategic study plans, effective time management, and seeking expert feedback can enhance your performance. There are more strategies to discover in order to excel in IB History.

In short

- Develop a thorough understanding of historiography and various interpretations of events.
- Master the art of essay writing, with an emphasis on building logical arguments backed by evidence.
- Select an engaging topic for the IA, supported by in-depth research and a clear presentation.
- Improve time management skills during exams, setting aside time for planning, writing, and reviewing.
- Participate in group learning and request feedback to enhance comprehension and enhance performance.

IB History Exam Structure

Grasping the structure of the IB History exam is essential for achieving the highest scores. This section will detail the components of Paper 1, Paper 2, and the Internal Assessment. It will also highlight differences between Higher Level (HL) and Standard Level (SL) courses, laying the groundwork for effective study planning. An in-depth analysis of the syllabus and marking criteria will equip students with the necessary knowledge to excel.

Paper 1 is a source-based examination, where students analyse and evaluate various historical documents. For HL and SL students, this paper tests skills in interpreting and understanding historical sources within a specific context.

Paper 2 requires students to write essays from a choice of topics, demonstrating their knowledge and understanding of historical themes and events. The essay topics cover a broad range of historical events, and the choice allows students to showcase their strengths. HL students are required to write more essays than those studying at SL.

The Internal Assessment is an independent research project that constitutes a significant portion of the final grade. It requires students to investigate a historical topic of their choice in depth, developing critical thinking and research skills. The distinction between HL and SL students in the Internal Assessment is primarily in the complexity and depth of the research question.

For those studying at HL, there is an additional Paper 3, which focuses on the in-depth study of specific regions and their historical developments over time. This paper demands a comprehensive understanding of the chosen topics and the ability to compare and contrast them critically.

In preparing for these examinations, students must familiarise themselves with the syllabus content and the assessment criteria. A strategic approach, focusing on areas of strength and addressing weaknesses, will be beneficial. Regular practice with past papers and feedback from teachers will also help in refining exam techniques and improving performance.

Analysis of Paper 1, Paper 2, and Internal Assessment

The IB History Examination consists of three main parts: Paper 1, Paper 2, and the Internal Assessment (IA), each aimed at assessing students' ability to understand historical concepts and skills.

The history IA, a crucial component of this assessment, allows students to carry out an independent investigation, showcasing their capacity to analyse and synthesise historical data. This aspect is assessed according to a specific rubric, with criteria emphasising the development of a clear research question, the effective use of sources, and the coherent presentation of findings.

Proficiency in these areas is essential for success in the IA, as it demonstrates the student's ability to apply historical methodologies and viewpoints critically and autonomously.

IB History HL vs SL: What You Need to Know

Choosing between Higher Level (HL) and Standard Level (SL) for IB History is a significant decision that influences the depth and breadth of the exam content students will face. The IB History course is designed to develop a profound understanding of the past, equipping students to contribute to their communities with well-informed viewpoints.

HL students, however, undertake a more extensive engagement with the IB history syllabus, covering additional topics and tackling more intricate historical essays. This requires a higher level of dedication to studying history.

Appreciating the distinctions between HL and SL is vital for students aiming to match their academic and community-focused ambitions with the right level of challenge and inquiry within the IB history course.

Thorough Curriculum Analysis and Grading Criteria

Analysing the detailed syllabus and understanding the rubric are crucial for doing well in the IB History exam. The syllabus outlines the key themes and study areas, while the marking scheme provides clear guidelines on how examiners evaluate performance. For those committed to advancing in education, mastering these elements is essential.

IB History requires more than just knowledge of historical events; it also involves conducting a thorough historical investigation and writing insightful extended essays. These tasks demand a deep understanding of the syllabus and a precise application of the rubric's criteria.

By carefully examining these aspects, students equip themselves with the necessary knowledge and skills to meet high standards and make significant contributions to their academic and professional environments.

Essay Writing for IB History

Essay writing is a crucial element of excelling in IB History, requiring not only deep knowledge but also a skilful ability to convey ideas effectively. This section will explore strategies for composing essays that can achieve the highest marks, focusing on detailed analysis of historical events and the importance of comparing and contrasting to demonstrate a thorough understanding. By refining these skills, students can significantly improve their performance and achieve a grade 7 in their exams.

Achieving excellence in essay writing for IB History requires a thorough understanding of the subject matter and the adept application of critical thinking skills. Students must be able to build logical arguments, supported by evidence, and present them in a clear, concise manner. Attention to detail is crucial, as is the ability to synthesise information from various sources to create a compelling narrative.

A successful essay in IB History often depends on the student's ability to compare and contrast different perspectives, events, or interpretations. This not only shows an understanding of the complexity of historical events but also demonstrates to the examiner that the student can think critically about the material. To do this effectively, students should structure their essays clearly, ensuring each paragraph flows logically from one to the next, and using topic sentences to introduce the main point of each paragraph.

Moreover, the use of specific examples and quotations to support arguments is vital. Students should make sure they accurately reference these sources, following the IB's guidelines for citations. This not only bolsters the credibility of their arguments but also highlights their research skills.

Lastly, revision is crucial in the essay-writing process. Students should set aside time to review their work, checking for grammatical errors, ensuring the clarity of their arguments, and confirming the accuracy of their references. Peer reviews can also offer valuable feedback, providing an alternative perspective on the essay's structure and content.

How to Write an Essay That Scores a 7

Crafting an outstanding IB History essay requires a strategic method in structuring arguments and presenting evidence. The key to successful essay writing is the careful selection of evidence that robustly supports your thesis, demonstrating an analytical depth that sets your work apart.

The Internal Assessment (IA) in IB History is a prime example of the importance of this analytical approach, requiring a well-argued thesis backed by compelling evidence. To excel, one must manage their time effectively, allowing adequate periods for research, writing, and revision.

This disciplined approach to time management enables the thorough analysis and integration of evidence, ensuring that each argument presented is not only persuasive but also deeply informed. Adopting these strategies will significantly improve the quality of your essay writing, setting you up for success in achieving a score of 7 in IB History.

Analysing Historical Events with Depth and Clarity

Analysing historical events with precision and depth is crucial for creating essays that stand out in IB History. To achieve this, students must engage with historiography, understanding varied interpretations of events to enhance their analysis. This involves critically evaluating the messages of sources, identifying any biases, and how these perspectives influence our understanding of past societies. Analysing historical events is not just about stating facts; it's about exploring the intricacies of past societies, recognising the causes and effects of events in a way that demonstrates a sophisticated understanding of history. By carefully comparing the information gathered from different sources without directly contrasting them, students can present a subtle narrative that captures the complexity of historical events, thereby providing the academic community with essays of exceptional insight and clarity.

Students should examine the credibility of sources, taking into account the context in which they were created and any potential bias. This applies to both primary and secondary sources, where the former offers direct evidence from the period being studied and the latter presents interpretations and analyses of those primary documents. A thorough review of these materials allows students to develop comprehensive arguments supported by a range of perspectives.

A key aspect of essay writing in history is the ability to argue cohesively and persuasively, presenting evidence in favour of a thesis while acknowledging counterarguments. This skill demands a deep understanding of the historical context, the ability to synthesize information from various sources, and the skill to write clearly and persuasively. Students are advised to present their arguments logically, backed by evidence, and to write with clarity and precision.

Comparing and Contrasting: Key Skills in History Essays

Becoming proficient in the skill of comparing and contrasting historical events is essential for creating engaging essays in IB History. This approach not only demonstrates a deep understanding of the subject matter but also showcases analytical skills, which are vital for achieving high grades in the history examination. Here are some tips for effectively applying this technique:

- Identify similarities and differences in the causes and outcomes of historical events.
- Structure your essay to clearly differentiate and compare various aspects.
- Support your analysis with evidence, emphasising the significance of each comparison.
- Conclude by offering insights into how these comparisons enhance our understanding of broader historical themes.

Make sure that your writing follows British English spelling and grammar conventions. The content should be informative, authoritative, and precise, suitable for readers at UK secondary school, A-Level, or advanced levels. Your paragraphs should be concise yet rich in factually accurate information.

The tone should be instructive, providing clear guidance to the reader. Use academic vocabulary that requires a solid grasp of terms and concepts. Write sentences of moderate length, using commas for effective separation of ideas. It is advisable to employ a variety of sentence structures, including both complex and simple sentences, to provide thorough yet succinct explanations. By following these step-by-step instructions, you will gain a comprehensive understanding of the topic.

Maximising Your Score in the IA

To excel in the IB History Internal Assessment (IA), it is essential to grasp the fundamental elements needed for success. The journey commences with choosing a captivating topic, followed by extensive research and development, and culminates with the tactical application of feedback. Each phase is pivotal in aiming for the top grade of 7, establishing the foundation for academic excellence.

Selecting a topic that not only intrigues you but also aligns with the IA criteria is the initial step. It should be specific enough to permit a thorough analysis within the word limit yet broad enough to offer ample scope for exploration.

Once the topic is chosen, the subsequent stage involves meticulous research. Utilising a range of sources, both primary and secondary, to gather data will fortify your argument. This phase necessitates a discerning assessment of sources for their trustworthiness and relevance to your topic.

Upon compiling your research, the drafting process commences. Here, conveying your findings in a clear, succinct manner is crucial. Your argument should be coherent, underpinned by evidence, and logically structured.

Lastly, feedback plays a crucial role in the IA process. Integrating constructive criticism from educators or peers can significantly enhance the quality of your work. It is vital to perceive feedback as an opportunity for refinement rather than criticism.

Selecting a Winning Subject for Your IB History Internal Assessment

Selecting a compelling and sufficiently focused topic is a crucial initial step in achieving a high score on the IB History Internal Assessment (IA).

- Adhere to the History Curriculum: Make sure your chosen topic aligns with the themes and periods covered in the IB history curriculum, showing relevance and compliance with the syllabus.
- Demonstrate Independent Study: Select a subject that allows you to display your ability to carry out independent research, demonstrating dedication and initiative.
- Explore Less Examined Perspectives: opt for a topic that presents a unique perspective or delves into a less explored event, distinguishing your IA from others.
- Fulfil IB Criteria: Choose a topic that enables you to meet the IB's specific criteria, including analysis, evaluation, and the synthesis of sources, ensuring a thorough and comprehensive investigation.

Navigating the Research and Development Phase

Upon selecting your topic, the next crucial stage is to fully immerse yourself in the research and development phase to ensure that your IB History IA stands out. This stage is vital for honing the skills required to identify unexpected connections, similar to the work of professional historians. Using both primary and secondary sources will enhance your analysis and argument.

Incorporating feedback to achieve a 7 in History IB

Having laid a strong foundation through thorough research and development, the next step towards securing a top mark in your IB History IA is to effectively incorporate feedback. This aspect is crucial in refining your work to meet the demanding standards of the IB History examination. Here is how you should proceed:

- Seek Varied Opinions: Ask for feedback from teachers, peers, and mentors to gather a range of perspectives.
- React Constructively: Evaluate criticisms objectively, focusing on areas that require improvement rather than taking offense.
- Apply Changes Thoughtfully: Prioritize adjustments that significantly enhance the coherence and depth of your argument.
- Engage in Reflective Learning: Regularly assess your progress, using feedback as a guide to enhance your exam preparation.

Ensure the content follows UK English spelling and grammar conventions. The style should be informative, authoritative, and precise, suitable for a UK secondary school, A-Level, or advanced reader. The text should be concise, with accurate details, and the tone instructional, providing clear guidance. The vocabulary should be suitable for an academic audience, with sentences varying in length and structure to offer detailed yet concise explanations. Instructions should be presented step-by-step for a comprehensive understanding.

Effective Study Strategies for IB History Students

To excel in IB History, adopting effective study strategies is essential. This section will discuss several methods, including creating a personalised study timetable, using flashcards and other memorisation tools, and the advantages of alternating between solo study and group learning sessions. Each method offers distinct benefits that, when combined, can significantly improve a student's grasp and memory of historical content.

Crafting a personalised study timetable allows students to allocate their time efficiently, ensuring that all topics are covered thoroughly before the examination. Using flashcards for key dates, events, and figures aids in memorising critical information. Furthermore, alternating study methods by sometimes studying alone to focus deeply on material and other times collaborating with peers, can enhance understanding through discussion and explanation, offering different perspectives on historical events.

These strategies, when applied diligently, provide a robust framework for mastering the complexities of IB History, leading to improved performance and deeper comprehension of the subject.

Creating a Study Timeline That Works
Crafting an effective study timetable is crucial for IB History students aiming for a top mark of 7. A carefully planned timetable enables optimum learning and ensures comprehensive coverage of the syllabus. Here are essential steps for creating a study timetable that produces results:

Highlight Key Dates and Events: Focus on important historical dates and events that need to be memorised.
Set Aside Time for Review: Schedule specific periods for revising material that has already been studied.

Plan Breaks: Include short breaks to prevent fatigue and enhance memory retention.

Adjust as Necessary: Regularly review and adjust the study timetable to match your learning pace and needs.

Using Flashcards and Other Tools for Memorisation

Flashcard systems and mnemonic devices are invaluable resources for IB History students aiming to improve their memorisation skills. Using these techniques together can help students in gaining a comprehensive understanding of the extensive content in IB History HL. Flashcards, in particular, provide a dynamic and interactive method for reviewing crucial dates, figures, and events, promoting active recall and aiding in the retention of information over the long term.

Mnemonic Devices

Flashcards and mnemonic devices are crucial for students who wish to excel in IB History HL, enabling them to recall vast amounts of information efficiently. By encouraging active engagement with the material, these methods significantly boost learning efficiency. Through the use of timelines, students can better understand historical events in their chronological context, enhancing their grasp of cause and effect relationships. Essay plans are valuable for structuring coherent and persuasive arguments, a skill essential for success in history examinations. Lastly, peer quizzes not only reinforce learning but also promote a sense of community and mutual support among students, making the learning process more enjoyable and effective.

From Independent Study to Group Sessions: Diversifying Learning

Moving away from solitary memorisation strategies, the integration of group study sessions offers a comprehensive approach to excelling in IB History. This method broadens the scope of learning and cultivates a supportive environment where students can prosper collectively. Here are some strategies:

Peer Tutoring: Students alternate roles as the tutor, reinforcing their own knowledge whilst aiding their peers.
Discussion Groups: In-depth discussions guided by IB history tutors can enhance understanding of intricate subjects.
Debate Sessions: These sessions promote critical thinking and the application of historical knowledge in practical scenarios.
Joint Research Projects: Working in groups can streamline the research process by combining resources and insights, leading to a more effective and thorough investigation.
This approach not only enriches the learning experience but also prepares students for collaborative work environments in the future.

Seeking Help: Tutors and Resources
To excel in IB History, seeking external support through tutoring and academic resources is vital. A tutor can offer focused advice and speed up the learning process, while access to specialised online content and books can deepen understanding and knowledge. This section will discuss how these components work together to help students achieve the highest marks in their course.

Utilising a tutor familiar with the IB curriculum can make a significant difference. These professionals can tailor their teaching strategies to meet individual learning needs, clarifying complex historical events and theories. Additionally, they can provide practice questions and mock exams, preparing students for the type of assessments they will face.

Academic resources, including journals, historical texts, and online databases, are invaluable for deepening knowledge. Students should engage with a variety of materials to gain different perspectives on historical events and figures. This approach not only aids in understanding but also helps in developing critical thinking skills, which are essential for success in History.

How Tutors Can Help You Achieve a 7 in IB History

Securing a tutor can greatly enhance your comprehension and performance in IB History, acting as a catalyst for achieving the highly coveted score of 7. IB tutors provide crucial guidance to students, particularly in developing the skills necessary to attain a 7. Their expertise is invaluable in areas such as timed essays, crucial for success in exams.

Online Resources and Books Every IB History Student Should Know

Securing a dedicated tutor and utilising online resources and key books are vital for any IB History student aiming for a top score. The IB DP history course is demanding, and understanding the perspectives of IB examiners can significantly improve your preparation.

Online resources like academic journals, specialised websites, and forums can offer insights and discussions that enrich your understanding of historical events and historiography. Additionally, accessing past papers is essential; they provide a clear view of the exam format and the types of questions asked.

Engaging with these resources promotes a deeper comprehension of History HL content, equipping students with the skills and knowledge necessary to excel in their exams and contribute positively to their academic communities.

Engage with a specialised tutor with experience in IB DP History.
Make use of online platforms that offer practice with past papers and expert feedback.
Join study groups to share insights and viewpoints.
Look for extra materials that offer a deeper understanding of historical events.
These steps can significantly improve your comprehension and performance, putting you on track to achieve top marks in IB History.

Exam Preparation and Time Management Tips
As the IB History exam draws near, it is crucial to grasp the content and excel in strategies for exam preparation and time management. Developing a personalised study plan that suits your learning preferences and aligns with the exam format can significantly impact your performance. Understanding what examiners seek and employing targeted techniques to meet these standards is vital for achieving a top score of 7.

Make sure your study plan incorporates a range of resources and revision methods tailored to the exam's demands. Practise past paper questions to familiarise yourself with the question types and enhance your time management abilities in exam conditions. Utilise feedback from teachers to fine-tune your approach and concentrate on areas requiring improvement.

Maintaining a balance between revision, breaks, and other activities is crucial for sustaining well-being and preventing burnout. Establish achievable goals for each study session and monitor your progress to keep motivated.

- Strategizing Your Study Sessions Before the IB History Exam
- Creating an effective study plan is essential for success in the IB History exam. Strategizing your revision sessions is key to mastering the material and understanding how each topic affects your overall score. Here are four vital strategies:

- Allocate Specific Times for each historical period to ensure a balanced review.
- Use Active Recall to test your grasp of key events and their consequences.
- Group Study Sessions with peers to debate historical interpretations, improving your analytical abilities.
- Prioritise Topics based on their significance and your level of understanding, concentrating more on areas that could greatly influence your performance in the history exam.

Managing Your Time Effectively During the Exam

Efficient time management during the IB History exam is crucial to make sure that each question gets the right level of attention. Whether you're sitting Higher Level (HL) or Standard Level (SL) papers, effectively managing your time during the exam is key to fully showcasing your knowledge and analytical skills. Here is a brief guide to help you allocate your time wisely:

Section	Time Allocation
Paper 1	60 minutes
Paper 2 (HL/SL)	90 minutes
Paper 3 (HL only)	150 minutes

Planning   10% of section time
Writing & Review   90% of section time
Devoting some of your designated time to planning before writing can greatly enhance the quality of your answers. Making sure you allocate the right amount of time to planning, writing, and reviewing can have a significant impact on your performance.

Examiners' Expectations and How to Meet Them
Understanding what examiners expect and mastering the art of meeting these expectations is essential for optimising your study strategy and time management skills. To achieve top marks in IB History, it's crucial to grasp what examiners are looking for and how to effectively present your knowledge within the constraints of the exam format. Here are four essential strategies:

- Stick to the Word Limit: It's vital to adhere closely to the word limit requirements, demonstrating your ability to express ideas concisely and effectively.
- Familiarise Yourself with the Marking Scheme: Focus your study efforts on areas that are highly valued by the examiners.
- Use Past Papers: Get to know the types of questions asked and what examiners expect.
- Develop a Coherent Argument: Ensure that every essay or response you write puts forward a clear, logical argument that directly addresses the question.

Following these strategies can significantly help in optimising your preparation and potentially enhance your performance in the exam.

31. Beating Biology

The sciences are fundamentally different, and it is this difference that makes one more difficult than the other. Biology is a game of memorisation; if you can remember everything then you are guaranteed a 7 as the critical thinking involved is minimal when compared to the other sciences. Nonetheless, it is extremely easy to lose marks for missing out on simple points, so practice a lot with the question bank and past papers and understand what the question is asking.

How to Guarantee a 7 in Bio

Here are a few tips that got me through HL Bio and might help you too.

As you may know Biology is a very content-heavy subject, but there are no complex concepts that you need to understand. It is just pure memorisation but there are some techniques that can make the HL bio trip less stressful and more enjoyable.

It is important that you make NEAT notes that are aesthetically pleasing. This may sound obvious but if your notes are visually appealing, you will have a better time looking at them. The more often you look at them, the better. As you go through the topics try to summarise all the information on a single A4 sheet. Condensing information will make you memorize more effectively. It is also crucial that you go over the topics more than once and you should make various different note sheets per topic as you move through the syllabus. You should never exactly copy the book.

Use different styles of study methods. It is important that you don't only stick to flashcards but also make yourself big summary sheets. Use drawings, colours, neat handwriting... Try and be as diverse as possible in order to transform the information from the book into something that is your own. This will really help process and remember all the information. Bio is also one of those subjects where if you have a friend who just makes really neat and awesome notes, you should try to get a copy from them if you can.

It's crucial that you familiarise yourself with the exam structure and style. I recommend getting the Questionbank even if there is a new syllabus. The more questions you do, the better. This is really important for the big 20 mark questions. Reading the questions and looking at the markschemes helps you understand how the examiners think. It is also imperative that you go through your answers using the markschemes after a biology test. The more you do this the better you will get at writing answers that are tailored to the question asked. Basically just try and do as many past papers as possible; it really does help.

Study from markschemes (for the 20 mark questions). Some questions like "explain the process of translation or transcription" just never change and are recycled every other year. I recommend doing this for a few big questions per topic so you can be sure that one will come up at least. However, this should be done close to the exam time.

Keep your notes on display in your room or bathroom. The more often you see your notes the better. Even if it's just 3 minutes while you are brushing your teeth. This is really important for diagrams as there are around 30 of them that you must memorize.

The best way to do well on your exams is to know the material, so lots of revision. Most importantly is to find a way that works for you. I personally find that re-writing notes to make them look more appealing works best for me. The other important part is being consistent, even if it's only twenty minutes a day it really helps to keep material fresh in your mind. The final piece of advice, given to me by my coordinators, is to try to make connections between topics and between subjects. So for instance in both Chem and Bio you do an organic chemistry unit, you can try to overlap knowledge there.

You need to know that there are three types of examination questions:

1) Multiple Choice Questions (Paper 1): You choose the answer from four possible choices. Read them all, eliminate any answers to narrow them down. Always give answers and never leave questions empty. Leave the hard ones till the end and focus on the straightforward ones.

2) Structured Questions (Paper 2 and 3): Each question is broken down into sections. Answers are written in spaces or on lines. If you run out of space, complete elsewhere on the examination sheet itself, but clearly indicate where you wrote the rest of the answer. In paper 3, you are allowed to have extra paper. The marks are allotted at the end of each question; useful for you to know how many points and details to include in the answers. An example of this type of question is the data-analysis question (beginning of paper 2). It requires you to analyse graphs and compare results. (See Data-Analysis Questions).

3) Free Response Questions (Paper 2): These questions require long and detailed answers on lined paper. You are the boss of the style of answer (best choice, tables, carefully annotated diagrams..). Usually the questions will direct you. Sometimes (Section B) you are given choices. Read them carefully to choose the question that best suits you and you know you can answer the best. Always follow a logical sequence in arranging your answer and avoid irrelevant information. Try to make your handwriting as legible as possible.

Basically, 50% of the questions require factual recall. So recharge your memory! These questions require direct answers: LIST, STATE, OUTLINE or DESCRIBE. The other 50% involves expressing ideas that are more complex or involve using your knowledge of things you haven't been taught.

These questions usually start with:

EXPLAIN - Sometimes it involves giving the mechanism behind things with a logical chain of events. It is a 'how' sort of explanation with 'therefore' being the keyword. However, sometimes it involves giving reasons or causes; a 'why' sort of explanation with 'because' being the keyword.

DISCUSS - Sometimes, you have to include arguments for and against something. Try to give a balanced account. Sometimes, you might include a series of hypotheses without making a final choice.

SUGGEST - Mostly never taught. Use your overall biological understanding to find answers. As long as they are possible, they will receive a mark!

COMPARE - refer to the previous section to see a detailed explanation.

DISTINGUISH - Include only the differences in your answer. Use 'whereas' to help.

EVALUATE - Assess the value, importance or effect of something. How useful is the technique/model? What are its impacts on others/environment? Use your own judgment and criticism as long as it's valid and biologically correct.

Other action verbs are more straightforward and you'll probably answer them easily.

Data-Analysis Questions

I know many of us suffer from these types of questions. Read the question carefully. Underline any keywords in the question (sometimes, there are hidden facts that examiners put to see if you pay attention or not). Always underline action verbs in the questions (discussed above). This helps in case you forget or get messed up.

Start with the question, see how many marks are allotted and solve accordingly (2 marks means at least 2 major points in the answer, and so on). In case of graphs, always read the title of the graph, each axis and its units. In case of calculations, show your working and always indicate the units.

Study the data presented carefully many times (but watch out for the time). Be familiar with it and start solving. Practice such questions in your free time. They might really be annoying, but it really helps in the long run.

Resources

I would suggest revising from a range of different sources - I prefer using Bioninja (http://ib.bioninja.com.au) and other online IB Biology websites to make notes from since the textbooks either have too much or too little of certain bits of the syllabus. If your teacher isn't great or you're just not able to concentrate in class, check out Alex Lee on Youtube – this channel basically got me through Bio HL. I-Biology.net is another holy grail of IB Biology resources.

To be perfectly honest, there is such a myriad of resources out there that you just need to spend a good couple of hours searching around and finding what you find works best for you. The official IB Biology study guides are also great, but you should make sure that your revision is always remaining active and not just reading/glossing over.

32. Cracking Chemistry

Chemistry is halfway between Biology and Physics. It combines large amounts of memorization with elements of critical thinking and analysis. What this means is that even if you know your theory inside out you will still struggle when it comes to certain complex problems, more so than in biology. I also suggest you use past papers and the Questionbank extensively to help you review chemistry.

Chemistry is one of those subjects that at first glance is extremely difficult, this is due to the fact that there is so much new content introduced. The amount of "stuff" you have to know is significantly larger in IB chemistry than in any pre-IB course. Concepts such as orbitals, quantum chemistry and modern analytical chemistry are completely new and might be difficult to understand at first, especially with such an interlinked subject as Chemistry. This means that you will need concepts you still haven't studied to understand those you are currently studying. It might be especially difficult for those of you who like to understand the fundamentals of principles (as I do), as you still haven't studied those principles.

There are a few ways to solve this issue and improve your understanding of chemistry. Firstly (the least suggested method), would be to simply memorize all that you are taught and hope that once you have gone over most of the subject things will start to come together (they usually do, however you will need to go over certain concepts). The alternative is to go above and beyond the scope of the course. This means reading ahead in your book and discussing what you have learned with your teacher to understand the basics and fundamentals and linking ideas together.

Once you are able to link concepts together (which usually happens by the start of the second year of IB chemistry), the subject becomes much easier. Don't take this as an excuse to not work during the first year, as a matter of fact you should put a lot of energy during the first year to gain a very solid grasp of the basics which will allow you to understand and perform better with more difficult concepts.

As always I suggest you download the Questionbank to practice what you have learned. Despite the change in course, the question bank is still very useful and I suggest that you start using it 3 to 4 days before any test. Go through all the questions and understand the concepts. When it comes to chemistry there is no better way to study than to take quick notes while reading and answering Questionbank problems at the end of each chapter/topic.

Look through the specification, there are some points that you actually need to rote learn as an example (like the medical uses of some isotopes). I can't stress this one enough. When you revise, look through the specifics and ask yourself if you understand every point. My teacher missed a load of spec points so I used Richard Thornley to learn them (check the YouTube channel, it is a lifesaver).

If you're good at rote learning / memorization, or have the time to do so, I strongly recommend learning all of organic chemistry. It's a heavy rote learning topic but if it comes up in the exam you can easily get full marks on any organic chemistry question since you don't actually need to apply many, if any, concepts at all.

Learn how to do the calculations. The Henderson-Hasselbach equation is very useful for the acids section, but it isn't in the specification. I recommend learning that equation off by heart, because I've seen some 4 mark questions where you can simply plug the numbers into the HH equation (there's a longer way to do it too if you're wondering why they're 4 marks)

33. Figuring Out Physics

Physics might be a subject which requires relatively less memorization; however, the concepts explored are multidimensional and the critical thinking required is advanced. You might be asked to prove things using formulas, or derive certain formulas, or explain unknown concepts through previously studied ones. It is natural that you use the Questionbank and past papers to supplement your studying. After completing a chapter in each topic, do a few questions, reflect and then continue with the next chapter. I suggest this technique with all the sciences but especially with physics.

To show the importance of practice I will bring up Pablo and use him as an example. He is a smart guy who got into Oxford, but if it wasn't for the 7 he received in HL physics he wouldn't have made it. He was predicted a 7 in History and Economics, however to his astonishment he didn't get them, yet his practice and hard work for physics paid off in the form of a 7. A few weeks before the exams Pablo would come to my house on Fridays (desperate times require desperate measures, such as not partying on Fridays) and we would get to work. There really isn't any way around it. I had always been rather good at the sciences so Pablo used me as a resource (don't worry I don't feel exploited). He would practice Question bank problems and if he ever encountered any issues he would ask for some help. I helped him where I could (this helped me solidify my own understanding) and where I couldn't help him I went and did the research (this helped me spot some gaps in my learning). We did this for a few weeks until he felt confident with his physics and both of us came out on top.

This example was meant to emphasize two points: firstly that there is no way around studying, and secondly that you should work with your friends when needed (two minds are better than one).

It's important to know what the question is asking of you, more specifically how much information you should include when extrapolating the age of the universe from the Hubble constant or how many data points you should test to determine whether the correlation of the graph is correct. To get good at this you should take a look at the science command terms. This can be achieved as easily as Googling "chemistry/biology/physics IB command terms". (Command terms apply to all subjects and I suggest you understand all the pertinent ones).

Be greedy, it's the IB and you need to snatch points wherever you can (this idea applies to all the subjects). In the sciences the best way to do this is to place particular attention to the internal assessments and paper 2 of the exams. If you put in the correct amount of attention into the IAs you can score upward of 90% (this sounds high, but remember to use all the resources at your disposal: teachers, friends, and the Internet). You should also get better at doing Paper 2's, as they bring you the largest chunk of the final grade (36%). This entails learning the command terms, getting good at structuring answers and time management. It also means picking up the book and learning thoroughly the data analysis techniques that will be asked of you in the first part of the paper. If you can accumulate points in these 2 parts (IA and Paper 2) then you are guaranteed a passing grade and achieving that 7 will be even easier.

The Physics IA
To accumulate said points, it is imperative to do well on the Physics IA which acts as a safety blanket if you mess up on, say,

the high-pressure Paper 1. For both SL and HL, the IA is a physics investigation on experimental data that you collect yourself.

Having a well-structured IA is half the battle, as this ensures that you include all the necessary calculations and information. Here is the structure that got me a 7:

Introduction – a short introduction to the overall topic of the IA. This can be a good opportunity to showcase personal engagement by mentioning any real-life interactions you've had with the topic (I wrote about pendula, so I mentioned playing childhood games with a pendulum) and/or any preliminary experiments you did prior to the investigation.

Research question – a one to two sentence question/statement clearly outlining the aim of your investigation.

Background information – a one to two page section detailing any background knowledge the reader will need to understand the physical phenomena you're investigating. Instead of sketchy physics websites, use your IB textbook!

Variables – a short explanation of the independent, dependent and constant variables in your experiment. For your constant variables, I'd recommend creating a table with column headings 'variable', 'how it will be kept constant' and 'why it must be kept constant'. This is a good way to show you're thinking about the experiment critically.

Diagram – a diagram of your experimental setup. I'd recommend making one online on chemix.org. If possible, include a photo of your setup as well.

Apparatus – a list of all the equipment you will be using throughout the experiment. If applicable, mention the equipment's unit and uncertainty e.g. 'stopwatch (s) (±0.01)'

Risk assessment – a brief explanation of any safety and ethical considerations you made to make sure the experiment is safe and sustainable.

Method – a step-by-step explanation of each stage of the experiment. Think of it as a tutorial or 'recipe' with the help of which anyone could replicate the experiment themselves.

Raw data – a results table of your collected data with all values given to the precision of your measuring instrument e.g. if your meter-stick has a precision of ±0.001m, give your length values accurate to three decimal places.

Processed data – a results table with all calculated values along with their absolute uncertainties that will be used for your graph. Also include one sample uncertainty calculation.

Graph – a graph from your processed data which shows some kind of relationship between the variables you are investigating. Don't forget your minimum and maximum gradient lines from which you will calculate final uncertainties!

Analysis – any final analysis/observations/calculations you must make from your graph to achieve the investigation's aim e.g. if you're using the graph to find a value for gravitational field strength, include the final calculation of this value and its uncertainty that you found using the line of best fit and your minimum and maximum gradient lines.

Conclusion – restate your research question and answer it using the conclusions you drew from your data. Don't forget to compare your conclusions to secondary published sources and, based on this, state whether or not your investigation can be deemed successful. This is also a good time to mention any anomalies as well as systematic/random errors that arose during the experiment.

Evaluation – this is the last and debatably the most important part of your IA. This is where you explain the strengths and weaknesses of your experiment with reference to how your results differed from the published value/relationship. It is also crucial to mention how the experiment could be improved and extended based on where it fell short. As I said, the evaluation is the make-it-or-break-it of your IA, so make sure it is at least a page long!

Revision Examples

The following test advice doesn't only apply to the sciences but all subjects you will do in the IB. Memory retention techniques at their core are very similar, so listen carefully to the advice below and extrapolate as much as you can.

Reading is never enough to memorize or understand a concept (unless you are a genius, and I'm guessing you aren't), you need to take that information and reformulate it and apply it. The more (and more often) processing your brain does of the information the better you will retain it. That's why learning is so dynamic.

Reading is not enough on its own. To ensure a full understanding, you have to take notes, scribble on the page, highlight and connect concepts you read about. I annotate things, draw arrows that link ideas and solve problems. I also fill in the blanks or steps that might have been skipped by the book in proving formulas. The point is to transfer your thinking process onto the page.

Taking notes is extremely important. However, copying the book isn't enough. You must add an extra level of processing to the copying. This may include rephrasing what you have read, underlining key words, creating your own examples, drawing diagrams or explaining to yourself concepts that you didn't understand before.

I invest time and energy into my notes, so that I may refer to them in the future when I have forgotten the topic and actually understand them. Evidently this is a time-consuming process, so be smart; prioritize subjects based on how much difficulty you have retaining concepts, how technical it is, etc.

Don't forget to pair your note taking with sessions of question answering (this is the most important step, never skip it). However before the exams (a few days) I suggest that you go over your notes, questions you did in the past and found difficult as well as all the material provided in the exams (data booklets and so on). Annotate your data booklet and make sure that you understand everything in it.

A trick I learned before the exams is that not all the useful formulas are included in the data booklets (this is more evident for chemistry than physics).

34. The Group 4 Project

The idea here is actually pretty simple: students are basically just split up into groups with representatives from at least two sciences and told to design, perform, and make a presentation on an experiment based on a given theme They're basically grading you on teamwork and how well everyone in the group understands the experiment and the concepts behind it, rather than the experiment design, outcomes, or anything like that. Ours was actually pretty enjoyable. As long as you work well with your group mates, everything should be fine.

The group 4 project is a piece of work that all IB students have to do – it is so important for you to do this, that you fail the Diploma if you do not do it (but it doesn't technically count towards anything…) As such, your school should be making you aware of this.

For those that do not know, the project is unusual in that the process you go through is far more important than the actual outcome. The idea is that you work with other students in a multidisciplinary way. This may sound a little strange so I would explain it in the following way: there are 3 phases to the project …

1. The Planning Phase.

The aim of this stage is for each small group of students (approx. 6) to come up with a suggestion for the Global Title of the G4 Project. The students in the Planning teams should cover the G4 subjects at the school wherever possible.

It is important that each and every person MUST contribute to this process. It is everyone's responsibility to consider what their subject could contribute to the suggested Titles. For example, there is no point suggesting a title if you can't think what the Physics students could do with it. In most schools, the G4 subjects are Bio, Chem, Phys, EVS, DT.

Examples of possible titles are:

<u>Concrete</u>

Biology: medical effects of dust

Chemistry: purity of limestone, additives, chemical attack, the setting process

Design Technology: composites, choice of material, reinforcement

Environmental Systems: impact of extracting and using sand, cement, aggregate

Physics: strength, composite theory, thermal properties

<u>Analysis of local and/or traditional building materials</u>

Biology: effect of removal on local environment, support of growth of organisms e.g. insects

Chemistry: acid rain, salinity, combustibility

Physics: mechanics, stress, heat transfer, ventilation, insulation

Effect of caffeine of physical performance

Biology: effect on respiration, blood pressure, heart rate, reflex time and   balance

Chemistry: sources and composition of caffeine, determining caffeine levels in these sources

Physics: measuring power output (stair climbing, cycles, speed rotations)

Ski project

Biology: skeletal structure, muscles, temperature loss, anthropometrics

Chemistry: snow quality, artificial snow, waxes, materials

Design Technology: buildings, materials

Environmental Systems: forest destruction, erosion, economic impact

Physics: aerodynamics, friction, gravity, structure, heat loss, insulation

Science in the theatre

Biology: reducing stress for performers

Chemistry: creating safe special effects

Design Technology: designing new sets, lighting

Environmental Systems: improving air quality

Physics: creating new lighting effects

<u>Factors influencing performance in a 400m race</u>

Biology: heart beat, biorhythms, sleep, fatigue, stress

Chemistry: isotonic drinks and diet

Design Technology: design and materials for track, shoes, sports drinks containers

Physics: elasticity, shock absorbance, wind, temperature

2. The Action Phase.

Usually students are put into small groups (approx. 3-4) to do the actual work. You will do a short piece of research as a team. You need to split the work up and every member of the team must take responsibility for this part.

It is vital to remember that the actual outcome is not important, it is the fact that the students actually worked together and made something happen.

3. The Reporting Phase.

This is where the school asks you to normally give a presentation to explain what you did and asks questions for a few minutes at the end.

Final Comments:

The one BIG piece of advice about the Group 4 Project is to enjoy it – do not try to avoid it or do nothing. Work hard because these strange moments do not happen that often. Enjoy the work and engage with what you are doing – it should then be fun and you should get excellent marks for it. Also keep in mind that it counts for **0%** of your overall grade (you just need to 'pass it') so don't sweat it too much.

35. Mastering HL Maths

The advice in this chapter is written primarily with Maths AA HL in mind – however almost all of it is applicable to all other maths courses.

There is simply no way around it; you have to study and practice. Knowing the theory isn't good enough, especially when you are doing Maths AA HL. Throughout the two years of mathematics, I was consistently scoring between 4s and 5s on my tests, and even scored a shaming 28% on paper 1 in the mock exams. It goes without saying I thought I was going to fail the IB, however I used this stress and panic to my advantage. I began very intensive studying and in a period of 3 months was able to clock in around 120 hours of math studying; that amounts to about an hour and a half of math each day, thanks to which I scored a solid 6 in my exams.

I organised my math studying as follows:

I used the Oxford IB Mathematics AA HL book, and did most of the problems from there (even the easy and repetitive ones, as these teach you small tricks). I also spent some extra time doing the more complicated problems and didn't give up too soon. This book allowed me to really learn all the tricks that you will need for solving impossible IB problems. I strongly suggest you purchase this book and use it as a primary source of practice.

Upon finishing each chapter, I would turn to the QuestionBank and create a mini test with relevant questions. You have to get used to the IB formatting and understanding how they might attempt to trick you (initially I could honestly only understand one in three questions but by the end I could understand every one. This however didn't mean that I could solve all of them). You should also understand how the mark scheme works, because if you do not show your workings you could lose marks even though your answer is correct. Finally your teachers usually give you questions from the QuestionBank, so if you are lucky some you have done might come up again (this always helps with the predicted grade). Any questions I didn't understand I would bookmark and ask my math tutor or class teacher for help. (I had a tutor all year round; I strongly suggest this if you can afford it).

Alongside the textbook, I also did tons of practice from questionbanks I found online, most notably Revision Village. Even though it's a paid service, it was a true game changer, as it provided me with heaps of resources all neatly organised by topic. This helped me focus on my weaker areas, as I was supported by the hundreds of detailed video explanations that Revision Village provides for every single question as well as all the key math concepts in the AA and AI syllabi.

Finally, attempt all the questions in the exam, even if you only know the first half of the problem still attempt to solve it. The IB mark scheme works in mysterious ways and you can always get a few points here and there. These points might be the difference between a 5 and 6 or 6 and 7.

54%. When your teachers said you are capable of taking Higher Level Mathematics AA, they never explained that it meant dropping from a "straight 7s" student to barely getting half the marks on a test. It is never easy to have your perception of ability shattered the way the first HL Math text does, and no one prepares you for the inevitable questioning of one's intelligence. As any HL Math student will tell you, we have all asked the same, age-old question during the 2-year course. *Am I good enough for this?*

The key to success in HL Mathematics AA, however, is to take the test with its big red 54% and put it on your wall. The key is to look at that score and to associate with it a sense of determination. *I will always be more prepared than I was this time.* At first it is difficult, to fall from being a model math student to scoring so low, but as with most weaknesses, the first step to improving is realizing that one has a weakness.

Even then, it is easy to say you will prepare, work and improve, but not follow through. The more difficult task is to decide on a course of action, and stick to it rigorously, rather than fooling yourself into a false sense of confidence. Remember, confidence alone scores about zero marks. Practice, on the other hand, is far more valuable.

04h30 A.M. The sun hasn't come out and the birds aren't singing because they, like the rest of your family, are asleep. Why aren't you? Sometimes it is very easy to not set aside enough time for practicing mathematics. Sometimes you are just too tired after basketball practice, or band, or just doing all of your homework, to sit down and tackle a problem that continually eludes you. Convenience and cognitive clarity are what make the morning perfect for mathematics. A solid 90 minutes of work every morning from 0430-0600 were the only reason I was able to surpass my 54% and attain an excellent grade in the final exams. By using a time of day when you are normally free and your mind is clear, you are able to reap the maximum reward in terms of improvement in your mathematics. It will be tough to wake up initially, but when your scores start rising, you'll appreciate every sleep-depriving minute.

General Tips

Studying tips:
- Your fundamental **understanding** is very important. Focus on learning the techniques you may need. There may be some techniques/tricks/solutions that your textbooks don't cover, and you can learn these from doing past papers.
- Complex numbers, vectors, planes and probability usually have big questions in Section B, and with a bit of practice, they're pretty straightforward. I would recommend learning those topics well. Calculus comes up a fair bit, but from my experience, complex numbers, planes and probability are the most common.

- I generally feel that the math textbooks do have some limitations - the questions you get in them and in real exams are quite different. I say this because I've learnt so many more 'tricks' to solving questions from exams than I have from textbooks. Because of this, it is often also better to turn to online questionbanks and services as was mentioned previously.
- When you first start revising, I suggest using the textbook and online questionbanks. Pick the topics you are **least** comfortable with and focus on them. When you're comfortable with them, you can start doing past papers. It's fine to repeat past papers to really drill them into yourself, some questions are kind of recycled with different numbers (e.g. complex numbers with binomial expansion). You'll get to the point where some questions are so easy that you

should just skip them and do the questions that don't look easily solvable.
- As always, make sure you're focused when you're studying. Remove any sources of distractions like your phone and work to create a boundary between your normal life and your study life.
- There are some tiny bits of rote learning you need to do, such as the equations for sums and products of polynomials. Make sure you learn the equations for them - if you get a question on it in the exam it'll most likely be very straightforward, but if you don't know them then you've just lost some easy marks.
- Work hard on your Exploration (IA) and try and get the highest mark you can for it. I got 17/20 on my IA which really helped me. It's good to walk into the exam knowing you have a good buffer.
- Work with friends. You may not always have the best, or even right approach to a question - and they might. Sometimes it's the other way around. However, if you can explain a question to a friend and if they can understand it, then it means you know the topic well.
- It is very difficult to cram maths and I would strongly advise against it. Start revising early so you're in good shape for the exam.

Exam tips:
- In the real exam, you get 5 minutes reading time. Use this time to flick through every question, and make a (mental) note of the questions that are the easiest. When you can start writing, do those questions first, then do the rest of the paper. Since you have seen all the questions briefly before you begin, your brain will think in the background about these questions. You

may have a sudden 'Got it!' moment for some of the harder questions even if you aren't on those questions. Two more reasons for doing this - you build up momentum and confidence and if you don't finish on time, you've maximised the amount of marks you can get.
- Don't freak out when you see a question you don't know how to do immediately, but skip it and save it for later. There was a question in my maths exam involving a goat which really tripped me up. I only did part of the question but looking back at it, it wasn't that hard a question, and I knew all the maths I needed to solve it.
- If you're stuck, flick through the formula booklet. Formula booklet is your best friend. You may see a formula that suddenly makes you understand what the question wants.
- Draw a diagram to help you picture the scenario - this is particularly helpful when doing trig, complex numbers, stats or vectors and planes.
- If you're ever substituting, which is very often, put brackets around what you have substituted in. This helps you avoid BIDMAS errors. Negative signs are a pain and doing this makes things a bit clearer. It's a good habit to get into.
- Learn how to use your GDC well. In the calculator paper there are some very easy questions if you know how to use your GDC. They're very quick and easy to do.
- Most importantly, **RTFQ. Read the full question..**

- **Full Guide on Getting a 7 in Math AAHL/SL**

Advice

I (M24) got a 7 in my final IB exams in Math AAHL, and here's how you can too:
- **1. Understand**
- **Don't just memorise - understand:** my math teacher emphasised *conceptual understanding* over memorisation, and this was a game-changer for me. It is faster, easier and more fun to **understand** math, instead of memorising formulas.
- Here are three steps to understand any concept:
    1. **Derive** the formula or rule. Try to prove it yourself (or with guidance online).
    2. **Research:** watch a video, read a blog, or ask ChatGPT *anything* that you are not clear about. There are no dumb questions
    3. Ask yourself "**Why?**" - "Why does this math exist? How is it used in the real world? What problem does it solve?". Answer these, and similar, questions to get to the bottom of the purpose of this math.

Helpful Resources:
- MrMacMaths - concise, handwritten notes: https://www.mrmacmaths.com/
- 3Blue1Brown - intuitive, visual explanations for tough topics: https://www.youtube.com/@3blue1brown
- ChatGPT - you can ask any question about math you want, and it can explain the math at any level you are comfortable with. Take advantage of AI.
- **2. Practice**

Practice is everything. Understanding alone won't solidify the concepts - you need to get familiar with how this concept is used to solve problems.

Best question banks imo (just these two got me very far):

- Revision Village - best $200 you'll spend on some math questions, trust me.
- SaveMyExams - yes the answers are paid, but the questions aren't. There are workarounds to get them.
- **How I Practiced:**

Our teacher gave use unit tests for *each* of the subtopics, both a Paper 1 and Paper 2, which were held every 4 weeks on average. A week before each test I would practice for 2 hours per day. That's ~140 hours of topic-specific practice - **not including past papers.**

- **Tips for Effective Practice**
- When solving the questions, think back to what you researched in the 1. Understanding phase. You don't have to create any revolutionary mathematical connections, but aim to notice the theoretical concepts you learnt about while solving the questions.
- **Always check the mark scheme** - even if you got the answer right. You might learn a new, faster method to solve this type of problem.
- Make sure to do this after **every** topic. If your teacher does not provide you with unit tests for each topic, you will have to discipline yourself to do practice on your own.
- **3. Apply**
- Once you've mastered the concepts and done enough practice per topic, it's time for **past papers.** These are your best tool for acing the exam.
- **Don't rush into past papers** if you're still not comfortable with certain topics. Solidify weak areas first.

Once you are familiar with all topics, you can move on. Past papers can be gotten from your school, if not then... well there's the internet, you do your research. Asking seniors or graduates can also be a helpful thing to do. When practicing, I recommend you to **time yourself**.

You will start off slow, that is okay. After 2 or 3 papers, you should be all good. Remember to practice both Paper I and II (I will write a separate post for Paper 3's later). Now, all you need to do is keep grinding out past papers, timing your completion time, and checking your answers. Remember, if you notice that you keep struggling with questions from a specific topic, go back and practice before continuing with past papers.

Useful tip: Break the paper into sections (e.g., Part A and B) if sitting for the full exam feels overwhelming, or you don't have a full 2 hours to study. Keep grinding until you can finish confidently under time pressure.

- **4. Conclusion**
- Stay consistent - with enough practice you will understand what is going on with any concept.
- Reach out for help to your classmates, teachers, or even me.

36. Mastering the Math IA [part I]

This chapter will help you achieve a minimum level 5 grade (such as 12/20) with relative ease. To score that magical mark of an 18/20 you will need to put in some effort. This guide will ensure that when you aim for those top grades that you do not lose any marks for not having conformed to both the implicit and explicit demands of the IB, no matter how small or large.

Another point to note is that this guide is written specifically for HL mathematics students but all of the points discussed also apply to Mathematics SL (I've checked and asked top scoring Mathematics SL students for their advice). I'll however add an extra section at the end highlighting the major differences between the Math HL IA and the Math SL IA.

Criteria A, Communication:

Achievement level	Descriptor
0	The exploration does not reach the standard described by the descriptors below.
1	The exploration has some coherence.
2	The exploration has some coherence and shows some organization.
3	The exploration is coherent and well organized.
4	The exploration is coherent, well organized, concise and complete.

This is probably the easiest criterion to score highly in, so follow the points below:

- **Readability, the art of making your work easy and fun to read**:
    o Proof-read your work; look for spelling mistakes and ensure that you keep your language concise and effective. Keep an eye out for the flow of the text and make sure that your sentences are well structured and easy to follow. I suggest that after you have proof-read yourself, ask one of your friends to go

over your work (tell them to keep an eye out for all the above).
- Use interesting language, but don't saturate your work with irrelevant and fancy terms that do not belong there.
- Keep things concise; don't go rambling on about random mildly related stuff. Try to avoid repeating yourself, and keep your work under 12 pages.

- **Structure, to stop examiners from getting confused:**
  - Have a table of contents, and learn how to use it in MS Word. This means you should get acquainted with Text Styles (e.g. heading 1, heading 2, title and so on…).
  - Use the in-built equation builder when you use maths in your IA. I also suggest changing the colour of the font (black for standard text, blue for math equations).
  - Intro, Content, Conclusion. The intro should contain the reasons behind why you are interested in the topic, your IA's aim, how your topic is important on the global scale and a general overview of it. The content should have all the meaty maths (obviously) and the conclusion should have a wrap up of the exploration as well as reflection.
- **Citations, to stop you from failing the IB:**
  - Be sure to use MLA citations (or other recognized methods by the IB) on any text or work you extract from textbooks, the Internet or whatever medium you employ.
- **Explain: show the examiner you know what you are talking about:**

- Nearly each mathematical step in the exploration should have at least one line of text explaining what you have done.
- If you use any non-IB mathematical knowledge be sure to spend some time explaining it.
- If you use any non-mathematical knowledge (e.g. physics or economics), make certain that you explain it thoroughly so that your examiner is on the same level of understanding.

Criteria B, Mathematical Presentation

Achievement level	Descriptor
0	The exploration does not reach the standard described by the descriptors below
1	There is some appropriate mathematical presentation
2	The mathematical presentation is mostly appropriate.
3	The mathematical presentation is appropriate throughout

This is where people lose stupid marks, so pay attention.

- **Make your work pretty, to stop any possible confusion:**
    - Be sure that you use Insert Equations option (learn to use it, it's pretty simple and straightforward).
    - Use different text for the math equations; make the text Italic and change its colour.
- **Use Appropriate Notation:**
    - Never use notation that some calculations and computer software employ to denote 10^x by Ex; instead write it as a power of 10. So 3E3.5 would become $3\times 10^{3.5}$

- - Just use correct mathematical notation and when in doubt ask around.
- **Label Everything:**
  - If you are using generic equations make sure you label them with a line of text. This label should contain the name of the equation (as well as anything else you find appropriate).
  - Be sure to label tables and graphs using the citation tool provided by MS word. The citation should denote each element cited by a unique tag and a short explanation (e.g. table1: data from plant growth experiment // figure 1: graph of time vs acceleration).
  - When you use a table or graph make sure that they are correctly constructed. (Think of your Science IAs)
    - Tables: All rows are correctly titled, units of measurement are given (if appropriate), and all data is kept to appropriate significant figures
    - Graphs: Label all the axes, title and give units of measurement.
- **Term Definition: define fancy and complex words:**
  - Define mathematical terms that are not common knowledge and other complex scientific or mathematical terminology. When in doubt, just define.

Criteria C, Personal engagement

Achievement level	Descriptor
0	The exploration does not reach the standard described by the descriptors below.
1	There is evidence of limited or superficial personal engagement.
2	There is evidence of some personal engagement.
3	There is evidence of significant personal engagement.
4	There is abundant evidence of outstanding personal engagement.

This criterion is a little more devious than it seems at first glance. 4 marks for showing that you care: really? Well this is how it works: if you show that you care and that you have put a lot of effort into your work you can score a maximum of 2-3/4. To get that extra four, your work needs to be solidly on point; not only do you need to show that you are "personally engaged", but your exploration also has to be of top quality. I would look at this criteria as the "holistic criteria", one in which the examiners can mark on a whim.

- **Interest is Gold (Show it or Pretend):**
    o In the introduction spend a few lines explaining why your exploration is important to you on a personal level and why you chose it. If you don't have any good answers, just lie and try to link the problem you are analysing with a personal anecdote.
- **Pick an Interesting topic: it makes it more interesting for you and your examiner:**
    o Don't select a standard textbook problem (for example solving a Rubik's cube or generic problems like that). Try to explore new problems and make your topic more interesting. By showing that you have taken the time to investigate something unusual you are demonstrating to your examiners that you are engaged and willing to learn,

scoring you well in this criteria. I'll come to selecting the thesis later on in this guide.
- Extend your mathematics beyond the obvious. Try to spend some time to see how the mathematics you are intending to use can be implemented. Show the generic solution (by generic, I mean "most obvious" or "standard" solution) and spend time attempting a non-generic solution. Even if you can't directly do the maths, talk about alternative methods for solving your problem and describe in detail how it would be done. This shows the examiner you are thinking above and beyond the call of duty. Trust me, do it.

Criteria D, Reflection

Achievement level	Descriptor
0	The exploration does not reach the standard described by the descriptors below.
1	There is evidence of limited or superficial reflection.
2	There is evidence of meaningful reflection.
3	There is substantial evidence of critical reflection.

You don't get more IB than reflections and evaluations. Be sure to be efficient with your words and constantly talk about any assumptions you make.

- **Improving the exploration:**
    - Discuss what limitation you came across when doing your IA. These limitations could be, but are not limited to the following: Time constraints (what would you have done with more time, what would you have expanded on?), lack of technology or software (how

would better tools have helped you?), limitations in math skills (if you were a super mathematician what would you have done differently).
- o Mention what other types of math you could have used to improve your explorations quality. Please note that throughout the reflection process you will have to explain things in plain English, but you should also describe and show small snippets of mathematics, here and there.
- Local and global application:
  - o You should expand on why you chose this topic and how it has implications to you personally, but most importantly, towards humanity in general. This section should be a detailed continuation of the rationale you started in the introduction (explaining why your exploration is important on a global scale), however this time include your findings from the exploration into the analysis.
  - o Explain in detail how the maths and the problems you have explored are applied in the real world. Use these terms to guide you: implications, applications, limitations, compare and contrast. Think of the past, present and future, and how your exploration has changed over time (both in evolving and relevance).
- Wrap it all up
  - o Create a swift conclusion that wraps up all your findings, connecting them with the reflection. The reflection will serve as a

conclusion in itself; that's why no more than a paragraph is required to wrap things up.

Criteria E, Use of mathematics

Achievement level	Descriptor
0	The exploration does not reach the standard described by the descriptors below.
1	Some relevant mathematics is used. Limited understanding is demonstrated.
2	Some relevant mathematics is used. The mathematics explored is partially correct. Some knowledge and understanding are demonstrated.
3	Relevant mathematics commensurate with the level of the course is used. The mathematics explored is correct. Good knowledge and understanding are demonstrated.
4	Relevant mathematics commensurate with the level of the course is used. The mathematics explored is correct and reflects the sophistication expected. Good knowledge and understanding are demonstrated.
5	Relevant mathematics commensurate with the level of the course is used. The mathematics explored is correct and reflects the sophistication and rigour expected. Thorough knowledge and understanding are demonstrated.
6	Relevant mathematics commensurate with the level of the course is used. The mathematics explored is precise and reflects the sophistication and rigour expected. Thorough knowledge and understanding are demonstrated.

This is the toughest criterion to break. Up until now you could theoretically score rather well without having much mathematical knowledge, however things here begin to change.

- **Selecting the aim**:
    - Selecting the thesis/aim of the exploration is one of the toughest yet most important parts of the IA. You must do one of the following (trust me, a failure to do so will result in poor marks): either select an original problem and solve it with traditional math, or select a traditional problem and solve it with original math (or an original problem with original math).
    - I suggest you take a problem and model it in real life (Calculus usually comes in handy

here). I modelled the fuel consumption of a rocket going into orbit, and I'm also certain that almost all my calculations were incorrect, yet I still got a 18/20. The fact is that it really doesn't matter if you get the right answer; how will they ever know (unless there is a well-known answer to your problem)? As long as your mathematics is correct, it's all good. I suggest you look at mainly the modelling problems. These are the best and easiest to score highly in (as long as you follow this guide).

- **Getting more than a 4/6**
  - You cannot score more than a 4/6 by applying HL textbook math (if you are an HL student). What I did in my exploration was use integration, complex and fiddly integration. Most importantly I self-taught integration (we hadn't gone over it in class yet) and made note of it in my introduction (I explained that I had self-taught as the IA was written before my lessons in integration) to show that I was going above and beyond. I suggest that you use advanced concepts that are taught in the course and apply them in an interesting manner. Alternatively you can learn new mathematical theorems and concepts and apply those (a problem is that most people learn new maths and don't explore it in enough depth causing low marks). If you do select a new domain of mathematics, be sure to research it well enough (you should be able to go beyond copying a Wikipedia page).

- - Don't overcomplicate your exploration for no reason. Randomly shoving formulas here and there won't help you. Actually, the randomness of these formulas will cause the flow of the exploration to break, which will cause your communication mark to go down.
- Mix it up:
  - Within one exploration you can try different mathematical approaches to solving a problem and compare them. This type of IA would score highly on reflection and if the math is good, it would also score highly in the maths criteria.
  - To mix it up in my IA, I combined both algebraic solutions with technological ones (using cool software). This is really good if done correctly (you must include solving by hand and algebraic solutions), however you will score extremely poorly if all calculations are done using a computer and brute force techniques.

HL vs SL

So everything is exactly the same between the two explorations in terms of IB requirements and the criteria you are targeting. The major difference comes with the mathematics you employ and their relevance. Something that would score highly on a SL exploration would not necessarily on a HL exploration (but HL will usually score extremely highly for SL). It is therefore important that you use appropriate mathematics and seek appropriate depth in your exploration. The mathematics you employ should always be on the upper difficulty limit of what you are studying, or even beyond it.

37. Mastering the Math IA [Part II: Example]

Let's take for example a modelling IA, one where we want to model the Formula 1 racing and calculate the optimal strategy for it. We would want to take two opposing strategies and model their behaviour, compare them and derive an optimal solution. Please note that the points below are only summaries of possible discussion themes:

Introduction:

- Why Formula 1 interests me or a personal anecdote - (you could lie)
- If better algorithms are developed for Formula 1, these are likely to have a global effect. Technology and innovations from Formula 1 are often used in commercial situations. If efficient driving strategies are found they could be applied to smart cars (especially now that driverless cars are coming out) – Note that I am trying to relate the importance of the subject to current events and a global scale.
- A general overview of Formula 1, its rules and history – No longer that four lines.

Overview:

- The variables that will be taken into consideration, and the things that will not be taken into consideration: pit-stop times, weight of fuel and its effect on speed, acceleration and deceleration at turns, speed and its effect on wheel aging (and its relation to the number of pit-stops). Things that won't be taken into consideration, overall exact path through the track (too difficult to measure), refuelling times (no longer permitted, all fuel has to be pre-loaded onto the cars). I talk about both things that are in my capacity to calculate and things that are not. I make sure to simplify the problem so that I can apply the maths to it. I can later reflect on the simplifications that were made and score points in the reflection criteria.

- Two distinct strategies will be created, strategy A and strategy B, these will then be compared and an intermediate strategy will be developed (the more optimal one). Note that we are clearly laying out the problem and saying what we are going to be doing. It is also a good idea to refer to the techniques that we will be using. We also discuss all the parameters we are going to use and how they are linked (brief overview).

    o Strategy A: The most fuel efficient speed will be chosen, its effect on fuel consumption, tire wear and pit stops will be considered. All this data will be aggregated into a time for an arbitrary lap. The strategy's effectiveness will be considered for different types of tracks.

    o Strategy B: The fastest speed will be chosen, its effect on fuel consumption (initial amount of fuel), tire wear and pit stops will be considered. All this data will be aggregated into a time for an arbitrary lap. Track length will also be considered. The strategy's effectiveness will be considered for different types of tracks.

    o Strategy C: Integration and optimisation will be heavily used to find an optimal solution for finishing with the optimal time.

Mathematics:
- Option A is considered. All the mathematics is applied. The mathematics I would apply in general would be calculus, particularly the domains of integration, derivation and related rates. I would have a look into Calculus options textbooks, and attempt to use the maths from there. I would also search the internet for interesting applications of related rates and calculus.
- Option B is considered.
- Evaluation compares A and B. Further maths are explored to combine the two strategies and develop an optional solution C. Breaking the problem down into smaller chunks and applying simple IB calculus to it can actually yield interesting results, especially when everything is brought together into a general model. This can score you highly in the mathematics criteria as you are showing deep understanding of the problem and are applying solutions in an original manner.

Evaluation:

- Discussing potential flaws in my findings, such as the fact that the values used for tire wear, fuel consumption curves might have been wrong. You have to be critical with your own investigation, take it apart. It is completely possible you say that your results were invalid, it shows that you understand the complexity of the problem (you will get many marks

for your critical thinking and actually conducting "research/exploration").
- Points that could be added to my exploration on Formula 1 racing strategy are path calculations throughout the track. If my mathematical abilities were better I could create an algorithm for path calculation. This is an art however and entire teams spend years optimising path strategies. You should discuss possible areas of expansion, even if they are not feasible. Make sure that you at least have two feasible points and one non feasible point of expansion.
- I would talk about the global application of my exploration. The efficiency algorithms could define how cars must move for optimal efficiency. This has possible application in smart cars (cars with cruise control and lane detection) or driverless ones. The algorithms for efficiency could also be applied to other intelligent systems that move, such as: robots, UAVs and so on... Link your exploration to one closely related domain and a few distant ones.
- Calculus used in this modelling exploration is used in many domains of movement modelling such as aeronautics, space travel and even ballistics. Discuss the general application of the maths you used in the real world. It should be short, no longer than three sentences.

Cite your Sources
- Cite sources – Use MLA.

How you approach the IA

Understand:

Read the criteria and all the information that has been provided by this guide. I suggest you read it twice to be sure that you know exactly what is expected of you. You should also consistently refer back to the guide and the criteria to refresh your memory. Try to get your hands on as many past IA examples as possible – online, or ask your school for help.

Brainstorm:

Think of your interests and hobbies, draw them out on a mind map and start connecting things together. Write down any ideas or domains of exploration that might be interesting. Once you have a few interesting problems written down, think of the mathematics that could be applied to them. Have a quick look through your textbook and the Internet to gauge the difficulty of the maths. If the maths looks too difficult and undoable, don't do the problem and select a different one.

An alternative method for selecting a thesis is to first select the mathematics you wish to use, e.g. a particular domain or theory. Once that's done, you should research how this theory can be applied or think of some real life problems that could be solved using this piece of mathematics. Try to think out of the box and come up with original ideas. You will have to sit down and spend some serious time thinking of a thesis (it's one of the hardest parts).

Research:

Spend a long time becoming an expert with both your problem and the maths you will be applying to it. I suggest you use the Internet to search around for the information on your particular problem. YouTube, online archive, Wikipedia (you know what to do). For the maths however I suggest you get information from the following sources: teacher, core course book, option books, YouTube, MOOCs, and other websites. It might take you some time to get familiarised with a new domain or mathematical theory, but be sure to understand what you are studying.

Maths:

Before you write the actual essay you must be sure to get the maths sorted out. Spend a few days working on mathematics. I suggest asking other maths teachers and even fellow students to review your work. To get a 7 or high 6 you need to spend a few days working on the maths, however if you are aiming for a 5, you can get through all the required maths in a few hours. If you can't solve the maths however, it's time to go back a few steps and select a different thesis.

Write it all up:

Before you start writing anything be sure to reread the criteria and the guide. Now apply all the information you have learned over the last few pages and right up your exploration. This is the most tedious, but also the easiest part of the process.

Conclusion

You should also be able to get at least a 5 without much effort if you follow the tips above. Not much relies on your mathematical knowledge. Just be sure to check all the boxes and you will be ready. As a matter of fact, the guide was structured as a checklist, so be sure to go through the guide and physically check off each bullet point!

I suggest that you keep an eye out for modelling problems; these can score really well as the mathematics used is not too complex yet can create depth in your Exploration.

All in all the Mathematics Internal Assessment is rather simple, follow the points discussed above and you will smash it. I suggest picking something that interests you, so that you may invest time into your work without getting bored.

38. Hacking Your GDC

The purpose of this chapter is to drill into your head that your graphing display calculator can be a tool of great importance – if you use it correctly and to its full potential. Unfortunately, because there are so many different types of graphing calculators, it will be difficult to go in depth about the secret functions of each one, but I will try to provide a resource where available.

The single best resource that can be found for all basic calculator uses in the IB (Casio fx-9860G, Texas Instruments TI-84 models, Texas Instruments TI-nspire models) is at the Haese Mathematics website. Google 'Haese Mathematics IB calculator instructions' to find a 30 page pdf document that deals extensively with almost everything you need to know about your calculator.

There is also another pdf document written by Andy Kemp that deals with the TI-nspire calculator model specifically. You can find it by googling 'IB Mathematics Exam Preparation for Calculator Papers'. The OSC also sell a book that deals with using the TI-Series in IB Mathematics, but you need to purchase this and it costs 16GBP (bit steep in my honest opinion).

There are also two excellent YouTube videos that are both 40+ mins but are essential viewing if you want to understand how to get the most out of your calculator. The first is by the HKEXCEL Education Centre and is called 'How to ace your GDC calculator for IB Math', and the other is by mathsl1 channel and is called 'IB Math SL GDC Techniques for Paper 2'. I firmly believe that every IB student should spend time watching these videos as they teach you almost all of the quintessential techniques.

Basic Calculator Tips

1. Graphs displayed on a GDC may be misleading – so make sure that what you see makes sense.

2. Be sure your GDC has new batteries before your final exams.

3. As you are not allowed a GDC on Math Paper 1, the questions on this exam will focus on analytic / algebraic 'thinking' solutions. You need to practice these and simple arithmetic and algebraic computations as you won't be able to rely on a GDC.

4. On Paper 2, if you solve an equation by means of a graph on your GDC you must provide a clearly labelled sketch of the graph in your work – and indicate exactly what equation you solved on your GDC.

5. Even though a GDC is 'required' for Paper 2, do not assume that you will need to use your GDC on every question for Paper 2.

6. Do not use any calculator notation in your written solutions.

7. If you use your GDC to obtain an answer for a question on Paper 2, be sure that you clearly write down the appropriate mathematical 'set-up' for the computation you will perform on your GDC.

8. There will inevitably be some questions on Paper 2 where it will be more efficient to find the answer by using your GDC as opposed to an analytic method. Do not lose valuable time by choosing to answer a question using a tedious analytic method when you could get the answer quickly with your GDC.

GDC in IA / EE

If you have the opportunity to use your GDC graphs in your mathematics exploration or mathematics EE (if you are doing one), I would highly suggest this. It looks very impressive, and it shows examiners that you are using the tools at your disposal. Your calculator should have come with a USB link to your computer and software to extract the graphs / calculations – explore these avenues.

Formula Booklet

I want to take a section of this chapter to also stress the importance of knowing your math formula booklet inside out. During exams it is absolutely essential that students know where to quickly find every formula. Saving time by knowing where to find necessary equations in the data booklet and how to perform shortcuts on the calculator allows for extra time to solve the questions themselves and double-check over work. You don't want to be spending extra time looking for that one equation only to realize that it's not in the formula booklet, or not know how to perform an essential function on your calculator.

Being familiar with the formula booklet is even more important considering that several useful equations are missing from the formula booklet, and several difficult-to-remember equations are included. Students should therefore know which equations they will need to memorize and which are easily accessible. For example, in the HL and Further HL formula booklet there is the formula for the angle between two vectors, but not between two planes or a vector and a plane.

39. Acing Visual Art

I got a level 7 HL Visual Art this year and I have some important advice. I was looking for it when I was working, all over the internet and all I got was a regurgitated syllabus (or maybe repetition of what teachers have said...). So here it goes:

1. Pretend you are not doing the IB or any equivalent of school work (if you did GCSEs, forget anything connected to the format or requirements.) The IB as you should know has no prescribed themes; teachers usually try to make you set yourself limits. Resist. It's the one good thing about the actual visual arts course.

2. Culture is such a big word in the IB, but it doesn't have to mean worship and political correctness. If you really are a 'world student' and a thinker and all those other IB don't be afraid to criticise another culture as well as your own. You will not be penalised for having a voice as long as you know what you are talking about. Also don't focus on it too much. I've seen a lot of people obsessing about the culture aspect and it is so false and forced. If you don't feel it, aren't really that interested in it, then do not do it. My work was all universal - apart from literally 4 sketchbook pages on voodoo.

3. Other Artists: mention many but I beg you, again, do not force or obsess. Some projects come from you! Why should everything be an inspiration by Picasso or Rothko etc. It shouldn't work like this - you are in the driving seat. When I mentioned artists it was usually because of how they worked - method or how they thought that was inspiring; I tried to explain this well, and also explain why my work looks nothing like theirs and is absolutely unconnected in theme. If you know

your art history and theory well by reading in spare time, gallery's etc. this can work for you.

4. Studio Work is what makes you get a level 7 or so I believe, this is where the goods and time must lie whatever Option you take. It's what makes a real artist- I know a girl who got a level 5 - I was shocked! Her sketchbooks were the most beautiful, original and amazing things I have ever seen (god I was jealous), have never seen better even on university level but the final pieces were average. I would recommend academic sculpting-it's very time consuming but I recommend you do this in year 13 if you are a confident painter/drawer, it's also something fun and gives you a break from the whole paper format.

5. SKETCH BOOKS. The most difficult part for me as I hated having to be in a prescribed format (I generally hate rules I didn't make up) and I am a horrible perfectionist. I will be honest with you; I ripped many pages, stuck many together and repainted over others. I don't believe mistakes are a very good thing. For me it is a weakness, the learning experience is when you learn to do the page better and when your next RWB has less of those mistakes (yes my teacher was angry - but doesn't everyone hate ugly pages? they are not ok). But do not make this mistake which I did: get obsessed about one page and do it 10 times over. Chances are after the second time it will not improve much and is just a waste of time.

6. If you too hate sketchbooks I have a recommendation, carry around a Moleskine/ small notebook where you really can have a diary/ note pad/ mini sketchbook with no rules. Scan the pages from it that are nice and pretty or have interesting ideas, insights into your work and stick them into your RWB. This went down a hit with every one, moderator, examiner. +

present the originals at interview, exhibit and send to moderator (if your school requires it like mine did) it counts as extra work and is very personal and shows you're serious.

7. The interview is not difficult - if you know about your subject, mine ended up being less about all my work than about my attitude towards art. You can steer the conversation in a direction you would like by talking about things that will make the examiner interested to question you further.

IWB Advice

One of the biggest problems I have seen students encounter in their IB1 and IB2 with IB Visual Arts is their **workbooks**. Below I wish to give advice on how to complete amazing workbooks pages that relate to your studio works. All of the information below is from my personal experience and from watching other IB students in visual arts who have received 6s and 7s for their final IB grade. Besides giving simple advice, I have reviewed the syllabus, and I will try to demonstrate how the advice and tips given relate to what is said in the syllabus about requirements, objectives, outcomes, etc.

Investigation Criteria for Full Markings (OFFICIAL IB SYLLABUS EXCERPT)

- Analyses and compares perceptively art from different cultures and times, and considers it thoughtfully for its function and significance.
- Demonstrates the development of an appropriate range of effective skills, techniques and processes when making and analyzing images and artifacts.
- Demonstrates coherent, focused and individual investigative strategies into visual qualities, ideas and their contexts, an appropriate range of different

approaches towards their study, and some fresh connections between them.
- Demonstrates considerable depth and breadth through the successful development and synthesis of ideas and thoroughly explained connections between the work and that of others.
- Demonstrates effective and accurate use of the specialist vocabulary of visual arts.
- Uses an appropriate range of sources and acknowledges them properly.
- Presents the work effectively and creatively and demonstrates effective critical observation, reflection and discrimination.
- Presents a close relationship between investigation and studio.
-

Workbook, not a Sketchbook

The IBO refers to the sketchbooks used for your IB Visual Arts, both Standard Level and Higher Level as a **Workbook** or **Investigation Workbook.** There is a subtle reason for this change in name. Typically, a sketchbook is filled with random sketches, drawings, paintings, etc.; meanwhile, the IB Visual Arts Workbook also **focuses on a writing aspect.**

Your workbook pages, no matter how creative, will not be solid if the pages do not also contain writing with explanations for your drawings, brainstorming, etc. Therefore, for **the amount of drawing/sketching you put into your workbook, you should have a solid amount of writing/explanation on the same page** to go with it.

In your recorded Interview, it is a good idea to present your IWB and flip through your pages as you explain your work. The camera can zoom to film close up of specific things you are talking about. Some people like to fill up a page with drawings from their brainstorming, and then write another page about it. But that is not the most effective way. When the interviewer looks at one of your workbooks pages he/she wants to be able to read about how your sketch(es) relate to your plan of working, inspiration, ideas, artists you are looking into, etc. It must be a TRUE INVESTIGATION. Besides your brainstorming, experimentation, sketches and drawings, Interviewers want to see that you have investigated the techniques you are using or artists you are imitating. Make sure that for every studio work you create, you have a solid amount of INVESTIGATORY EXPLANATIONS in your workbooks.

The purpose of the investigation workbooks is to encourage personal investigation into visual arts, which must be closely related to the studio work undertaken. The relative importance of the investigation workbooks depends on whether the student has chosen option A or option B.

The investigation workbooks should incorporate contextual, visual and critical investigation. They should function as working documents and support the student's independent, informed investigation and studio practice. Investigation workbooks provide an opportunity for reflection and discovery and they play a key role in allowing ideas to take shape and grow. They should contain visual and written material that addresses contextual, visual and critical aspects of the investigation. They should also reflect the student's interests and include wide-ranging first-hand investigations into issues and ideas related to visual arts. There should be a balance in the investigation between analytical and open-ended discussion, illustrating the student's creative thinking.

Quantity AND Quality

Many students think that they can get by with minimal sketchbook pages, as long as the quality is sufficient. If you want to score 4, that will work.

If you want to score over 4, you must do MORE THAN THE MINIMUM. When you present your studio works and investigation workbooks in your video, the examiner will want to be able to see more pages than just the ones you turned in as your main pages. They want to see investigations, experimentation and drawings that you looked into, **even if you did not use** those newly learned skills or factual information in your final studio works. This demonstrates to the interviewer that you are not just meeting the criteria from the IB Visual Arts Syllabus, but you are going the extra mile. For a certain studio work, you may turn in 3 pages from your investigation workbooks about it, but the interviewer will want to see more. Even if you have one extra page, two, five or fifteen, **displaying extra knowledge that you did not turn in is vital.** After all, you are turning in your main pages, not all of the pages related to one of your main studio works.

You should be completing about 2 workbook pages a week. So let's do the math: if there are approximately 36 weeks in one school year, and the IB Visual Arts Program is two years, you have 72 weeks of school. 72 x 2= 144. Therefore, you should have a minimum of about **144 workbook pages** when it is time for your art interview! This is a lot, but it is doable if you stay on track!

AREAS TO CONSIDER

- There are five common functions of art: **Personal, Social, Spiritual, Educational and Political**. Your studio works should strive to encompass more than one of these areas, but you are not required to do all of the areas.
- **Personal Relevance:** to express personal feelings. Perhaps the artist wanted to remind viewers of personal family tragedy, or perhaps he just wanted to tell them to appreciate what they had, and to live each day as if it were their last.
- **Social/Cultural Relevance:** to reinforce and enhance the shared sense of identity of those in family, community, or civilization, for example, festive occasions, parades, dances, uniforms, important holidays or events.
- **Spiritual Relevance:** to express spiritual beliefs about the destiny of life controlled by the force of a higher power.
- **Educational Relevance:** symbols and signs to illustrate knowledge not given in words
- **Political Relevance:** to reinforce and enhance a sense of identity and ideological connection to specific political views, parties and/or people.

This is how I generally set the workbook pages for my studio works. It is an easy outline to follow, and it keeps me organized. It also demonstrates to the interviewer that I have a consistent train-of-thought when I pursue new studio work. This is from my personal experience. No such outline is recommended or required by the IBO. Also, if you have found your own outline that works for you, this one is not necessarily better. The final outline is up to you. Your teacher is asking for about TWO solid, good, creative workbook pages a week with a project every FOUR weeks, therefore I designed my own outline to give me 6+ sketchbooks pages. The remaining pages I usually fill with other artists, random experimentation, etc. (depending on what I feel I am lacking in my workbook)

Outline and Explanation:
1. **Introduction Pages**- Introduce the ISSUE/IDEA/THEME that you plan on exploring, investigating, brainstorming and creating. Explain why you are interested in that idea. This may include a definition of the issue, background information, a few minor sketches of how you visualize the issue/theme/idea.
2. **Inspirations (Artist) Pages**- Introduce the artists that are inspiring you. Not all studio works will have the artists page because you may use one artist inspiration for more than one studio piece or you may not have had a specific artist that inspired you for that specific studio work. You may also find yourself inspired by a historical event, a field trip, a collection of photos, a current event….. Briefly write factual information about the artist (this writing should be in the minority). Sketch out some of his/her works or glue in pictures if it is too difficult to imitate their works. Explain how their art has inspired you and how you plan to use that inspiration in your studio work(s) (this writing should be in the majority). You do not have to imitate the artist's technique to use them as an inspirational figure. You could have been inspired by the themes they target, sizes of art they create, their morals and/or beliefs, etc. Make sure to mention what aspect about the artist inspired you!

3. **Brainstorming Pages**- brainstorm your ideas. The brainstorming pages should turn into 3-4 pages depending on how simple or complex the studio work idea is. Write about technique ideas, media ideas, area(s) you wish to target, etc. Give about 3+ different compositional ideas you have in your mind about creating the studio work and how you envision the final piece. Another good idea is to draw out the materials you are thinking about using, instead of gluing in pictures of them. At the end of the brainstorming page write about which ideas you are looking into pursuing the most. Use colours, underlining, etc. to indicate minor ideas versus major ideas.
4. **Experimentation Pages**- Experiment in your workbook with the mediums/colour schemes/techniques/ your wish to incorporate into your studio piece. The experimentation page typically turns into two or three pages. Make the experimentation the main part of the page and leave a corner or strip of the page to explain yourself (do you like the media/technique, how did the experimentation go, define what you mean by bad or good experimentation, do you plan on using this technique for your studio work or have you decided on another, why or why not have you chosen this media/technique, etc.). Write your explanation in paragraph or bullet-point format. Do not write out questions you are answering and then the answers.
5. **Process Pages**- have someone take pictures randomly throughout your creation of the studio work so you can glue them onto your process page. Reflect on the pictures (what are you doing in the photographs, are

you having trouble, are you doing well, are you satisfied with your progress, etc.)
6. **Reflection Page**- Once your studio piece is complete is it good to have a reflection page about your work. Take a picture of your final work and glue it in, then write your thoughts. Speak about the good things and the bad things, difficulties, your likes and dislikes, how you have enhanced your skill in a certain media or technique, if you are satisfied with your work and why or why not, what would you do differently if you had to do the studio piece again, etc.

When you are writing in your IWB, don't forget that IB is an ACADEMIC course and that your written notes should reflect that. Describe your feelings, thoughts, successes and failures, comment upon your own progress and your ideas but DON'T use slang or informal English. Remember that this is your IWB – it's not being written for friends – an IB examiner will be reading it.

THE LANGUAGE OF ART

People throughout the world speak many different languages. To learn a new language, you need to learn new words and a new set of rules for putting those words together. The language of visual arts has its own system. They are arranged according to basic principles. As you learn these basic elements and principles, you will learn the language of art. It will increase your ability to understand, appreciate, and enjoy art, and to express yourself clearly when discussing or producing artwork. In your investigation workbooks, you should be demonstrating an increase in knowledge about the language of art. This is done through investigation pages and experimentation pages. Your investigations and experimentation do not always have to be related directly to the studio piece you are working with. They could simply be for further knowledge and possible ideas for future works.

Elements of Art:
- line
- color
- form
- space
- value
- shape
- texture

Principles of Design:
- pattern
- balance
- proportion
- variety
- emphasis
- rhythm
- movement
- unity

Properties in Art
- **Subject**- is the image viewers can easily identify in a work of art. The subject may be one person or many people; it may be an event, an object, a symbol, etc. In these types of works, the elements of art themselves become the subject matter.
- **Composition**- the way the *principles* of art are used to organize the *elements* of art
- **Content**- the message the work communicates. The message may be an idea or a theme, such as family togetherness, or emotions like love, loneliness, happiness, pride, etc.

Your investigation workbook should demonstrate, **over time**, a high quality of understanding of the language of art, with respect to the elements or art, principles of design and the basic properties/features of an artwork. Do not expect to have amazing vocabulary and understanding right at the beginning of your time in IB Visual Arts. These are skills you will develop over time. The interviewers **want to see a development in your skills**. So how do you go about demonstrating an increase in knowledge about the Language of Art?

Tips for Developing your Knowledge about the Language of Art:

Investigation Pages- when investigating an artist, look up new vocabulary (artistic words related to the form of art you are looking at). Create an investigation workbook page about it and write about it. One thing I always added in was a corner in the page called: "New Glossary Terms", where I would list new words I learned and their brief definition. Feel free to create investigation pages throughout your workbook that are unrelated to your current studio piece you are working on.

Experimentation Pages- when experimenting with a new technique or medium, make sure to check up the actual terminology for them. Like the investigation pages, write up the new vocabulary and their brief definitions. This will demonstrate to the interviewer that you recognized new vocabulary linked to a specific medium and technique and that you have taken note of it. Make sure to use that new vocabulary throughout the rest of your investigation workbook if you use that technique or medium. The interviewer likes to see how you have learned new, important words, and strive to use them when explaining your own art.

GUIDED QUESTIONS FOR ANALYZING OTHER ARTISTS' ARTWORKS

First Reaction- write down your first response to the artwork
- Did you like it?
- How does it make you feel?
- Does it remind you of anything you have seen before?

Description- list what you can see in this artwork
- Figures, colours, shapes, objects, background, etc.
- Imagine you are describing it to a blind person. Do this in as much detail as possible

Formal Analysis- write down your observations in more detail, looking at these specific aspects of the artwork:

- **Color:**
    - Which type of palette has the artist used: is it bright or dull, strong or weak?
    - Are the color mostly complementary, primary, secondary or tertiary?
    - Which colours are used most, and which are used least in this artwork?
    - Are the colours used different ways in different parts of the artwork?
    - Have the colours been applied flat (straight from the tube), or have different colours been mixed?

- **Tones:**
    - Is there a use of light/shadow in this artwork?
    - Where is the light coming from? Where are the shadows?
    - Are the forms in the artwork realistically modelled (does it look 3D)?
    - Is there a wide range of tonal contrast (very light highlights and very dark shadows) or is

the tonal range quite narrow (mostly similar tones)?
- **Use of Media:**
  - What medium has been used?
  - How has the artist used the medium (applied thick or thin? How can you tell?)
  - Can you see brushstrokes, markmaking or texture? Describe the shape and direction of the brushstrokes/marks. What size of brush. pencil was used?
  - Was it painted, drawn, sculpted quickly, or slowly? What makes you think this?
- **Composition:**
  - What type of shapes are used in this artwork? (rounded, geometric, curved, etc.)
  - Is there a mixture of several types of shapes or are all of the shapes similar?
  - Are some parts of the composition full of shapes and some empty or are the shapes spread evenly across the artwork?
  - Are some shapes repeated or echoed in other parts of the artwork?
  - Does the whole composition look full of energy and movement, or does it look still and peaceful?
  - How did the artist create this movement or stillness?
  - What is the center of interest in the composition?
  - How does the artist draw your attention to it?
- **Mood/Emotion:**
  - What do you think the artist wanted you to feel when you look at this artwork?

- What has he/she used to create a mood? (think about the colors, shapes, tones, etc.)
- How has he/she succeeded in creating this mood?

Interpretation- your personal thoughts about the work

- What do you think the artist is trying to say in this artwork? What does it mean?
- What is the main theme or idea behind this piece?
- If you were inside this artwork, what would you be feeling / thinking?
- Does the artwork have a narrative (tell a story)? is it a religious artwork?
- Is it abstract? Is it realistic? Why?
- How would you explain this artwork to someone else?

Evaluation- based on what you have observed, give your opinion of the artwork with reasons

- Is it successful or not? Why?

GUIDED QUESTIONS FOR REFLECTION ON YOUR OWN STUDIO WORK

- How do you feel overall with the studio work?
- Define what you mean by "good" or "bad" studio work?
- What difficulties did you encounter?
- How did you overcome these difficulties?
- Does the studio work look like how you imagined it?
- What would you do differently if you could do it over again?
- What is your favorite part about your final studio piece?
-

EXTRA PAGE IDEAS

When I first entered the IB Visual Arts program, I was really confused as to what different things I can put into my workbook. At the beginning of IB1, I experimented a lot with different types of pages to see what comments I would receive from my teacher. By the end of my first semester, I compiled a list of good types of workbook pages that received good comments. I continue to utilize that list whenever I feel that I am missing something in my workbook. For all of you who are not quite sure what you can include into your own workbooks, here is the list I compiled, so it may give you some useful ideas:

- **Artist Page**- a page in your sketchbook researching a specific artist of your interest. This page usually contains a creative title (decorated artist's name, decorated piece of works name, etc.), a brief biography, reasons you chose the artist, how you plan to use the knowledge you have learned from that artist in your future works, sketches or pictures of the artist's works, etc.
- **Art Analysis Page**- this is not an "Artist Page". It focuses solely on one work from a specific artist and analyzes that work in-depth. This page is typically mostly writing with a brief sketch of the work being analyzed and a picture of the original work. See the "Questions for Analyzing Artwork" for guidance on this page.
- **Technique Experimentation Page**- this is a page filled with your experimentation with one specific technique. Commonly, this page turns into 2 or 3 pages. The reason for this is because sometimes you can experiment with the same technique using different mediums, so you may choose to experiment with 2-3 different mediums, each on its own page. Make sure to reflect on your experimentation on each page, not just the last one!
- **Medium Experimentation Page**- this is a page filled with your experimentation with one specific medium.

Commonly, this page turns into 2 or 3 pages. The reason for this is because sometimes you can experiment with the same medium using different techniques, so you may choose to experiment with 2-3 different techniques, each on its own page. Make sure to reflect on your experimentation on each page, not just the last one!

- **Research Page** (other than artists)- this page is similar to the "artist page", but instead of investigation/researching one artist, you are researching one symbol, object, person, theme, etc. On this page you will, generally, draw the object, symbol, etc. being researched and write out new information you have learned about it. A good way to go about your writing on the "research page" would be to give various definitions of the object being researched- common dictionary definition, word origin and history, medical dictionary, science dictionary, famous quotes using that object, etc. Finally, form your own definition out of the researched definitions to demonstrate how you plan on using the object, symbol, etc. in your studio work(s).
- **Practicing Page**- similar to the experimentation pages, yet is related to one studio work. If you plan on using a new medium you are unfamiliar with for a studio work, it is a good idea to have 1-3 experimental pages of that medium or technique before you begin your actual studio work. If the experimentation is too large to be done in your workbook, then take pictures while experimenting (e.g. if you are experimenting with clay) and glue them onto one page in your workbook. Make sure to reflect on the experimentation!

- **TOK Link Page**- for students who are on the IB Diploma Program (not certificate program), it is important to connect your IB Visual Art experience to your TOK class. This page is simply a page with you writing about a position you take on a certain debatable/controversial topic concerning art, giving arguments, giving examples of artworks to defend your arguments, and giving a conclusion. The example artworks you use can be both in the form of pictures or sketches. Of course, sketching is always more preferable, but sometimes it is difficult to imitate artworks, so feel free to use photographs. Generally, you should have a couple of these types of pages in your IB Visual Arts years. If you have 2 or 3 by the time your interview takes place, that's perfect!

Some Ideas for TOK Questions for you TOK Link Page:
- What is Art?
- Is art original?
- Is it important for artworks to be original? Why?
- Life imitates art far more than art imitates life. Explain.
- Is art a Lie or Truth? Explain.

GOOD HABITS

Work in your IWB EVERY DAY! Get into the habit, starting today! Several good IWB pages spread out over a few days' work is always better than hours of late night rushed work late at night. Researching, drawing and designing your IWB pages will be an excellent creative break for you from other types of academic study – you should enjoy it! That's why you've chosen this course, right?

When you finish an IWB page, put the date including the year. This clearly shows your progress throughout the course. When you write in your IWB use a black pen and write clearly. We have to photograph pages to send to the examiners

– and they have to be able to read it. It should be an easy pleasurable read (think picture books when you were a kid… what did you like to read??!)

When drawing something from observation, automatically write down where you were and why you chose to draw that. Make notes on the weather or lighting if appropriate. Take photographs as well and attach them to the page.

When you use a book or the internet for info or pictures COPY the URL immediately. The same goes for magazines, newspapers, films, etc. You have to reference EVERYTHING.

Your IWB should reflect your personal approach and style. They are not scrapbooks or sketchbooks. Don't throw out weaker pages as this prevents your teacher and the examiner from seeing your progress. The examiners are not looking for a beautiful finished presentation, but a well worn, well used, well considered journal. Even if you don't like the results of your study, you can learn from your mistakes. And this, actually, will be more interesting to the examiner, instead of pretending that you did everything perfectly the first time around. You will need to use most of your class time for STUDIO work. Expect to do most of your IWB work outside of class.

TO GET STARTED…..

Choose an A4 sketchbook with reasonably thick white cartridge paper. This is the best size as it easily fits into your school bag and the pages aren't big enough to be overwhelming. Make sure you choose a spiral-bound or hard cover sketchbook (spiral is the best). Gummed sketchbooks will quickly fall apart.

Put your name and address on the inside front cover. Also a phone number – if you lose it... you will want it back!! Remember to DATE and NUMBER each page, as you work along.

LAST WORDS OF ADVICE
DON'T:

- If you mess up a page in you sketchbook do not tear it out, instead write about it, on the same page, about what you did wrong and why it failed and what you learned
- Do not feel like your art needs to based off of some deep, philosophical topic, or some huge event in society (ex. global warming, racism, rape, women's rights, etc). It is way overused and sometimes you run out of ideas, but if you have lots of ideas for something like that, go for it. For instance, I sat around for ages trying to think of a topic the interviewers would think was deep and profound, in the end, I found a simple topic where I could look into the history, society and connect it personally. I ended up taking "coffee" as a theme I use over and over again, and it allowed me to look into how it developed, social problems, addictions, etc.
- Don't use glitter in your IWB. It's not considered professional. If you want something to look shiny, find some specific paint or try to make the effect on your own.

DO:
- Always leave 1-2 pages at the beginning of your sketchbook blank in order to make a table of contents. Some students leave it at the end, but don't do that. The IB interviewer should be able to open your sketchbooks first page and find what he/she wants
- Make sure to number your pages once you are done with your sketchbook
- **Put dates.** They are getting stricter in IB about having dates on each page. They'll be looking for it.
- **Reference everything**. Anything you get from books, online, etc. need to be references. Just write the name of the book, or the internet URL underneath the picture or info you are quoting or summarizing. I sometimes just put the references in a small box at the bottom of the page.

40. Excel at the Extended Essay [Part I]

Those two dreaded words. Extended Essay. The EE. Satan's Essay. Whatever you want to call it, there's no denying that amongst all the responsibilities that the IB student is expected to juggle, the compulsory EE is by far the most feared and hated. This 3,500 to 4,000 word mandatory research paper raises many eyebrows when first introduced to IB students. This is usually followed by a tiny voice in your head telling you "4,000 words on ANYTHING over two years? That's easy!" Well, you would think so, wouldn't you? Why, then, do so many IB students find themselves in the beginning of their final year without a draft, without an outline, without even a title idea?

Let's do some simple mathematics. Let's say, hypothetically, that you are given exactly a one-year deadline to finish your EE (it's around that). That's 365 days. Now let's say you are an overachiever and want to write 4,000 words (the upper limit of essay length). According to my calculations, that's 4,000 divided by 365 or around 10.95 words per day. That's it. If you write 10.95 words per day for a year, then you will have completed your extended essay. I hope most of you can manage eleven words a day.

Now, don't be fooled – I'm not suggesting you spread your EE writing exactly over a one year period – I am merely trying to show you how little 4,000 words over a year really is. As part of my Economics and Management degree at Oxford, I was required to write a 3000 – 4000 word essay per week. Yup, that's right, an EE per week, and after having done it for the first few weeks, it became easier and easier up until the point where 4,000 words seemed like nothing. The IB, in an attempt to prepare you for this, generously gives you well over a year to write your "masterpiece."

So what is the problem then? Why do so many students struggle to write what seems to be a simple "extended" essay in such a great amount of time? Well, there are a few traps along the way, and hopefully the following guide over the next few pages will teach you how to avoid those traps and have your EE ready in no time.

What Subject?

Now, although there are no real restrictions on the nature of your essay, it must fall within a subject the IB has on offer (published by the IB in the *Vade Mecum*). Please don't be a wise-guy and try to write an essay on a subject that you do not take. Yes, it is actually allowed and I have seen it happen, at times with mediocre success, but usually with utter failure. A typical example: you are obsessed with WWI history, but your school does not teach history at all, yet you insist that your external reading you do in your own time will give you a great idea and basis for an essay. You spew out 4,000 words of something you believe is truly brilliant and hand it in to your middle school history teacher to mark. They think it's great. You then send it to the IB only to find out you completely missed the History EE guidelines and end up getting a generous grade D.

Another, more common, example is someone who is really passionate about religion and wants to do a paper in world religion. You will most likely end up being incredibly biased and perhaps say very controversial things. I'll probably regret saying this, but the EE and the IB don't deal directly with religion (unless it's the simple appreciation and acceptance of others' beliefs). Some schools have simply begun to ban their students from writing outside of their own subject areas (probably because of the lack of supervisors available). Look, you do six subjects so is it really that difficult to find something that interests you ever-so-slightly within those six?

Make sure you take a look at the detailed package of documents that the IB offers for the Extended Essay, which will include information on what you should expect in writing each essay. I'm not going to outline what the IB documents say because 1) I don't want to source things you can look up yourself and 2) you can look it up yourself! Once you have chosen your subject, you should print out the relevant guide and read it carefully. Also make sure that you have a supervisor available to oversee your EE in that subject area.

So, which Group should you be looking at then? Well, as my personal advice, I would tell you to stay away from any English or language essays unless you truly have a passion for literature and have been published or somehow rewarded for truly excelling in your writing. The reason is quite simple: writing an excellent literature essay is incredibly difficult because it's simply too competitive and many students who believe they are excellent writers and have been told so by numerous teachers are, in fact, quite average when compared to kids outside of their school. Do not become one of those students who say: "Hah! I'll just take one of my grade A English papers I wrote on *Doll's House* from last year, add 2000 more words and - viola! Extended Essay complete!" It does not work like that. The EE isn't really an extended essay – you can't simply elongate your normal run-of-the-mill English analysis of a literary work and expect to do well. The problem with Group 1 essays is that many will fail to reveal much personal judgement and overuse historical and biographical information. A very subtle balance is required, and this is often very difficult to maintain. EE reports show that students use secondary sources in place of personal opinions and vocabulary is often a problem, along with structure and quotations. The EE is supposed to be a piece of research, which is why I would suggest you stay away from literature because there is little research to be done.

Group 3 topics seem to make very popular EEs – and perhaps with good reason, too. There are virtually no limitations on what you can write about in Geography, Economics, Business Management, History, and so on. If you take a Group 3 topic that you are truly interested in, see if there is anything you have always pondered over but never really researched in depth. Talk to your teachers and coordinators about the success rates in these topics. For subjects like Economics and Business Management there is always great demand; however, success is varied. I remember an Economics teacher of mine told me that although it is easy to get a B or C in an Economics EE, you have to come up with pretty good material to get an A. Please, don't fall into the trap of "Oh, my dad has his own company, so what better way to do research in business/economics than to write an essay about his company!" Just because you have access to thousands of documents for a firm of a friend or a relative does not mean this will help you write an excellent essay in Economics or BM.

A common trouble area with Economics essays is that there is little personal research and not enough analysis of economic theory. Also, as you would with your Economics coursework, don't forget to define all the key economic terms (either on the spot or as an index). At all costs avoid subjective "What if.." questions because this just does not fit well with the EE's

Assessment Criteria. And please, for your own good, make sure to narrow the topic down to a sort of small case study.

With regards to History essays, the problem is as you would expect: reliability of secondary sources (probably would be a good idea NOT to use too many websites). Don't forget that your bibliography for a History essay will probably be twice as long as the bibliography in any other subject – so get ready to do some serious citing. Avoid the traditional "arguments for" followed by "arguments against" approach and then a conclusion consisting of "both sides of the argument are equally valid." Yes, it would be worse to produce a one-sided argument, but avoid being too neutral as well.

What about Group 4 then, the sciences? It seems at first that the task would be akin to a middle school science fair project or simply a longer-than-usual lab report. Don't get your hopes up. Writing an EE in a science is very demanding, as it not only requires you to have the literary ability found in any other EE, but you also must be able to master the process of conducting experiments, taking data, and providing top-of-the line analysis. My personal advice: if you are an excellent laboratory scientist with plenty of experience writing up lab reports and doing numerous research projects and you have an idea for an EE topic that is not discussed in much detail in the syllabus, then go for it. Perhaps more so than with any other group, writing an EE in Group 4 requires that you have a clear idea of what you want to research. You need to know exactly what you are doing and have a pretty good idea of what will happen. Sounds a bit demanding, but there's no point in looking at "the effect of sunlight on erection length" if there's clearly no relationship between the two variables! You would be wasting your time starting to write an EE about a scientific relationship that you doubt actually exists. The flipside, however, is that you would be wasting your time doing an experiment for which the outcome is already well documented in standard textbooks. Hence, you face a dilemma.

Moreover, it is very difficult to write an essay that is distinctly a chemistry essay, not shifting over too much to biology or physics. You could end up with an essay that relates very little to your specific science subject. Again, official IB EE reports state that many science essays lack a satisfactory degree of personal input – perhaps using sophisticated lab equipment limits how much personal input one can have. You also face the risk of reaching a somewhat too general conclusion, and analysis of sources and methods used is often too weak because of the high level of sophistication.

Ah, an EE in Group 5: mathematics, computer sciences, perhaps the most overlooked EE subject area. As I have relatively little knowledge about computer sciences, I will primarily be concerned with an EE in mathematics, so any computer science students can look away now. Also, unless you are taking HL Mathematics, you can forget about writing an EE in maths as well. Now, if you are a HL Mathematics student who is not struggling too much with the material and actually enjoys mathematics, then follow my advice and do an EE in it! Trust me, it will probably be the best decision you will make in your IB experience. Yes, it seems a daunting task – how can one write 4000 words on a subject that is primarily concerned with numbers? But once you do a little research, read several past mathematics essays and convince yourself that writing an EE in maths will be no more or less challenging than any other subject, you should begin to worry less about the whole concept. You will not be expected to make a contribution to the knowledge in the mathematical world.

Don't worry, they won't expect you to find the next largest prime number or solve Fermat's Theorem.

There is an unbelievable amount of resources available for anyone interested in doing an EE in mathematics. It really does shock me how few students give it a go, let alone think about doing it. In my year, it was me and only one other student that attempted the EE in mathematics (in our school). It was perhaps the most enjoyable and, at the same time, most demanding piece of work I had to do for the IB – but at the end of the day, it was something I could honestly pick up and be proud of. You don't need a Bachelor's degree in mathematics to be able to write an essay in maths. It might well be more demanding than an EE in other subject areas, but your willingness to challenge yourself will not go unrecognized by the EE examiners. Keep in mind that the minimum word limit is altered for EE in mathematics to around 2500 words (which is nothing really) but you do need a significant amount of actual maths in the text as well (which could be a problem).

What about Group 6? Well, I don't know many who have done an EE in visual arts, theatre arts or music, but if you feel you've got a mini art-critic living inside you, then give it a thought. If you plan on pursuing a university degree involved in the arts, then this may well be an opportunity to see what it would be like doing detailed research and analysis in that area. Remember that there is a great element of creativity involved, so if you're finding your Group 6 classes and assignments uninteresting, then perhaps it would be a good idea to stay away from an EE in that area. Don't think that for your art EE you can just analyze the history of graffiti or that for your music essay you can write 50 Cent's biography – it has to be of a quality expected in the IB program.

The bottom line is that you need to take a long and hard look at your HL classes and decide which subject will suit your essay needs best. I know that the emphasis on EE and subjects differs from school to school, so if you are at a school that is really science-intensive and lacking in mathematics, then it would probably be better to follow that route. You should ensure that you write your EE at HL, not at SL – simply because you will have not learnt the subject in enough detail. If you are doing HL Mathematics, I once again strongly suggest that you at least consider writing an EE in this subject. If not, my next best bet for you would be to look at your Group 3 subjects and choose something from there. If you're more of a scientist than a social scientist, then by all means go for the Group 4; however, be warned of the obstacles and traps that you may have to overcome. Unless you are a truly naturally gifted literary critic and have extraordinary analysis skills, I would strongly advise to stay away from Groups 1 and 2. Similarly, unless you are obsessed with your Group 6 subject, I would not recommend doing an EE in the arts.

Topic Choice

Once you have done the easy part of choosing under which subject your EE will fall, you must begin thinking of a topic or a range of topics that you could write about. Pick something that actually interests you and is motivating. Don't get too excited if you can find a truckload of information online about your topic of interest – that's usually a bad sign. Pick a topic that has barely any research already done on it and is unique in its nature. Remember, however, that this is a research topic and not your ordinary book review – you must have a question, which you can argue and answer.

Also remember that it needs to be very specific – you don't want a topic that is too general. Please, understand just how important your topic choice really is – it will make or break your essay. Choose something that is silly and unprofessional and you will suffer incredibly. Before you decide on a topic, talk to your friends about it, Google it, see if there's an appropriate approach that you can take. A paper on "Economic Monopolies" is far too general, but a paper on a specific type of company monopoly, analysed at a more in-depth level, is more appropriate. It is critical to have a focused research question – talk to your supervisor and see if you can narrow your topic even further. A good topic is one that asks something worth asking and that is answerable within 4000 words. Remember also that your topic should not be something that is taught in relatively good depth already in the syllabus (for example, if you are doing a specific English book in your A1 class, you cannot use the same book for your EE).

Another piece of advice about choosing an EE topic is to choose something that is relatively unknown. If your examiner has no clue as to what your topic is about, then you will be able to educate him/her; how much can the examiner criticize you if he/she knows nothing about it him/herself? And, as I said before, if you choose a topic for which you think you will find almost no information, you are in a much better situation than someone who has a multitude of sources from the go.

The title of your essay (your topic question) does not necessarily have to be in question form. Nonetheless, the title is of incredible importance (see Assessment Criteria). You need to make sure it's precise, concise and clearly shows the focus of the essay. The sooner you get this done, the better – it will drive your essay in the right direction. Remember that the exact wording of your research question is not set in stone; you will be able to go back and modify it later on.

Time Management

Some schools suggest that you spend about 35 - 40 hours on your EE, the IBO suggests approximately 40 hours as well, other schools encourage 80 to 100 hours. No matter where you stand, you can see that a great deal of time will be spent on your essay, which is why you need to manage your time well. I was once amongst those who didn't understand why we had to follow a timeline for our EE and couldn't just do things in our own time. Well, I hate to admit it, but the timeline that the IB sets out ensures that you don't mess up and fall behind. This way, if there are any problems with your essay, they can be detected in the early stages, so that you don't waste your time writing an entire EE only to have it rejected.

Do yourself a favour and ignore any stories you hear from seniors who tell you how they wrote their EE in one sitting, a few days before it was due and got an A for it. Unless you have some magic ability to work productively non-stop for a good 80 hours or so, you will not be able to complete your EE in one sitting – or even in a few sittings. Take my word for it, taking small steps, one at a time, is the key to success. There are limits to this as well, however, so don't fool yourself into thinking that by adding a sentence or two to your essay you have done enough work for the week.

Your IB coordinator should ensure that you more or less follow the deadlines. Make sure you know all the important dates and keep them in your agenda (if you have one) or print them out and post them on your board. There will be dates for having your topic ready, finding your supervisor, getting your outline and bibliography ready and so on. Remember that if you risk falling behind on one of the dates, it could have a domino effect and some serious repercussions.

You will be writing your EE primarily outside of the classroom on your own time and, unlike with school homework, it is unlikely that there will be any check-ups to verify that you are doing the work. It is 'strongly recommended', but not 'required' that your school sets internal deadlines for the stages of completing your EE. Take some responsibility. I know that the workload in your other subjects will be heavy, but don't forget about your EE. I highly recommend finishing the bulk of it over the summer holidays (between IBY1 and IBY2). Also, I wouldn't rely too much on the dates that the coordinator "suggests" you follow – the more ambitious and independent of you should make your own agenda and stick to it. Set yourself specific goals, and if you fall behind, then make sure to catch up at the cost of perhaps even missing some schoolwork or failing a few tests (EE points are a lot more important than your everyday school work). Also, contrary to popular belief, working on your EE over the weekend is not a crime.

Supervision

The role of the supervisor is very clear. They are strongly recommended to spend between 3 and 5 hours with you working on your EE. They are not there to write your essay for you, and you shouldn't protest against them for not helping you enough. There is a set of guidelines that supervisors must follow (once again, see IB documentation) in order to ensure that each student in every school gets an equal chance to maintain fairness. They are mainly there for support and encouragement, along with making sure that you keep up with the deadlines and don't plagiarize. They will also need to give you advice and guidance on undertaking research. The words "encouragement, support and reassurance" do not mean that they will write sentences for you. They will also decide on a set amount of time that they can devote to your EE (which is a good reason to choose a supervisor who doesn't have his/her hands full all the time).

Your supervisor is your friend. Remember that it is not an obligation for a teacher to supervise an EE – so make sure you don't abuse that privilege. Treat them like trash, and you will get trash in return. Don't be too demanding, but then again, don't let them get away from their promises. Once again, have a good read of what the IB suggests the supervisor does, and if your supervisor isn't up to standards, then you make the case to your coordinator to reach a solution.

Look, let's be realistic. The more experience the teacher has with the IB and the EE, the more they will be able to offer in terms of what to do and what to best avoid. I know this is a problem in many schools that are just starting the IB program and where almost all the teachers have zero IB experience. But, if you have the opportunity to work with a teacher who has been teaching the subject for more than a few years, then I would strongly suggest you go for that. Trust me, you don't want to end up complaining about your new A-level accredited chemistry teacher just because he has no idea what an EE is in the first place.

Remember that it is your supervisor who has the final say on whether or not your essay will even get a passing grade. So if you choose a supervisor who is clueless about what a pass is, then you risk failing your entire IB diploma if your paper ends up not satisfying the examiners' requirements for a passing grade. Your supervisor should have you rewrite your paper if you are borderline passing (however, if you have been following this guide, this should not be the case!).

Find a teacher who will best match your subject and perhaps give you sources (books, websites, magazines, etc.) that others cannot. They need to be able to provide you with constructive criticism and guidance. Remember that you are not tied down to your supervisor with regards to help and advice. You can consult your seniors and friends for general EE advice. If it is topic specific, then make sure you source the person in your bibliography. At the end of the day though, your supervisor is the one who needs to complete all the formalities that are described in the EE guide.

Getting Started / Research

There are few things in life that compare to looking at a blank page, struggling to come up with an eye-catching introduction. My best advice for you (and advice that is usually given to beginner writers) is simply to put the pen to paper and jot your ideas down. The introduction might not be the best place to start, so start jotting down your research in clear, coherent form, and eventually you will be able to start structuring your essay properly.

Your best bet before putting the pen to paper would be to conduct some serious research. Hopefully, your school will have given you a brief introduction into how to write a research paper, but there are a few things you need to keep in mind while researching. Depending on your topic, it could be that research is either incredibly easy or incredibly hard. The latter is probably the better situation to be in. For my EE, I wrote a paper on a 2,000-year-old mathematical riddle called

"Alhazen's Problem." Googling it got me almost nowhere. Yes, I found some news articles here and there and some definitions and outlines, but in terms of raw research done, there was almost nothing. I didn't worry too much, because the internet (as great as it is) doesn't hold the answer to everything.

As an IB student, you need to learn to become very enquiring about what you are learning. There are several search engines designed specifically for research papers that you might need to consult (JSTOR, SSRN and Proquest to name a few). Yes, some are free, but some have a subscription fee. You need to figure out what it is you really want. Alternatively, you can try popping down to your local city library (because you've already gone to your school library, right?) and see if they have anything of interest. Be creative with your research. I remember having to email an Oxford professor to see if he could provide me with any information (unfortunately he totally ignored me!). Don't give up though, and keep in mind that all the other students are doing exactly what you should try and avoid. As great as Wikipedia, Bized and Dictionary.com are, you will not stand out amongst the crowd if your research does not go beyond that.

Whilst on the subject of research, make sure you take a look at as many EEs you can get your hands on in your subject area (preferably good ones). I don't mean read them from beginning to end, I'm just saying you may get some ideas about where to start once you see what a good EE is supposed to look like. The IB have now launched a collection of 50 great EE's (all of which were awarded a grade A) available in CD/DVD format for about a hundred dollars. Hopefully your school will buy a copy of this to keep in the library. If not, then try to get your hands on it by some other means (perhaps chipping in a fiver with twenty or so friends). It's not essential you look at many past EE's, but I would highly recommend it. By reading previous essays, you can identify common pitfalls as well as strengths in various topics.

41. Excel at the Extended Essay [Part II]

Topic Choice

Once you have done the easy part of choosing under which subject your EE will fall, you must begin thinking of a topic or a range of topics that you could write about. Pick something that actually interests you and is motivating. Don't get too excited if you can find a truckload of information online about your topic of interest – that's usually a bad sign. Pick a topic that has barely any research already done on it and is unique in its nature. Remember, however, that this is a research topic and not your ordinary book review – you must have a question, which you can argue and answer.

Also remember that it needs to be very specific – you don't want a topic that is too general. Please, understand just how important your topic choice really is – it will make or break your essay. Choose something that is silly and unprofessional and you will suffer incredibly. Before you decide on a topic, talk to your friends about it, Google it, see if there's an appropriate approach that you can take. A paper on "Economic Monopolies" is far too general, but a paper on a specific type of company monopoly, analysed at a more in-depth level, is more appropriate. It is critical to have a focused research question – talk to your supervisor and see if you can narrow your topic even further. A good topic is one that asks something worth asking and that is answerable within 4000 words. Remember also that your topic should not be something that is taught in relatively good depth already in the syllabus (for example, if you are doing a specific English book in your A1 class, you cannot use the same book for your EE).

This is your perfect opportunity to research that little thing that you have always wondered about but that seemed too complicated to ask. Whether it be specific casino techniques to win at blackjack (mathematics) or Hitler's secret homoerotic sex life (history), find something that has great depth and actually interests you. Don't become one of those students who picks a topic that "sounds good" but has no real meaning – you will end up regretting it. If you pick a topic that actually interests you, then there is a greater chance that you will actually work on it! 4,000 words may be difficult if you are summarizing the Bible, but 4,000 words on your favourite television program seems a lot less demanding (DO NOT write about that). You may want to write outlines for several plausible topics, and then see which one would work best.

Another piece of advice about choosing an EE topic is to choose something that is relatively unknown. If your examiner has no clue as to what your topic is about, then you will be able to educate him/her; how much can the examiner criticize you if he/she knows nothing about it him/herself? And, as I said before, if you choose a topic for which you think you will find almost no information, you are in a much better situation than someone who has a multitude of sources from the go.

So how do you go about finding a final topic? Well, it will depend from subject to subject, but usually you will need something to inspire you. For this very reason, you need to start flipping through books concerned with the ideas you plan to write about. For example, if doing an EE in maths, I strongly recommend as a good starting point to look at a book about "100 greatest unsolved mathematical problems" and see if there is something there that interests you. Don't stress out yet! Just because it has not been solved doesn't mean that you will have to solve it! It just means that you can do a good research paper on it – find out what others have been writing and develop your own method at solving the problem. Try contacting some university-level professors and see what they have to say (this doesn't only apply to math, but also to history, economics, the sciences and so on).

The title of your essay (your topic question) does not necessarily have to be in question form. Nonetheless, the title is of incredible importance (see Assessment Criteria). You need to make sure it's precise, concise and clearly shows the focus of the essay. The sooner you get this done, the better – it will drive your essay in the right direction. Remember that the exact wording of your research question is not set in stone; you will be able to go back and modify it later on.

Time Management

Some schools suggest that you spend about 35 - 40 hours on your EE, the IBO suggests approximately 40 hours as well, other schools encourage 80 to 100 hours. No matter where you stand, you can see that a great deal of time will be spent on your essay, which is why you need to manage your time well. I was once amongst those who didn't understand why we had to follow a timeline for our EE and couldn't just do things in our own time. Well, I hate to admit it, but the timeline that the IB sets out ensures that you don't mess up and fall behind. This way, if there are any problems with your essay, they can be detected in the early stages, so that you don't waste your time writing an entire EE only to have it rejected.

Do yourself a favour and ignore any stories you hear from seniors who tell you how they wrote their EE in one sitting, a few days before it was due and got an A for it. Unless you have some magic ability to work productively non-stop for a good

80 hours or so, you will not be able to complete your EE in one sitting – or even in a few sittings. Take my word for it, taking small steps, one at a time, is the key to success. There are limits to this as well, however, so don't fool yourself into thinking that by adding a sentence or two to your essay you have done enough work for the week.

Your IB coordinator should ensure that you more or less follow the deadlines. Make sure you know all the important dates and keep them in your agenda (if you have one) or print them out and post them on your board. There will be dates for having your topic ready, finding your supervisor, getting your outline and bibliography ready and so on. Remember that if you risk falling behind on one of the dates, it could have a domino effect and some serious repercussions.

You will be writing your EE primarily outside of the classroom on your own time and, unlike with school homework, it is unlikely that there will be any check-ups to verify that you are doing the work. It is 'strongly recommended', but not 'required' that your school sets internal deadlines for the stages of completing your EE. Take some responsibility. I know that the workload in your other subjects will be heavy, but don't forget about your EE. I highly recommend finishing the bulk of it over the summer holidays (between IBY1 and IBY2). Also, I wouldn't rely too much on the dates that the coordinator "suggests" you follow – the more ambitious and independent of you should make your own agenda and stick to it. Set yourself specific goals, and if you fall behind, then make sure to catch up at the cost of perhaps even missing some schoolwork or failing a few tests (EE points are a lot more important than your everyday school work). Also, contrary to popular belief, working on your EE over the weekend is not a crime.

Supervision

Before you start writing your EE you will need to have a member of faculty "supervise" your EE so that there is someone to make sure you follow IB guidelines. Be quick and reserve your supervisor first because usually the more popular teachers are filled up with requests within a week – especially for the social science topics such as IB History and IB Economics. I strongly advise getting your subject teacher to be your supervisor because 1) they should know most of the material that the subject encompasses inside out and 2) they will be familiar with the IB program and will know what to expect. For your own good, try not to get a supervisor who does not teach the IB or who is unfamiliar with the demands of the program.

The role of the supervisor is very clear. They are strongly recommended to spend between 3 and 5 hours with you working on your EE. They are not there to write your essay for you, and you shouldn't protest against them for not helping you enough. There is a set of guidelines that supervisors must follow (once again, see IB documentation) in order to ensure that each student in every school gets an equal chance to maintain fairness. They are mainly there for support and encouragement, along with making sure that you keep up with the deadlines and don't plagiarize. They will also need to give you advice and guidance on undertaking research. The words "encouragement, support and reassurance" do not mean that they will write sentences for you. They will also decide on a set amount of time that they can devote to your EE (which is a good reason to choose a supervisor who doesn't have his/her hands full all the time).

Your supervisor is your friend. Remember that it is not an obligation for a teacher to supervise an EE – so make sure you don't abuse that privilege. Treat them like trash, and you will get trash in return. Don't be too demanding, but then again, don't let them get away from their promises. Once again, have a good read of what the IB suggests the supervisor does, and if your supervisor isn't up to standards, then you make the case to your coordinator to reach a solution.

I hate to say it, and this might come as an unfortunate shock to most of you, but I would say that your EE's success depends about 75% on your input, and 25% on your supervisor's. Although they don't actually write anything that goes into your essay or give you that much advice, the report that they submit to the examining board (which includes his/her personal comments) is incredibly important. Pick a clueless and incoherent supervisor and you will not only pay the price in terms of feedback, but also you risk having all the formalities that are involved with the submission of the EE to be incomplete. This is why I strongly suggest finding a supervisor who is confident with the IB Diploma system and who has at least a year or two of EE experience. I wish I could tell you that no matter how poor your supervisor is, you can still get an A, but due to the increasingly important role they play, this is not the case.

Look, let's be realistic. The more experience the teacher has with the IB and the EE, the more they will be able to offer in terms of what to do and what to best avoid. I know this is a problem in many schools that are just starting the IB program and where almost all the teachers have zero IB experience. But, if you have the opportunity to work with a teacher who has been teaching the subject for more than a few years, then I would strongly suggest you go for that. Trust me, you don't want to end up complaining about your new A-level accredited chemistry teacher just because he has no idea what an EE is in the first place.

Remember that it is your supervisor who has the final say on whether or not your essay will even get a passing grade. So if you choose a supervisor who is clueless about what a pass is, then you risk failing your entire IB diploma if your paper ends up not satisfying the examiners' requirements for a passing grade. Your supervisor should have you rewrite your paper if you are borderline passing (however, if you have been following this guide, this should not be the case!).

Find a teacher who will best match your subject and perhaps give you sources (books, websites, magazines, etc.) that others cannot. They need to be able to provide you with constructive criticism and guidance. Remember that you are not tied down to your supervisor with regards to help and advice. You can consult your seniors and friends for general EE advice. If it is topic specific, then make sure you source the person in your bibliography. At the end of the day though, your supervisor is the one who needs to complete all the formalities that are described in the EE guide.

Getting Started / Research

There are few things in life that compare to looking at a blank page, struggling to come up with an eye-catching introduction. My best advice for you (and advice that is usually given to beginner writers) is simply to put the pen to paper and jot your ideas down. The introduction might not be the best place to start, so start jotting down your research in clear, coherent form, and eventually you will be able to start structuring your essay properly.

Your best bet before putting the pen to paper would be to conduct some serious research. Hopefully, your school will have given you a brief introduction into how to write a research paper, but there are a few things you need to keep in mind while researching. Depending on your topic, it could be that research is either incredibly easy or incredibly hard. The latter is probably the better situation to be in. For my EE, I wrote a paper on a 2,000-year-old mathematical riddle called "Alhazen's Problem." Googling it got me almost nowhere. Yes, I found some news articles here and there and some definitions and outlines, but in terms of raw research done, there was almost nothing. I didn't worry too much, because the internet (as great as it is) doesn't hold the answer to everything.

As an IB student, you need to learn to become very enquiring about what you are learning. There are several search engines designed specifically for research papers that you might need to consult (JSTOR, SSRN and Proquest to name a few). Yes, some are free, but some have a subscription fee. You need to figure out what it is you really want. Alternatively, you can try popping down to your local city library (because you've already gone to your school library, right?) and see if they have anything of interest. Be creative with your research. I remember having to email an Oxford professor to see if he could provide me with any information (unfortunately he totally ignored me!). Don't give up though, and keep in mind that all the other students are doing exactly what you should try and avoid. As great as Wikipedia, Bized and Dictionary.com are, you will not stand out amongst the crowd if your research does not go beyond that.

Whilst on the subject of research, make sure you take a look at as many EEs you can get your hands on in your subject area (preferably good ones). I don't mean read them from beginning to end, I'm just saying you may get some ideas about where to start once you see what a good EE is supposed to look like. The IB have now launched a collection of 50 great EE's (all of which were awarded a grade A) available in CD/DVD format for about a hundred dollars. Hopefully your school will buy a copy of this to keep in the library. If not, then try to get your hands on it by some other means (perhaps chipping in a fiver with twenty or so friends). It's not essential you look at many past EE's, but I would highly recommend it. By reading previous essays, you can identify common pitfalls as well as strengths in various topics.

42. Excel at the Extended Essay [Part III]

Plagiarism

Simple. Don't do it. Yea ok, it's unethical, it's unfair, it's bad – all of that is true. More importantly, however, you will get caught. I have seen it all: plain copy and pasting off the Internet, the purchasing of essays for ridiculous amounts of money, and even getting specialist friends of your parents to write your paper for you. Even if the anti-plagiarism computer software (which has advanced incredibly over recent years) fails to catch you, it's your tutor's job to decide if the work is yours or not. Turn-it-in.com has been somewhat of a breakthrough in the way research papers are monitored these days. Keep in mind you will have to submit an electronic version of your EE – so spare yourself the drama and make sure you don't copy and paste.

I always say that the only person dumber than someone who knowingly plagiarises is the person who does it unknowingly. Fail to include a proper bibliography and cite certain sources "by accident" and you will taste the same consequences as the kid who did it on purpose. Don't make that mistake.

Now look, if you have been writing poor essays for as long as you can remember, and then all of a sudden you hand in a Doctorate-worthy masterpiece, flawlessly written and organized to perfection – your tutor (unless he's like you) will notice the sudden change in writing style and will question you extensively. Nothing looks worse than a student unable to answer simple questions about a paper he/she supposedly wrote. Reward is just not worth the risk, considering you are capable of producing something of a greater quality.

Come on now, it's only 4,000 words! Are you really telling me you are not able to write 4,000 words yourself without cheating and plagiarising? If that's the case, then good luck with university or whatever career you choose to pursue after high school.

Finished?

My teacher once said that your EE will never really be a finished product – there will simply come a time when you must hand it in. Keep this in mind whilst proofreading your essay and more importantly writing your conclusion. Please, under no circumstances write as your final sentence "In conclusion, there are .... The End" – the IB does not expect you to know every single detail about your topic and give a concrete and flawless answer. If you still have unanswered questions relating to the topic, then make sure you say so (and, if possible, suggest how you would, given more resources and time, go about answering these questions).

Now you think you're done? Well think again. Go back constantly and make sure you have done everything as best as you can. They are handing you an opportunity to get an A. This is not an exam for which you need to study; it is a piece of work that you can take as many hours as you need to complete. Go online and find an EE checklist, make sure you hit all the nails on the head before you hand in anything.

If you're still convinced that you have completed your final draft, then I suggest you hold up your EE and ask yourself the following: is it something that I am proud of? Are you not embarrassed to read it? Is this your best work? If you can answer "yes" to the last question then you're probably ready to submit.

The Viva Voce

The IBO recommends supervisors and schools to conclude the EE process with a short interview, called the Viva Voce. It is a recommended conclusion to the extended essay process.

The point of the Viva Voce is to eradicate any suspicions of plagiarism as well as provide an opportunity to reflect on what has been learned from the experience. The whole interview will last 10 to 15 minutes and you should be ready to answer any questions your supervisor may have about your essay, including questions on specific sentences, citations, references but also on why you chose the topic, your high and low points of the process, and what interested you the most.

It may be possible that you won't have this interview, as it is not obligatory per se. Nonetheless, I would recommend you prepare yourself to answer questions about your methods, choice of topic, conclusion, and skills you learned during the process. Remember however that you will not be graded on this interview as there is no grading criterion for it and it's not compulsory.

To be honest, this interview should not pose any threat to the success of your EE. It is really just used as a way to catch students who are suspected of plagiarism off guard. Unless you have serious short-term memory loss, you will do fine. The process should end positively and is a nice conclusion to the completion of such a major piece of work.

Additional Resources

When I started the IB program, there was some material available on the Internet with regards to help with the EE. Now, having a quick look around, it seems as if there has been an incredible shift in interest and an increase in information with regards to the Diploma Program. This guide is supposed to help you survive the EE – but by all means, don't let your research end here. Make it your primary goal to gather as much information as you can. Find out what others are writing about the EE, ask your peers, keep Googling "Extended Essay help." No matter how hard I try, there's only so much I can put into this guide. You need to understand that there are hundreds, if not thousands, of good websites, books, and other resources out there that can complement this guide and your quest for more information. Keep checking the IBO website store to see if there is anything worth purchasing (or begging your school to purchase) with regards to the EE.

Don't exaggerate the difficulty and magnitude of the Extended Essay. Take it seriously, but don't get obsessed with it (if that makes any sense). Just remember what the real aim here is: to get an A or a B in order to boost your chances of getting all three bonus points. Three points is less than half of what just one of your courses can potentially give you (seven points). That being said, they are probably the easiest three points to obtain as there is no examination involved (so you can work your butt off and guarantee yourself the points). Don't make the EE more overwhelming than it really is.

Remember that if you mess up your EE, then you can wave two years of hard high school struggling bye-bye. It's not optional – it's mandatory. To be quite honest with you, after having completed the EE, I can understand why the IB would want you to write a 4,000-word essay. You won't find the same or any close equivalent in the A-level program or AP's, and if you go on to university, you will be able to separate the kids who did IB from the non-IB kids almost instantly by their ability to write long, well-structured essays. The EE, if written correctly, will give you a massive advantage later on in your further studies – trust me.

Since the IB suggests that the EE should take around 40 hours to complete, you could, in theory, leave the EE to the last weekend before it is due. There's a funny old saying about this extensive deferment of work – "the best way to get something done is to start it today." Start your EE the weekend it is assigned, finish it by end of Christmas break, and have it fully cleaned up and edited by end of Easter break – do that and you can take the rest of the time off laughing as your fellow IB peers continue to fool themselves.

43. Tackling TOK: The Essay

Boring. Useless. Naptime. "Wannabe philosophy" – just some of the words I have heard students use to address the TOK component of IB. My own opinion is not of importance, but let's just say I have felt very mixed feelings when it comes to Theory of Knowledge. As with many things in the IB Diploma, TOK has its upsides and downsides. The bad news first: it's controversial, at times utterly boring, and you might struggle to accept what the course is trying to teach. The good news: it's less work than the Extended Essay if you want an A grade and there is almost no academic ability involved. Whether you are an A student or an F student it doesn't matter – *anyone* can do reasonably well in TOK.

TOK is the only course taken by every IB diploma and certificate candidate around the world. The implications of this are immense. Your work is being compared to the other 200,000 or so IB kids taking it every year. So why do so many students hate the course? I don't really know where to start – it could be the lack of quality teachers, the "incompleteness" of the syllabus, or the fact that not a single other high school program being taught around the world has anything that even remotely compares to TOK. Moreover, it is frustrating for students how subjective the course can become. It can easily be the case that two teachers in the same school will teach and mark in completely different manners. The classes can become tedious as you start to find yourself questioning things such as your own existence and having endless repetitive debates about "how we know" something. The subject material found in TOK is mostly unfamiliar to both teachers and students, therefore making it all the more difficult to teach.

Out of all my classmates, I probably disagreed with the course more than anyone else (ironically getting the top grade for my essay/presentation). Get this into your head now: no matter how much you hate the course or disagree with it, it should have no impact on your ability to get a top mark. Yes, some will tell you that if you're positive and interested in the material then you will be more successful. This guide, however, will teach you exactly what to do (and what not to do) in order to succeed – regardless of your personal interest in TOK.

One of the reasons I find TOK so controversial is that some teachers insist on teaching TOK as the (ultimate) knowledge course. As if it's accepted worldwide that there are four Ways of Knowing and a concrete seven Areas of Knowledge. The fact of the matter is, outside your TOK class, no single other non-IB educated person will know what you're talking about. Philosophers have debated for millennia on knowledge issues and will continue to do so. It might be a sad truth, but the TOK diagram is almost "fictional" in the sense that it's made by the IB, for the IB. I'm not trying to take away the valuable lessons in knowledge that TOK does offer; however, I want you to understand that there is so much more depth and so many more interesting things to learn about knowledge outside the IB course. Just to show you how ambiguous and intangible the course is, in recent syllabuses the "perception" Way of Knowing has been replaced with "sense perception." This shouldn't concern you too much, but just keep in mind that whilst you are trying to ace your essay and presentation, there is much more to philosophy and knowledge than TOK tries to teach.

So what will it take? Well, the TOK component consists of a 1200–1600 word essay and a roughly 900 word written 'exhibition'. I have to admit that both are probably going to end up being extremely dull, but at least you should be happy about the fact that you will be getting very high marks.

As of 2022, the maximum scaled mark for TOK is 30 points, with your essay being 20 of those scaled points (but actually being marked out of a raw mark of 10) and the rest being your exhibition (also marked out of 10). This is probably a good thing as the essay is externally assessed (no matter how much you irritated your TOK teacher throughout the years, he/she can't get revenge on you). You should be aiming realistically to get at least 22 points for a guaranteed A, which is not that easy. I have outlined several tips below that will guide you in the right direction.

The essay will require you to show your TOK assessment skills in a prescribed title that you probably would have never chosen if you could have come up with your own essay title. Examples will play a key role in your essay as well as a TOK-based analysis of those examples.

Half of the work in writing a good TOK essay involves choosing a good essay title. Out of the list of six that the IBO provides, there will be one or two that have potentially more marks up for grabs than the others. Do not make the easy but fatal mistake of saying, "Ah, screw those long questions. The shorter the question the easier it is." I would actually argue the other way around. Shorter questions tend to carry a lot of ambiguity, whereas with longer questions, you know exactly what you are supposed to write about.

Look for questions that have a lot of TOK terminology in them and ones that will give you an opportunity to provide a lot of "interesting" TOK arguments. Remember that the essay will demonstrate your ability to link knowledge issues to Areas of Knowledge and Ways of Knowing. Don't go for the questions that you think are interesting to write about; instead, go for the questions you think your TOK teacher would find interesting to read. Anything that specifically asks you to compare, contrast, explain or describe an Area of Knowledge or Way of Knowing is much better than a question that lacks TOK material. If you don't think that the title suggests problems found in knowledge, then it is best to choose another one.

Take your time when choosing the title. Titles usually come out very early, and you usually don't need to make your final choice until your second year. Think long and hard about which question will allow you to demonstrate your TOK knowledge best and one that will let you critically assess. As a rule of thumb, the more TOK key words in the title, the better. Also, avoid questions that could have ambiguous meanings. Remember that you will be paying close attention to the terminology in the question and that you will be expected to address every aspect of the question.

Make sure you know exactly what you are being asked to do. Questions that require you to "evaluate" and "assess" a certain claim will require you to provide arguments for and against. Don't oversimplify the question and make sure to take into account all possible "grey areas." Furthermore, you need to understand every single word that is part of the question. You may think you know what is being asked, but make sure you look up different interpretations of the word (it's unlikely that you would include this in your writing, but at least you will be more prepared when you start writing).

If you're choosing a question that *kind of* sounds like something you could do a great essay on and you're hoping you can just edit the title just a tiny bit, well, think again. The title must be used exactly as given, without any form of alteration. If you fail to follow these instructions, you risk obtaining a failing or incomplete grade. Work with what you are given and focus on the title at hand.

Last but not least, don't be a sheep. Do not think that by choosing a topic that is more popular you will be able to get some good ideas from your friends doing the same topic. Since the essay is capped at 1600 words, there will be literally pages and pages of material to write about, which you will need to filter. Don't worry about not having good enough examples or arguments. And also, if you were to "borrow" an idea from a friend's essay that would probably be plagiarism anyways.

Where to start

My best advice to those who are just about to start writing their TOK essays would be to get your hands on as much official IB-TOK material as possible and highlight everything that is relevant to your essay. With TOK, you are limited with the information you can find on the Internet because the nature of the course is too specific. You can try Googling "perception as a way of knowing" and you will find two types of information – stuff written specifically for the IB TOK program, and stuff that other philosophers/writers have to say. Only the former is of any use to you. As you will find out later on, these "Areas of Knowledge" and "Ways of Knowing" are by no means world acknowledged. Only in the IB program will you find such specific classifications.

Nonetheless, do a fair amount of research on your topic within the realm of TOK. Hopefully your school has some TOK books lying around in cobwebs and dust – get those out and make notes on your question. This is the best type of resources, because they are written by the type of people who will be marking your exam – the true believers of TOK.

Unfortunately, you will have to be pretty good at convincing your examiner that you know what you are talking about. You need to show strong evidence of the Problems of Knowledge, Areas of Knowledge and Ways of Knowing. My best advice for you is to read the official IB TOK books that have been issued over the years. There is a lot of "fun" activities and rubbish in them, but you'd be surprised at how often you will find a quote here or there that will fit into your essay perfectly (of course not plagiarised).

Organization and Structure

My help here is going to be extremely limited. I'm sorry, but nothing I say will really make you write in a more structured manner or teach you how to organize your thoughts – it is something that you must learn and perfect over time. That being said, make sure you keep the essay title with you at all times on a separate piece of paper. Keep glancing at it from time to time and if you ever think a paragraph or sentence is simply too irrelevant, then take it out.

When you start the actual writing process, be sure to type out the question exactly as it is written, word for word, at the top of your paper (including the question number). Throw everything into quotations and in a bold font. This saves the examiner any confusion as to which question you are doing.

Your structure will largely depend on the nature of your question. If it is a simple compare and contrast between two Areas of Knowledge, then you could spend three or four paragraphs explaining how they are similar, and follow that up by the same treatment of how they differ, leaving a few paragraphs at the end for final analysis and conclusion. If you are asked specifically about different Areas of Knowledge, your approach may be to go through each one and explore how it relates to your topic question. Eventually you will end up forming some sort of concluding argument. Keep in mind that there is no single optimal way to write the essay, you need to use your judgement and decide what suits your essay best.

When your paper is complete, you should be able to read it and applaud yourself on your good transitions and structure. Have some rhythm and don't jump paragraph to paragraph talking about completely unrelated matters. If you are still struggling, consult an English book that guides you on how to have smooth transitional paragraphs.

Essay or socratic dialogue?

Talking about structure and organisation, here's a secret that only some IB students know: your essay can actually be written as a dialogue. Yes, you heard that right. Instead of using a standard essay structure, many TOK teachers actually recommend writing the essay as a 'socratic dialogue' in which two characters argue about the prescribed title.

The socratic dialogue will realistically have a very similar structure to a standard TOK essay. Depending on the question you select, there will still need to be a series of arguments and counter-arguments to create a balanced discussion of the question with reference to at least two Areas of Knowledge. There will also have to be some sort of conclusion that the two characters come to after their debate. However, what is good about writing the essay as a socratic dialogue is that you don't have to overload your brain thinking up fancy academic phrases and transitions. Instead, when, for instance, presenting a counter-argument, you can express disagreement between characters just as normal humans would in a conversation. This (especially if you struggle with academic writing) can actually make your essay clearer and easier to understand for both you and your examiner.

Personally, not one student I know of that wrote their essay as a socratic dialogue got less than an A or B as their final TOK grade, but it is ultimately up to you and your circumstances to decide whether or not this structure is for you. If your TOK coordinator is unfamiliar with the idea and seems opposed to it, maybe just stick with the standard structure for which they will likely be able to give you more constructive feedback. If, though, you know you struggle with academic writing and perhaps have experience with writing scripts or other creative text types, the socratic dialogue may just be your saving grace.

Writing

The actual writing process should take far less time than the research and the post-writing procedures you have to go through. 1200 words is nothing really. As you would with the EE, try to push yourself closer to the 1600 target and further away from the minimum. If you have done your research and thought about the essay enough, writing it should not be an issue. Rarely will a 1200 word paper get a grade A – show the examiner that you are not a minimalist student.

Don't mess around when it comes to essay length. You can try and outsmart the IB by lying about the word count; however, that would be incredibly stupid as an electronic version is included. Remember that the word count includes the main parts of the essay along with any quotations. It does not include acknowledgements or references given in footnote form, or the bibliography. At the end of the essay, you should indicate your word count in bold to signal to your examiner that you followed the guidelines.

Your introduction should capture the reader's attention and summarize what the bulk of your essay will argue. Keep it short but well-written. Avoid any grossly meaningless opening statements and get into it straight away. Remember that you can't really afford to have a long introduction given the word count limitations, so be sure to establish your topic and provide clarity. Discuss the key concepts and include an insight into the major arguments of your essay. Also, while writing, keep in mind that it is probably best not to expand ideas too far – if you still have words to spare at the end, you can always go back and develop arguments in more depth.

As far as definitions are concerned, be rational. Don't give the Oxford Dictionary definition of "knowledge" – let about 10,000 other kids make this very mistake. You should know better than that. In fact, don't use the dictionary unless it's absolutely vital. When describing concepts such as "knowledge" or "proof," you are better off using the words of various intellectuals, coupled with your own interpretations rather than a wordy dictionary definition. Don't be fooled into thinking that by providing a definition, you have cleared up all ambiguities and complications associated with the concept – that would be stupid.

Some will tell you it's better to write a lot about a little instead of a little about a lot, whilst others will suggest you include as many TOK concepts as possible. The optimal, my experience has shown, is somewhere in between. If there is any specific terminology in the prescribed title then it should be clearly defined, addressed and discussed in the essay. You do need to make sure you tick off an adequate number of Areas of Knowledge and Ways of Knowing, otherwise, the examiner will not know how comfortable you are with the course. At the same time the word limit will not allow you to go through each one by one. Filter out the best material to discuss. Don't sacrifice quality for quantity. If your essay lacks depth of analysis, your examiner will remember this shallowness in treatment when marking your essay. Clarity is the key – think and write clearly.

Also, a top tip to wrap the examiner around your finger: in the beginning of your essay, mention any assumptions you can spot in the prescribed title. For instance, for the 2023 title *"Does it matter if our acquisition of knowledge happens in "bubbles" where some information and voices are excluded?"*, a clear assumption is that in these 'knowledge bubbles' some information and voices are indeed 'excluded', which may actually not be the case in real life 'bubbles' of scholars and knowers. Although this may seem obvious, it's actually a good way to show the examiner you're analysing the question critically and to give your essay substance and direction from the very start.

Some teachers may warn you against using "I" or "me" in an essay of this sort. This becomes very difficult to do when you discuss your personal experiences and your own beliefs. Try to get around this by avoiding amateur statements like "I believe that... I think that..." and replace them with statements like "judging from my personal experience.... Having witnessed something similar myself..." Catch my drift?

The conclusion is probably the best place to present your personal opinion. Here you are allowed to take a stand because you have already gone through all of the arguments and counterarguments in the body of your essay. Again, avoid being too narrow-minded and show an awareness of a variety of opinions. Also, if you haven't yet convinced your examiner by the time he gets to your conclusion that you have shown personal engagement, then at least you can achieve this in the last paragraph he/she will read.

Always go back and clean up your essay, making sure you have no elementary spelling and grammar mistakes. Although you will not get punished specifically for having any of that, it can potentially interfere with your structure and the "flow" of your essay.

Nothing Controversial

Ok, this is going to be very difficult to write, but it needs to be put out there. The name of the game is: tell them what they want to hear. Look, I know how you feel. It's that feeling of wanting to rip your hair out if you hear another person mention their WoKs or AoKs. Now, you can either be a rebel and fight the entire IB system and argue that all of this is complete nonsense. Or, you can be smarter and use this "flaw" within the course to your advantage.

I spent a good year or so arguing with my grade-eleven TOK teacher that much of what we are taught is simply the IB's attempt to implement an element of philosophy into the syllabus. I would sit there and laugh at questions such as "How do we know?" and "What is knowledge?" – I honestly found it a joke. Then eleventh grade came to an end. My teacher gave me a C for the year and marked my controversial mock oral presentation a pathetic seven out of twenty. I had to learn from my mistakes.

The lesson here is that you are not doing anyone a favour when you try to deny what TOK is trying to teach – you suffer, your classmates suffer, and your teacher will get fed up with you as well. I know it sounds horrible, but it's one of life's most valuable skills – the ability to tell people what they want to hear. You need to understand that you are only in this course for a few years, so you might as well suck it up and try to get through TOK as successfully as you can – whether you believe the material or not. That is what truly separates the top TOK student from the bottom. It's not what you know, it's what others think you know.

Here's an example. For my TOK essay I chose a title about the boundaries between various Areas of Knowledge and whether they are permanent. Initially, I wanted to argue that the AoKs are somewhat superficial, and that there exist tens if not hundreds of other methods of classifying knowledge areas into categories. Basically I was arguing that the Areas of Knowledge that we learn about are not exactly *correct* – they are simply an "IB" classification. After having a talk with my TOK teacher, it became clear that this was not going to sit well with most examiners. While I could have potentially written a wonderfully creative essay about various interpretations of the Areas of Knowledge and what other intellectuals believe, I would not score very high. I needed to focus on what the TOK syllabus is talking about - I needed to write in their language.

This is hard to swallow, I know. I'm not happy that it's this way, but there is little you can do to change it. Your best bet would be to just play along and outsmart everyone else. Leave your controversial arguments at home and get ready to talk a lot of TOK lingo in your essay. This includes avoiding bias at all costs. Even if you think your country/religion/sex/race or whatever is truly the best in the world – avoid saying so and keep it professional. Your essay needs to constantly focus on knowledge issues, no matter how non-TOK the essay title may seem.

While on the subject of controversial statements, another common pitfall for TOK students writing the essay is to make generalizations. "Muslims do this," "Americans eat that," "Women want this," – avoid making these oversimplifications. You should know that no two people are alike, so don't make false statements about a group/nationality/country that have no real basis except your own stereotyping. This just reeks of an anti-TOK way of thinking and you don't want the examiner to know that you are that close-minded. You are going against the whole IB concept of making you an open-minded individual. Be very careful when using words such as "all," "mostly" and "usually." To be fair, you are more likely to write these statements by accident, which is fine, as long as you can spot and rephrase them before you send off your essay.

Examples

The factor that will separate your essay from other students doing the same essay will be your use of examples. Now, this being the IB, you need to make sure your examples are personal, unique and ethically correct. You need examples from other cultures and countries, and they need to appear researched and not just made up.

One of the reasons I strongly suggest that you refrain from sleeping in your TOK class is because you might miss out on potentially good examples brought up by your classmates or teacher. Keep one eye open for anything that could be put into your essay. Go over your notes (if you bothered to make any) and remind yourself of some of the stuff that was discussed in class. Gather examples from newspapers, magazines, Internet or any other relevant source. You will need to filter this by throwing away the "poor" examples and carefully but rigorously summarizing the "good" examples.

Remember that you will be given credit in your essay for not only tying all the relevant ideas and arguments together, but also for drawing on your own life experiences and personal analysis. Make sure you throw in a few cultural and internationally diverse examples here and there. If you've lived in hundreds of different countries and speak ten languages, use that to your advantage. Include not only your own experience but also examples from other cultures with which you have become familiar. Your essay could end up in the hands of an examiner living anywhere from Poland to China. Use a wide variety of sources, but more importantly, make sure that they actually clearly portray the point that you are making. Avoid superficial examples that all high school students think of: Galileo, Francis Bacon's dictum, Inuit words for snow and embryonic stem cell research are worn-out examples – be original!

You will often be advised to find linkages in your IB subjects and you are encouraged to point out these connections. In the TOK essay this is also the case. If you are writing about something and then a little light bulb goes off in your head to tell you, "Hey, we actually discussed this in biology class," then make sure you mention that one way or another. You are likely to be reading great literary texts in your IB English class and learning about some of the most influential people in your history class, so why not see if there is any TOK-related stuff to talk about there.

As far as actual quotations go, I would not overestimate their importance. It's impressive to show the examiner that you appreciate what some of the greatest minds in the world have had to say about your topic, but another person's opinion is only worth so much. Use these more as a stylistic device, rather than as a method to prove a point. As a general rule, you can either start with a quote to set the mood or summarize with a quote to have a lasting and memorable impact on your reader.

As long as we are on the subject of examples, I would also warn you to avoid using examples which are not clearly connected to the topic in question. If you have included an example that you doubt has any real significant impact on the essay, then you're better off taking it out. Similarly, if you can't remember why you placed that example there, then it means it's not proving a point – take it out!

Marking Criteria

As with almost everything else that has assessment criteria in the IB program, the marking criteria is of the highest importance. Read the official IB instructions over and over again. Once you have come close to finishing your essay, sit down and pretend you are the examiner. Give yourself what you think you will get out of 10 points.

Do you have evidence to prove that you know enough about problems of knowledge and that you have experience as a "knower"? Have you included enough examples to illustrate your points? Have you answered the question as it is stated? Did you score 8+ points when you graded yourself against the assessment criteria? If you gave your essay to a fellow TOK student in your class, would he mark it +/- 8 points as well (something I recommend you do if you have helpful friends)?

Make sure you can answer yes to those questions. Pay extremely close attention to the descriptors for top marks in each category. Does that sound like your essay? Can you get at least 7 or 8 points?

Bibliography

Make sure you cite all your work and use a well-known citation method to ensure your bibliography is 100% correct. Remember, even one mistake (such as misuse of quotation marks or italics in the bibliography listings) could cost you one or two marks.

I know it is perfectly feasible to write an entire TOK essay without consulting a single source. While I would normally tell you that this is OK, stay on the safe side. Don't think, "Oh man, I don't have a single source, which means no bibliography, which means they have to give me all 10 marks, because there can't be any mistakes!" Unfortunately, it doesn't work like that. There is still the possibility that you will lose marks for not having sources when you really should have. Do the wise thing and make the effort to include a proper bibliography. The IBO does warn that, "Essays which require facts to support the argument, but omit them, will be awarded zero." Don't take that risk.

Keep in mind this is not a research paper – the *Theory of Knowledge Guide* provided by the IB states that 'neither the [TOK] essay nor the exhibition is primarily a research exercise'. Anything in excess of five sources for a 1600 word essay in TOK is a bit sketchy, because you are expected to rely on your own experiences and analysis more. Keep sources to a minimum but make sure you have something there. Please don't mess up and "accidentally" forget to source an entire statement that you just ripped off from a newspaper article. You will probably get caught – and you will definitely feel dumb. That being said, if you don't bother to look up information, you take the risk of making statements that are clearly false. For example, if you can't exactly remember what year Columbus discovered America and write carelessly 1294 (instead of 1492) you risk losing a point or two for your lack of research (note: I highly recommend you DO NOT use that example). It's not a research paper, but if you do use specific sources, then please include a bibliography just as you would for the EE. All the works that you consulted, whether it be online, book, journal or television, should be included in the bibliography.

There is no guarantee that you will get 10 marks out of 10. My advice is to aim for right about there, and hopefully you will end up with 8+ points. If you follow the directions and marking criteria, there is absolutely no way that you should be getting anything less than 7. Make sure you get the easy points and try your best for the harder ones.

44. Tackling TOK: The Presentation

The following Theory of Knowledge (TOK) presentation structure has been designed very carefully. (It's taken several years of conversations!) It's easy for you to follow and ticks all the boxes.

I'm going to tell you how many slides to have (nine), what text should go on each slide (less is more) and what you should talk about while each slide is up (focus on the interesting parts).

A clear structure like this is essential because it helps the audience follow what you're saying. It also keeps you from wasting time, both during your presentation and in your preparation phase. There are a few things I need to go over before we get into the slides.

The Development Section

When you get into the Development section (where the knowledge question is explored and analyzed with reference to the AOKs and WOKs), you'll see that **we use a Claim, Counterclaim, Mini-Conclusion structure**. We do this (claim, counterclaim, mini-conclusion) for each of your developments (AOKs or WOKs), so we do it 3 times in total.

Here's an example, for one of your developments:

-Your **claim** might be that emotion is reliable when trying to achieve new knowledge art and you show this using some theory (evidence) you learned from your teacher or your pal Google.

-Your **counterclaim** is a problem (a limitation) with your claim, or an opposing idea in the same perspective. It might be that emotion can sometimes lead to unreliable insights in the arts (i.e. creating or interpreting art). You show this using (as evidence) an example from your own life experience or some other kind of evidence.

-And then, in the **mini-conclusion,** you basically have to find a way to draw together the two opposing sides. You have to somehow synthesise these two insights to arrive at a more insightful understanding or some kind of summary. So you might say that emotion can be both reliable and unreliable at the same time, or perhaps there are situations where it's pretty hard to know whether emotions are helping or not (in terms of achieving reliable knowledge). So your MC (mini-conclusion) is a possible conclusion to your KQ (Knowledge Question).

In the final conclusion of the presentation (I call that your Big Conclusion) you will try to combine (draw together/synthesize) the insights of this mini-conclusion as well as the other ones (from the 2 other development sections) to show a really sophisticated/developed answer to your KQ.

Using Evidence

Use evidence for each of your claims and your counterclaims. It will make your talk much more compelling.

Evidence can be:

-Examples of from the course or from your research. For example, stories of real scientific experiments or how society responded to a certain piece of art.

- Personal examples. Specific and realistic examples from your own life experiences are really powerful in presentations, because if they're true (and the audience can normally tell) they are normally really convincing. If you processed your break-up grief by creating a powerful piece of art and you can talk about how you did that (how much this knowledge-generation was coming from emotion).

Now let's go through the structure of your presentation, slide by slide. (The suggested timings in green are **assuming you're in a group of two**, so you'd have 20 minutes). Don't work by yourself.

- **The TOK Presentation Structure**

Slide 1: Title Page (1 minute)

Text on this slide:
- The title of your presentation.
- Your group members' names

What to say:
- Explain what you thought about the real life situation (RLS) when you first encountered it.
- Explain why it's significant to you.

Slide 2: Decontextualization (1 minute)
Text on this slide:
- Some of the thoughts or questions you had about the real life situation. Start explaining the situation in a ToK sort of way --using some of the key terms from the course.

What to say:

- Explain a few of the things we can know about the RLS and how we know it. For example, our senses may provide some insights, while emotion provides other ones.
- Explain that there may be limits to what can be known about your RLS.
- Basically, show us your thought-journey from the RLS to your KQ.

Slide 3: Knowledge Question (1 minute)

Text on this slide:

- Write down your KQ -List the AOKs and/or WOKs you will use to explore your KQ and how they are related to your KQ

What to say:

- Mention 2 KQs that you considered and the one you are investigating.
- Explain how this KQ will help you to explain the RLS.
- For each of your AOKs/WOKs, preview how they can help to answer your KQ.
- Explain any assumptions you've made about your KQ (if any).
- Explain any key terms that need to be explained in order for us to understand your KQ.

Slide 4: Development #1 (3.5 minutes)

On the slide:

- Very briefly, state your claim for WOK/AOK #1 (see development example above). State how it is supported by evidence (i.e. a scientific theory).
- Very briefly, state your counterclaim for WOK/AOK #1 (i.e. an opposing idea in the same AOK/WOK). State how it is supported by evidence. - State your mini-conclusion.

What to say:

- Explain the claim and how it is supported by evidence. Make it clear how it would answer the KQ.
- Explain the counterclaim and how it is supported by evidence. Make it clear how it would answer the KQ in a different way than your claim did.
- Explain your conclusion and how it ties together the claim and counterclaim.

Slide 5: Development #2 (3.5 minutes)

On your slide:

- Very briefly, state your claim for WOK/AOK #2. State how it is supported by evidence.
- Very briefly, state your counterclaim for WOK/AOK #2. State how it is supported by evidence.
- State your mini-conclusion.

What to say:

- Explain the claim and how it is supported by evidence. Make it clear how it would answer the KQ.
- Explain the counterclaim and how it is supported by evidence. Make it clear how it would answer the KQ in a different way than your claim did.
- Explain your conclusion and how it ties together the claim and counterclaim.

Slide 6: Development #3 (3.5 minutes)

On your slide:

- Very briefly, state your claim for WOK/AOK #3. State how it is supported by evidence.
- Very briefly, state your counterclaim for WOK/AOK #3. State how it is supported by evidence.
- State your mini-conclusion.

What to say:

- Explain the claim and how it is supported by evidence. Make it clear how it would answer the KQ.
- Explain the counterclaim and how it is supported by evidence. Make it clear how it would answer the KQ in a different way than your claim did.
- Explain your conclusion and how it ties together the claim and counterclaim.

Slide 7: Conclusion (3 minutes)

On your slide:
- Write down your conclusion.
- Write down a possible flaw in your conclusion.

What to say:
- Explain your conclusion.
- Explain how this conclusion is supported by the insights you've drawn along the way (in your mini-conclusions).
- Explain the possible weakness or a flaw in your conclusion.
- Explain an example of someone from a different perspective (a different gender, age, time, or culture) who might disagree with this conclusion.

Slide 8: Link back to the RLS (3.5 minutes)

On your slide:
- Write 2 interesting ways that your conclusion applies to the RLS.
- Write down two other real life situations (which are perhaps related). If possible provide pictures for these two other situations, so they can be quickly understood. One of these should be personal to you (something one of you encountered) and another which is more of a shared experience.

What to say:
- Clarify how your conclusion applies to the RLS.

- Explain how this conclusion can help to explain 2 other real life situations you have on your slide.

Slide 9: Bibliography (0 minutes)
What to say:
- Just leave this one up on the screen as the class erupts in thunderous applause. Some people will want autographs, but try to be cool about it. You were once just like them.

Of course you are not required to follow this structure (unless your teacher says otherwise), but it is recommended. Everything in this structure is there for a very good reason.

Footer

I also recommend that **every slide from #3 onward should have your KQ written on the bottom of it**, as a footer. This will make it easier for the audience to relate your various insights to the knowledge question.

Also (to be completely honest) sometimes we don't hear you when you quickly said your knowledge question. We were writing something down or thinking about lunch.

Signposting

Finally, to help to make sure that the person marking you gives you full credit, it's useful to do what we call signposting. This means, using the exact key words the marker was trained to look for. Professionals do this all the time. Their use of specialist language signals to their colleagues that they know what they're talking about. So try to speak like a TOK teacher basically. In this case, your marker will respond favourably if you use a fair amount of terminology you learned in the course. For example, use the term perspective. So you might say, "**from the perspective of** a historian.." rather than saying, "Historians believe that…" --just to get that word in there.

45. How to get a 45

This chapter contains a collection of random titbits of advice from IB Redditors who have **scored a 45.** Some of it may repeat advice you already encountered in this book, but that just means that you should really listen to what is being recommended!

1. u/bigbluetony (2024)

Hey M24s, this is just gonna be some quick advice from a N23 who was feeling terrible before exams and procrastinated until the final month.

My subjects: HL AA, Physics & Chemistry SL English, Geography & Lang B

I wouldn't say that I am very smart, but I do acknowledge that I had decent/strong foundations to work with. I genuinely procrastinated all study until the final month (did not take mock/trial exams) and for some subjects, I had not even learned 50% of their content.

The main idea is not studying long or all day, but studying effectively. Personally I tried to study as much as possible, but I'd always get distracted by tiktok or other things. I found that my deep, focused studying helped the most. So everyday (assuming you don't have school) maybe just spend 6-8 hours on studying. Personally, I spent around 6 and still burned out. You genuinely do not need to be spending 10+ hours per day. Focus on understanding and internalising the content.

Maths AA, Physics & Chemistry (or other STEM subjects)

PLEASE USE SAVEMYEXAMS

Literally saved my exams, and was the best revision/learning resource out of everything available to me. Genuinely I learned a lot from Savemyexams, but make sure you also have the subject syllabus guide up when you're reading/learning. Identify each dotpoint in the syllabus and make sure you're keenly aware of which dot point you are learning about when you are reading savemyexams. Every hour or few hours, make sure you blurt what you remember for each dot point, and fill in the gaps when you re-read. Re-read the PDF many times,

DO NOT RELY ON REVISIONVILLAGE SCIENCES

(absolutely sucked in my experience, but RV maths is ok). Make sure to read through the whole pdf for each subject multiple times, making sure you can explain each concept to yourself and work through the example worked questions they have. It is SUPER important you properly understand this content. Once you understand a concept/topic, work through real past paper questions on that topic (find the official questionbank, iykyk, and sort by topic.

USE REAL PAST PAPER QUESTIONS, NOT RANDOM QUESTIONBANKS

Some of them suck. Don't take that risk. But make sure you don't exhaust every practice question (leave some for you when you do a real past paper in exam conditions). Just do enough to make sure you know that topic well.

Once you have read through each subject's PDF and done a thorough amount of topic-related past paper questions, you're ready to take a real past paper under exam conditions. Take it timed, closed-book (there should be no reason for open-book since you should've already learned the content from savemyexams) and record your score. Mark all your mistakes and UNDERSTAND them. See what you did wrong and correct it. After you've finished that, write ONE TAKEAWAY (one weakness from that paper that you need to improve on). This part is really important.

As you do a few past papers, you should see your grades start increasing. Well done if that's the case.

Geography (and other humanities I suppose)

If you're like me you didn't pay attention in class and don't know the content. Oh well! There is no time to read the textbook. GO ONLINE. Find a good set of notes to use on each core topic and the options. I found some good notes on clastify (really hit or miss sometimes). The important point here is to make sure you've highlighted each syllabus dotpoint. Make sure you memorise content relating specifically to the syllabus dot points. If the syllabus asks for 2 case studies, make sure you have them memorised really well. If you forget them in the exam, literally just make them up lol.

Language B

Big struggle for me. For lang B, I just crammed a vocab bank the week before ngl and it worked out fine. I can't really offer good advice for lang B, other than do lots of past papers, make sure basic vocab is learned and try to "game" the papers. I remember in one reading article that I thought was about innovative robots was actually about highways but I still got 9/10 because I had done so many I could find the patterns and fluke the paper.

English

Fucked me up good. I did not read ANY except 1 of my books. If you're in this position, try to use poetry for paper 2. Personally I feel that poetry is extremely versatile (memorise and pre-analyse a few diverse poems) and can adapt to many questions. In my case, I could only do poetry for one of my works. Now, you have to use pre-written guides.

USE ATARNOTES

It was the night before my exam and I kid you not, I was still choosing my second text because I simply had not read any of them. I ended up choosing a play but THANK GOD FOR ATARNOTES, because their guide allowed me to skim, read, analyse and memorise quotes/themes/arguments literally all the night before the exam. Atarnotes is great, but what would be even better is if you could nab a good document of notes from a smart classmate or online (unfortunately I was out of time). My advice for both papers is literally just analyse a lot. Always talk about techniques and their effects (try to synthesise and produce some coherent arguments).

The next morning before the exam I basically just panicked looking at the past paper questions but all was well in the exam. I thought I did really bad in the exam (like ofc because that was literally the first paper 1 and 2 I had ever written) but it turned out fine in the end.

Overall, don't be nervous everyone!! You still have so much time left (more than I had) and you aren't as far behind as I was (hopefully). Yes, I did end up getting a 45 and I'm VERY grateful, but I'm just showing you all that you can too with some calculated studying and good strategising.

Best of luck to you all!

2. u/Illosa

Hey everyone,

The r/IBO subreddit has been one of my most indispensable tools during the IB period. Now that it is all over, I'd like to help others on here just like previous generations have helped me. Just for laughs, this was me last year.

So firstly, free tutoring. I did English A Lit, German B, and History (Europe/Middle East) at HL. Chem, Bio, and Maths at SL. EE was in History. I will teach any of these subjects to you/help you with proofreading IAs and assignments, basically whatever a normal tutor would do. I am available on Skype (can video call) and you can WhatsApp call me in cases of emergency. I can also email or PM you or whatever. Because lots of people need help, I will be giving preferences to serious cases who really want to improve. If you need help, comment or PM with your current IB year, subjects needed (hopefully ones I've done, haha), what your current grade is, and what you want it to be. I will share my own work and my special IB spreadsheet as examples. All my notes are pen and paper so if you want 'all the notes for maths please', I am going to disappoint you. My time zone is GMT + 10 so keep that in mind.

I'm not doing this to 'spoil the market' but because I believe that education should be free. Many IB students go to private schools and are relatively well-off, but going to a school where someone got tuition from the person who wrote the Chem textbook, I don't want anyone to feel disadvantaged because they don't see the point of paying $100 an hour to do something that they honestly can do with a little help.

Now on to my guide to getting 45. I'm sick of top scorers going to those stupid education companies and appearing in their books for study success. It's a gimmick and we all know it. Though my individual stand may not mean much, I want to make it all available...again for free. So I'll write my guide in parts and post it. Let me know if you think I'm just bullshitting (IB habits die hard) and I'll change it. If this is boring, let me know too.

Guide Part 1: Choosing your subjects
Most of you are too late for this, but if I could change anything in my IB life, it would be my subjects. Now, in 'The Art of War', Sun Tzu says that 'knowing thyself' is important for victory. In the case of IB, you need to make a choice. Are you the kind of student that a) MUST get 40+, or b) wants to explore interesting subjects? There is no shame in wanting to get 40+ by the way; many uni courses require it. Also, a and b are not mutually exclusive sets, but just pick one.

Armed with your category, you now need to seriously consider how compatible your choices are. Go look at the statistics reports for IB worldwide, first link on this page and see what percentage of each student in your subject gets a 7. Again, use your critical thinking; just because 100% of people in Amharic A got a 7 doesn't mean it's easy, it just means that only really good Amharic speakers took the subject. This is relatively accurate as a predictor of difficulty with common subjects though.

Subjects that I would personally warn against UNLESS you are in category 'b' are: History HL, Chem HL unless on the engineering track, Language B HL unless you are a fluent/native speaker.

Really, History HL is damned hard. In my experience, it is the only subject where time limits in the exam are too short. Maths is challenging but you at least have a decent amount of time to panic in the exam. In History Paper 2, one minute of panic will really cost you.

Subjects that are good to study (again, depends on your personal talents, but if you are inclined towards any of these areas you will have a good time): Theatre, Business Studies, Maths Studies. The reason why Maths Studies is a controversial inclusion into this territory is because people who do maths studies tend to believe that they are no good at maths. This is untrue; it takes a whole new sort of thinking to do well in Studies. As someone once explained to me, Maths SL is 5 units 'calculus' and 1 unit 'statistics', while studies is the other way around. If you're bad at statistics, do not do Studies thinking that it will solve your problems! Generally though, Studies IS indubitably easier to 'study' than Maths SL, due to the nature of statistics vs calculus.

Of course there are strategies against panic, but more on that next time. Also, when it comes to choosing subjects...make sure you choose your HLs strategically. I fared slightly better at this; I chose Chem and Bio SL because these were content/practice heavy subjects, and I needed time to do History HL. If I had chosen History HL, Bio HL, and Chem HL, I would have had a very bad time. It has been done, people have gotten 7s all around from it, but...again, consider what you want and whether you can sustain the workload at a stressful time.

Another important aspect of subject choice which may not be too late for you is the EE and TOK presentation. Do your EE in a humanities subject if possible! Eco EEs seem to be hard to score well in. If you do History SL (the best kind of history, really) do your EE in History, it's fine. Consider Language B if you are fluent, though you do have to write your EE in that language. Also, English is an overlooked EE subject.

The reason why science EEs are dangerous is because many of us are procrastinators. When you do a science EE, 9/10 times, your own research is expected. You need to spend time setting up the study, growing plants or preparing controls, and it's basically a monster IA.

Math EEs can be very good ideas if you are mathematically inclined, as it is a lot easier to write a super detailed Math Exploration than it is to do 3 IAs at once while actually struggling with the workload of 3 IAs. Business EEs are good ideas.

As for TOK, do not overestimate yourself. I cannot stress this enough. TOK seems like crap to a lot of people but...it can cost you one of those 3 points. I never paid attention in TOK class and I was really in danger at the very end. Remember to rehearse your presentation, preferably WITH the teacher...the more you see your teacher, the better things will be for you in IB. Go see your teachers in all subjects! Also, for the essay, borrow a bunch of those TOK textbooks that nobody reads and seriously copy the style shown in the books. They want you to sound friendly and factual at the same time. It's weird.

Alright, that wraps up today's guide. Hope I can have some feedback as to what aspects of the DP you want to hear about. Future segments planned are CAS tips, study strategy for DP1 and DP2, IAs in sciences and humanities, the IOP/IOC, Language B tips, Maths SL practice guide, exam skills, and general timetabling...

PS: I have always done 'timetabling' for friends and acquaintances. If anyone needs help drawing up a study timetable (I use a certain system), I'm here to help. The offers in this post will remain open until I edit due to lack of time, but I'm waiting till September before uni starts so I should be pretty available.

3. u/HNN_N

The IB score is not an index of intelligence.

With that, it's not impossible to score 45 points in the International Baccalaureate. I've done it. Others have done it. And here's how you'll do it.

To begin with, you need to get familiar with the task at hand.

It's a simple fact that it takes a lot of mental work and preparation to conquer a big project. The International Baccalaureate is just another one of them. Therefore, it'd be unreasonable to undertake it without a concrete plan. Whilst it probably wasn't your choice to get involved with it, don't simply reduce it to an insuperable mission leaving you drained of all your resources.

Though it may not seem worthy of reverence to you at present, in hindsight, I'll sanguinely say the I.B can be rewarding. It's a career with prospects; It awards you with a sense of worldliness and set of helpful academic, social and emotional skills that will serve you well later in life.

If you're only just choosing your I.B subjects, you might as well be on the brink of a decision that'll either make or break your next two years. Where you can, compensate. If you've already identified your university and course of choice, find out which subjects are either required or not. Select subjects at standard levels unless high levels are mandatory and if you can, only pick subjects of genuine interest.

To put it mildly, the IB is an ongoing saga of challenges with endless implications. You'll probably struggle, you'll probably cry, but here's the kicker: you'll get through it.

My (unexpected) success persuaded me to compile a host of strategies that helped me in my experience. Though you may find some of these strategies somewhat repetitive, trust me – there is no simple formula for success in the IB.

I consider the following techniques the key drivers behind my personal success. In the spirit of sharing, I believe you too can gain from them to muster the motivation and perseverance needed to get through the IB. No need to wind up woefully looking back at your IB career on results day.

Don't wait until your ship comes in. Swim out to it.

1. Visualise. Set goals. Put them into perspective.
Goal setting is a testified technique to promote productivity. It allows for a long-term vision that'll help you organize your time and resources effectively. Begin by asking yourself some questions:

How many points do you need to achieve in order to get into your university of choice?

What do you want to see when you receive your results?

What is it, that you want to gain from your IB experience?

This will give you an overview that'll signpost your way through the programme. Taking the headfirst approach leads to the inevitable pattern so many IB students befall: feebly scrambling to scrape through deadlines as they go. Determine the score that you want, and plan to work accordingly. If you're a high achiever, simply have faith in yourself. Know it has been done before – so you can succeed too.

If you're not, don't worry. There's always room to improve.

If you know you won't be able to handle the workload alone, don't hesitate to ask for help. There are plenty of tutors that dedicate themselves to helping students in your position. Be an active communicator, make use of your teachers and mentors by asking plenty of questions – they make their living by helping you learn. Stay proactive, think about your strengths and weaknesses – do you work better in study groups? One-on-one with a tutor? Or by yourself in general?

Once you have an overall view of how and why you want to work in the IB, you're off to a good start.

2. C.A.S – Creativity, Amusement, Spirit.
Perhaps you're naturally sporty, a social butterfly or charitable at heart. Provided, you wouldn't consider completing C.A.S a struggle even if you tried.

If, like most, of us, you're not as lucky, adopt the golden rule: only to commit to what you genuinely enjoy. It'll ultimately spare you of a lot of wasted time and effort. Do you want to learn a new skill? Join a club, or start one with friends?

It's worth putting all your stock into long-term projects. They'll turn out more beneficial than short-term projects here and there. Not only are they more fulfilling, but you'll be thankful when you garnish your CAS portfolio or university application with an artfully selected array of activities, making you stand out. Don't entirely eliminate the prospect of short-term commitments, though they may do little to embolden your leadership qualities.

Once you've decided which projects you want to engage in, make sure they align with the three aspects of the programme – creativity, action and service (incomplete hours are an IB fail condition!) Your school will be a particularly useful resource in this respect: it offers swathes of opportunities for long-term projects.

Most importantly, allocate a specific time in your schedule for updating your portfolio – you'll avoid sleepless nights come the final closing stages, having dodged the failing condition, or a rejection from your dream university for an inadequate extracurricular profile.

Don't let CAS undo all the other hard work you put into the IB.

3. Look before you leap into TOK and the EE
When it comes to the Extended Essay, pick a subject you're well practiced and authentically interested in.

No matter how generic, this is the most significant advice out there.

The best essays are born from a unique collision of passion and sustained effort. The EE and TOK are key determiners of your I.B score, bumping your mark to the pinnacle if you tackle them well. The EE is a task you'll be dwelling on for weeks, and if somewhat enjoyable, the sense of enthusiasm shows through your writing, brings an incredible nuance to your content, and will undoubtedly spellbind your examiner.

Contrary to probable assumptions, it doesn't matter if its contents match the subject you'll be studying at university.

What matters is whether it returns an A.

With a genuine interest in your subject, you'll find yourself forming an argument incessantly and writing your essay in no time.

You must devote some of your summer holidays to your EE. This is the last time you'll have an abundance of free time, which lends itself ideally to the planning stages of the EE. Use it to structure your essay by breaking it down into manageable tasks, contact necessary primary sources (which return higher scores for quality research), and writing a full draft. Returning to school with your essay will leave you more time for editing with your supervisor.

Although TOK Essay titles are prescribed, opt for your preferred subjects when constructing your thesis and you'll be met with more content for your arguments. In the end, you'll find TOK rewards you with a new perspective, no matter how tedious or lackluster it may be.

4. The Early Bird Catches the Worm
It seems every teacher possesses an unprecedented capacity to pile study material, assessments, and I.As on you in concurrence with others. If you're only getting started with the I.B, the deadline schedule is your holy grail.

Plan ahead and be proactive, set your I.A deadlines earlier in your personal calendar. Allocate specific times for tasks during the week, though leave room for relaxation too. Quite frankly, holidays are virtually non-existent in the I.B. Indubitably you should spend time with friends and family, but strike a balance between studying as well. Even if you take just a few times to reread or rewrite your notes – practice makes perfect in the long term.

5. Running the Mile….
There is one simple link that binds all Olympic gold Athletes together: sustained training. Just as this daily practice becomes intrinsic to them over a period of years, you must treat revision as such: ensure it becomes an integral part of your day weeks before the exams.

An invaluable skill is note-taking by hand. Mundane, but information is better retained through active note taking in contrast to typing up the teacher's words. Although typing up lectures verbatim has its short-term tactical advantages, it's still a passive form of learning and fails to stimulate the brain in the way that deciding what to note down yourself, would. Although you might have understood and notated something in class, weeks later you'll forget.

Tapping into your long-term memory facilitates information recall when you're taking your exams. Revise as much as you can, prepare flashcards and summaries to look over briefly, even if only for a few minutes, then use class time to clarify any inquiries. Make regular revision a habit by doing it on the go. Check your flashcards when you go somewhere, make small handy notes to whip out anytime. That way, you'll make sure the information is engrained.

There's power in visualizing yourself taking your exams in the hall: mental preparation can combat intense emotional fears around the prospect. Only do practice tests once you've completed your notes and revision for a subject. Experiment with note taking styles (visuals, mind maps), but place an unrelenting emphasis on making sure your notes correspond with the learning outcomes/ objectives in the subject syllabus, as mark schemes tend to be pedantic.

In studying for essay-based subjects, write practice essays and mark them according to the criteria. If you get something wrong, make sure you know why. Revisit the error to ensure you're not lured into the same trap again once when taking the actual exam. Completing as many past papers as possible (also, under time pressure) will help you gauge what examiners are looking for: e.g use of quotes with complementary justification in essays, subject-specific vocabulary or methods to solving equations, among many others. Practice drawing diagrams, graphs and other visual material required as well.

Don't simply study the material, study the exam.

…Or Doing Sprints?
There's a fine line between effective and ineffective studying. Identifying which areas require most effort is imperative to effective study. If you're short on time, hone in on aspects of the subject that may be contenders for this year's exam.

Luckily, the IB is quite repetitive in nature, especially when it comes to exam content. You can expect topics that have been left out for one to two cycles to make appearances on the upcoming exam.

Then, focus on consistently practicing and reviewing these areas instead.

7. Time is Money.
It is a cliche for a reason. Think about it; Although the I.B may have you falling on hard times, it'll only take up two school years, (four semesters) of your entire life. It's essentially a fleeting period, a wrinkle in a fabric.

You're then eternally liberated from anything I.B related .

so why not work hard while you must?

Let's dispel some misconceptions about the I.As. No Internal Assessment can be completed in a matter of one day, despite any veneer of hard work – no high scoring I.A, that is. No matter what former students or your friends may tell you, although feasible, the resulting piece of work will never supersede adequate. When you are first introduced to the assignment, calculate how much time you might need for each section. Honestly, grab a pen and paper and scribble down some rough estimates, then pencil them in on your calendar. Our brain is naturally inclined to overestimate the effort required for big tasks we set ourselves. We visualize the crux of the workload, in turn releasing stress hormones that perpetuate procrastination.

However, there's a route beyond this psychological impasse:

Create a schedule. Allot a specific window of time for each section of the I.A. If you're unsure how much time you might need, ask a teacher or former I.B students for their opinions.

You have enough time to finish it all. If you feel like you don't, reevaluate your current schedule. Small, hourly habits (such as checking social media platforms) might collectively amount to precious minutes you could use on your I.A.

Read, re-read, and proofread again. Check every aspect of your I.A, whether that be calculations, spelling, grammar or fact-checking. Leave yourself enough time to critically examine your own work before you hand it in. Take your teachers advice seriously. Remember they've seen plenty of I.As, they're well practiced in separating the needle from the haystack.

In preparation for your exams:

Begin by creating a study schedule. The clock is ticking in your final year; the second half of the IB programme is the preparatory run leading into final the exams.

The best thing you can do for yourself is to start revising early in the school year. Make revision a daily or weekly habit – make it a rule to allow nothing to pile up until the very end. Identifying which subjects might require more/less studying, and plan accordingly.

Be specific: clearly identify the days you'll be studying which subject, chapter or even subchapter. Pinpoint the days you'll be summarising your notes, and when you'll be revising.

When studying, apply the Pomodoro technique. It's consistently recycled advice for a reason. Passively trying to keep track of study times will cease to give accurate results, as we often don't realize just how much time is gone to waste on small distractions. Actively tracking time using a timer gives you a clearer overview of just how much you have studied for the day/ must study the next.

8. Stay organised

This is the true key to success in the I.B. This piece of advice may be simple, but it can take a whole load of failure to wise up to this fact.

Avoid it through developing persistent note-taking and reviewing habits. Class notes covering content from the onset of your IB programme are solid gold when it comes to the final stages of revising for exams. Allocate specific colors to specific subjects, organize them using folders, and keep your work in a space solely dedicated to it in your room.

An organized schedule with study time allocated for each subject every weekend will carry you through the programme. Dedicate certain blocks of time, perhaps 1-2 hours or 30 minutes to certain subjects every day, and plan accordingly for holidays. If you can't stick to your study schedule one day, don't worry about it. Simply move the study blocks in your schedule around and refocus as soon as you can. The plan should be flexible, not restrictive, merely functioning as a backbone for support.

9. Consistency is always key

It's easy to simply say you're going to do something. Perhaps its Saturday and you've set yourself the task of starting an assignment.

But suddenly its 8pm on a Sunday night and you haven't left your bed yet.

More often than not, starting something may just very well be the hardest part.

Well begun is half done. Use the oldest trick in the book: Set a timer to 20 minutes, in which you force yourself to start. Watch yourself break the ice and discover it might not be as hard as you'd imagined it to be. Even if it is, you'll be happy you ended up getting something done and left with more knowledge than you had at the start, perhaps in terms of following steps.

You may discover you need to ask for help or allocate more time for the task in your schedule than you initially thought. That way you won't abandon it, then surprise yourself with an unmanageable workload one day before the deadline.

10. Learn From Others
You're never alone when you're struggling with your work.

Active communication is a discipline that concurs with comprehension. Your school community is filled with people who've either dealt with this experience or are there to help. Perhaps, your friends are equally as stuck? Get together and form a study group, in which the exchange may raise new insights into a task you didn't understand before. Not only that – vocally reviewing notes and quizzing each other will reinforce your understanding of the material.

Ask your teachers. They'll be happy to explain anything you might not have understood during that one class. Visit youtube. There's a multitude of qualified educators which might explain a subject better than your teacher did, and your understanding will consolidate naturally.

11. A Balancing Act
Remember, the I.B shouldn't enslave you or rob you of your social life.

It's simply excessive and altogether unsustainable to stay on top of your work without weaving in a mental break during the IB. It's at your discretion what you make of it, and it'll only treat you as such if you don't prepare and stay organized.

There's enough time for friends and family on the weekend, fun during holidays and activities after school. Just make sure you avail yourself to the time you've allocated to studying as well. If you feel overwhelmed, take a break and do something fun. If you're of the over-achieving kind, keep in mind that overworking yourself is counterproductive.

Nobody will execute you for having a bit of fun.

12. Go on Hiatus
I positively ascribe my I.B results to bursting my social media bubble just before the exams. Trust me, I have this one pegged.

Although undoubtedly a nightmare for most millennials, ridding yourself of the social media is easier than you think. I deactivated what I considered the most distracting of social apps for weeks before my exams and almost instantaneously, felt a vast expanse in time to spare for leisure activities still within the realm of my study plan.

I got in hours of work daily, simply eliminating the accumulated sum of moments in my day, otherwise spent checking social platforms, then rescheduling accordingly. Ridding yourself of the unnecessary mental clutter also frees up bandwidth for enhanced concentration. You'll be finding yourself subconsciously recycling study material mentally, as opposed to social media related thoughts. This translates into an effective technique to reinforce your memory so you can recall things with greater ease during exams.

Once you get to the actual exam, you'll notice a strengthened ability to focus and less distraction when recalling information.

13. Mix up the scene

It's worth separating your study space from space for recreation. When it came to final exam preparation, I spent days in the library as an alternative to working at home.

Your room is an environment rife with distractions. Its subconscious capacity to lure the brain into a state of relaxation is a direct assault on productivity.

Additionally, a cluttered desk is said to foster a cluttered mind. If you're not one to enjoy tidying up, find a study space elsewhere, perhaps your local library or a quiet area in school. Each night before you go to sleep, re-read the study material of that day in the comfort of your bed.

A host of research suggests, that strengthened memory retention is directly correlated to sleeping right after learning, as your brain rewires neural connections when you sleep to process and cement new memories. Simply put, success hinges on sleep. However, this only counts for memorizing: struggling to grapple with new concepts late at night, cramming or prioritizing studying over sleep is altogether ineffectual. If you didn't manage to complete your studies that day simply accept it, sleep and move on.

Give yourself time to recover and let your brain solidify that which you were able to cover during your studies that day – don't stress about what you didn't cover.

As aforementioned, balance is a vital aspect of your lives, especially when it comes to maintaining an active social and productive work To study well, you need the freedom to think well – and that's not within the comfort of your personal space of relaxation, with a bed inviting you for a nap.

4. u/SurviveTheIBDP

Hello there! We are two IB students who have just started year 2 of the IB programme. We went into the IB knowing basically nothing about and we want to save you some of the troubles we had by giving you a beginner's guide to this programme. We want to mention here that we talk a lot more about futures in STEM than for example humanities. This is because STEM is generally much more rigorous in terms of applications and requires more consideration and planning. We mean no offence to those who don't see themselves in STEM, we just figured that it deserved relatively more details.

- What subjects do you have to take?

The first thing you have to do, before you even start the first year, is to choose your subjects. The IB requires you to choose 6 subjects and do 3 mandatory "components" (more on them later in this post!). Out of the 6 subjects, you need to choose 3 that you will take on HL (higher level - more content, more difficult but also counts more towards college admissions) and 3 which will be on SL (standard level).

We will explain the choices you can make a bit later, but let's first set some ground rules for choosing subjects:

1. Find out what your university course needs from you. This should be your absolute priority - after all, the reason why

you do the IB is to get into college. Take a peek at the website of your dream uni course and the details should be there. If you don't have a specific uni in mind yet, look at the best unis in your desired country which offer the course you want.

2. If you aren't sure what you want to study in the future, don't just choose the easiest subjects. Doing this will certainly make your two years in the IBDP easier, but applying to college will be difficult because the "easy" subjects simply won't compliment eachother very well. If you really have no idea what to do, ask yourself - what kind of person are you? If you're detail oriented, maybe look at something STEM related. Like working with people? Maybe medicine will be for you. This process is much more complicated than we make it sound here, but you need at least a vague idea what to do in the future.

3. If your university doesn't specify what they want in a certain subject group, go for what interests you. For example, we both want to study medicine. Medical universities in our country simply don't care about humanities. In such a situation, you need to remember: even if there are no specifics, you still need to pass that subject and probably get a decent grade (many unis look at all the grades you got, not just the specified subjects). We promise, it is so much easier to accomplish when you have at least a little bit of passion for that subject and aren't bored to death during every class.

- First subject - "Studies in Language and Literature"

The first subject you choose will belong to this group. In short, these are language courses, which don't teach you the language as much as they teach you how to work with it. Therefore, it is best that the subject you choose here is based on a language that you know well - preferably your native tongue so that you don't need to catch up on grammar and vocabulary.

- Second subject - "Language acquisition"

This subject group focuses on teaching you a language that is not native to you (at least that's the assumption here). This group can be divided into three types of courses: Classical Languages, language B and language AB initio.

• Classical languages are exactly what it sounds like and they include classical Greek and Latin among others. These are rarely a formal requirement for any university course, so we'd recommend them only if this is something that really interests you.

• Language B is the "standard" second language course. Here, it is assumed that you have the basics of that language covered. In language level terms, these usually start at B1 or higher (on the A1-C2 scale). From anecdotal experience, such courses should be rather easy if you have worked with the chosen language before (such as in primary/middle school).

• Language AB initio is the course that teaches you a chosen language from the very basics. This should be the course you take if you just want to learn another language. Beware, this course is quite unlikely to teach you a new language on a level that may be required by a foreign university (where courses are in that language).

• Third subject - "Individuals and societies"
This subject group includes humanities and economy-related subjects.

• Business management (BM) is often considered a rather easy option for undecided individuals.

• Economics is also called quite easy (especially economics HL compared to other HL subjects). Both BM and econ can be good choices for anyone who envisions a future in finance or business.

• Geography has more essay writing than you'd expect. At least in our school, this is considered an easy "filler" subject (one that you take when neither you nor your university cares about this subject group).

• Global politics has split opinions in the community. Some say it's easy, some say it's hard. This is not a very universal subject - good for very specific courses, but may not be credited that well elsewhere. We'd recommend it only if you know it fits your dream university course.

- History has A LOT of content to learn. Importantly, HL history has relatively few people scoring the highest grade. We both take and enjoy history, and from our perspective, this will be a great choice for those who like it and a rather painful one for those who have no interest in history. Keep in mind, IB history relies a lot on your essay writing skills.
- Philosophy is cited as having rather simple content. Similarly to history, how you do in this subject depends a lot on how much interest and aptitude you have for theoretical and abstract discussion.
- Psychology has split opinions. Generally, the content requires a lot of content to learn (memorize). So, if you're a fan of Freud and making shit up, this may not be exactly for you. Still, we believe that this can be a really good choice if you like psychology, so we'd recommend you take a look at the subject guide if you're undecided (can be found easily just by googling).
- Fourth subject - "Sciences"

This subject group contains what you'd expect - science subjects.

- Biology requires memorizing a lot of content. Notably, the exam markschemes (the instructions for teachers how to decide on whether you get a point for your answer) are a kafkaesque nightmare. We might be a little biased as we both take HL biology and we both absolutely hate it (or at least how it is conducted in our school), but the mountain of content to learn remains a fact. Generally, this is a useful subject for STEM and a must for medicine.
- Chemistry relies a lot on your understanding of the content. This is something that some people will just "get" and others will have to put considerable effort into. We are a little

biased as our teacher is amazing, but the content here is not very difficult. However, it requires you to apply theories correctly in practice, which may be difficult for some. This is a very universal subject for STEM.

- Computer Science is very specific. Very few people who are undecided take it and it just seems to be a subject that requires your interest. It is important to note that the Internal Assesment (we will elaborate on what that is in a bit) which every CompSci student has to do is said to be very difficult.

- Environmental systems and societies (ESS) is widely regarded as the easiest IB science class. However, it doesn't really fill the usual role that sciences do (such as in STEM applications). Can be a good choice if your future is more humanities oriented.

- Physics, especially on HL, is statistically the most difficult IB subject (not just in this group!). It is similar to chemistry in the sense that it also requires understanding of the content. However, it requires significantly better math skills than any other science class. Overall, this is possibly the most useful subject for STEM. Outside of that, we can't recommend it due to its difficulty.

- Fifth subject - "Mathematics"

Ah, the bane of every high schooler's existence. In the IB programme, there are two types of mathematics courses:

- Applications and Interpretation (AI) is the course more focused on applying math knowledge to concrete problems. This type of IB math is generally regarded as easier, especially AI SL. It leans more on using your calculator to solve problems and contains more applied math such as statistics or modeling. However, this course is poorly credited by some universities (or in some cases, not even considered in math-heavy course applications). If you don't need math for college, AI SL is a great choice. If AI HL seems interesting, make sure it won't be a disadvantage compared to AA math when applying to your desired course.

- Analysis and Approaches (AA) is closer to pure math and places more emphasis on abstract problem-solving. Generally, the AA SL course, while harder, should be manageable for most and is worth considering. AAHL, while statistically not as hard as physics, is often the source of horror stories in this subreddit. Even if you consider yourself a math person, this is still a rather difficult course. One of us takes AA HL and the comments on how difficult it is are generally rather overblown. Sure, it requires a lot of practice, but with enough consistency, it is managable for most people. AAHL is the most useful math course for STEM, just make sure you have decent foundations before undertaking it.
- Sixth subject - your choice!

Theoretically, this subject group also allows you to take an Arts course (such as Dance, Film, Theatre, Music or Visual Arts). However, it is hard to describe these courses objectively. Many schools (such as ours) don't offer them at all and the people who take these are usually already somewhat experienced in that area. Overall, if any of these seem interesting to you and if choosing them won't be a disadvantage in applying for your dream university, consider researching them yourself (again, subject guides can be found very easily on the internet).

If you aren't keen on any of these, the sixth subject can be almost anything from any other subject group (excluding mathematics and group 1). This can be a good "boost" towards certain courses. For example, combining two sciences is almost a must for STEM. We, for instance, both take biology and chemistry. Overall, this is your opportunity to enhance your diploma's appeal for very specific courses.

- A note on non-standard subject configurations

The IB allows you to do some manoeuvring outside of what we've described when choosing your subjects. Here are a few exceptions to the rules that might interest you:

1.   Four HL subjects: instead of the standard 3-3 HL/SL configuration, the IBO allows you to do a 4-2 HL/SL diploma. Generally, unless you are sure this will benefit your uni application significantly, we would not recommend it. You will simply need to cover a lot more content while getting the same diploma with the same maximum score in the end. If it just seems "fun" and you want to take the subjects that interest you on HL, don't do it. You will need to work a lot harder, and a standard 3-3 configuration doesn't prohibit you from developing your interests anyway. One of us takes four HL's and it's manageable mostly because one of these is language B (our school required it) in which I am essentially a native speaker. If you need the four HL's for university, we'd recommend taking an easier course for the SL subjects just to not get overwhelmed when exam season comes around.

2.   Irregular diploma: that's a tricky one. Basically, you can ask the IB (you NEED their official approval to do this) to for example take three sciences and omit a language course. Similarly to the four HL's dilemma, this should only be considered when you know this will be beneficial in the context of applying to college. For instance, triple sciences can help when applying for medicine or some specific STEM courses. Otherwise, sciences already tend to be more difficult, and studying something you don't have to for "fun" in the IB tends to give you a lot more work and a lot less satisfaction than you'd expect. If you need this, make sure to talk to your IB coordinator as early as possible.

- First mandatory component - "TOK"

Now we are getting into the areas where IB gives you no choices. Theory of Knowledge (TOK) is the first (and arguably the most noteworthy) case here.

In short, TOK is a dumbed down epistemology course. Epistemology is a branch of philosophy concerned with knowledge. Generally, this part of the IB programme gets a lot of hate and it's easy to see why. A lot of our friends who aren't too keen on abstract discussions simply feel baffled by how "pointless" this subject feels a lot of the time. Personally, we enjoy philosophy, but from our perspective TOK often feels too flat, restrictive and infantile.

On a positive note - it's easy! There is really no perscribed content here. The course instead focuses on teaching you how to think in a certain way and how that's done depends on your teacher. Also, there are no exams for this subject - you are assessed based on two assignments done at home. Overall, it takes some time to adjust to TOK, but it's a pretty chill subject. And if you absoutely hate it, there is some good news too: it is nowhere near as important as the six subjects you choose in the context of your overall diploma score (more on that in a second).

- Second mandatory component - "Extended Essay"

The Extended Essay (EE) is not a subject, but an assignment. Basically, you write a 4000 word work on the subject of your choosing. This part of the IB programme is here to teach you how to do academic writing, how to be analytical and how to use sources.

Although you're given freedom in choosing the subject and topic of this work, it's not that simple. Generally, the EE's in sciences or math tend to do a lot worse in terms of scores. On top of this, they require a lot more work (such as conducting experiments). Overall, an EE in the sciences is just a bad idea - a lot of extra work for (likely) worse results. Even if you are extremely well educated on a specific topic, you can still score poorly. I've heard stories of undergraduate level math EE's getting average grades due to them being too specialized and advanced for examiners.

Another important thing is that you choose a supervisor for your EE. This is just a teacher of the subject which your EE is based in who is meant to guide you during the writing process. Keep in mind, there is a limit to how many students one supervisor has (it depends a lot on the individual school and teacher, it's best just to ask).

Overall, it has surprisingly little relevance in the context of the whole diploma. In the end, it's coupled with TOK for a maximum of 3 points (one subject that you have exams in can give you up to 7). We will elaborate on how points on the diploma work in a post next week.

- Third mandatory component - "CAS"

Creativity, Activity and Service (CAS) is the least like a subject out of all these components. There are no grades or exams here and the assessment is conducted on a pass/fail basis. Essentially, CAS requires you to document your extracurricular activities in the three strands:

- Creativity - what you do for yourself - your personal interests, hobbies, etc; unlike the name suggests, this applies to not only "creative" or artistic extracurriculars, but to practically anything you do to develop yourself in your free time
- Activity - what you do for your physical wellbeing - exercise, walks, sports, gym, etc. This category is very simple and straightforward.
- Service - what you do for others - participating in communities, helping people in need. This is quite broad yet difficult to define.

There are two specific things IB requires you to do for CAS:

- CAS project - something done in collaboration for at least a month (including preparation). This includes things such as organizing an event.
- CAS portfolio - a documentation of what you do for each of these strands. This looks differently based on your

coordinator and school. We, for example, have a portfolio in the form of a google calendar.

Overall, there are very few formal requirements for CAS. As such, your CAS coordinator generally makes the rules. Questions like "does XYZ count as service?", "how many hours of creativity do I need?" can only be answered by your CAS coordinator - they are ultimately the one who decides whether you pass CAS.

- There is still a lot more to be said...

However, this post is already crazy long. Soon enough, we will publish part 2 of the newcomer's guide which will focus on assessment in the IB programme - exams, assignments, etc. Until that comes around, feel free to ask any questions in the comments!

- The Extended Essay

What is it? - A written work in a subject of your choosing meant to simulate the process of writing an academic paper. The word limit here is 4000. You choose a teacher (of the subject you are writing in) to be your "mentor" here.

Is it difficult? - It depends. You certainly need to develop new skills for it, most notably knowing how to properly cite sources and maintain a bibliography. The difficulty relies mostly on the subject you choose. As a rule of thumb, language EE's are much easier compared to just about any other topic. Most teachers agree that an EE in sciences will require more work often for a worse result.

How important is it? - It depends. The EE is graded on an A-E scale (where E is the failing condition). This does not give you any points on the diploma by itself. Instead, it is evaluated alongside your TOK grade (which is also on the A-E scale) and this evaluation can give you up to three points on your diploma (out of the 45 possible points). For more information of how this is done, just google "IB bonus points matrix". Whether that's important depends on whether your uni considers total points (our, for example, does not). If it does, getting three points instead of two can make all the difference and allow you to fit the admissions requirements.

The assessment criteria, very shortly explained:

1. Criterion A [6 points]: Is your topic well-explained? Is your research question connected answered in the essay? Did you choose your methods and sources well? - Generally, when assessing this criterion, the examiners will focus on your introduction and bibliography. Importantly, they don't care how advanced your work is here - just whether it's about what it says it is and whether you approached it appropriately

2. Criterion B [6 points]: Do you understand and know what you're talking about? Do you use your sources well? Do you use subject-specific terminology well? Do you demonstrate your understanding? - Here, the examiner looks mostly at whether your work is suited to the standards of your subject. The keyword here is demonstrate - is it clear that you are knowledgable on this topic? You can show this through (for example) specialized language and terminology.

3. Criterion C [12 points]: Is this relevant to the research question? Is your work analytical? Do you evaluate the research appropriately? - This is the most important criterion. The keyword here is analytical, which in the IB context essentially means developing arguments and arguing instead of describing facts and events. The examiner wants to see you drawing reasoned and logical conclusions here. The question the examiner will most likely ask themselves here is "So what?" - you'll be punished for points which don't clearly connect to an argument or for excessive descriptions where details don't add anything to your reasoning.

4. Criterion D [4 points]: Is the work structured as expected for this subject? Does it follow conventions? Is your layout and formatting good? Does the structure help the reader

follow your reasoning? - This is probably the easiest criterion to score well in as it's mostly focused on the technical details of your document. Your document, not your essay. Here, the examiner focuses on whether your EE roughly resembles an academic work in this subject in terms of the structure, layout and bibliography. The best way to score well here is to search for academic publications in the subject you're writing in and see how they do it.

5. Criterion E [6 points]: This criterion focuses on the reflections form. It's a separate 500-word document attached alongside your EE where you are meant to reflect on the writing process at three different times (before starting, during the writing and once your final draft is done). Here, the questions are: Do you demonstrate the ability to plan ahead and adapt to adverse circumstances? Do you show the difficulties experiences and how you've dealt with them? Importantly, the examiner generally looks at this in the broader context of your work, so feel free to include specific examples of troubles you've overcome here. Overall, the keyword here is demonstrate - you have to be as clear as possible when writing this! Generally, the reflections are supposed to be done with your EE supervisor, so they should be able to guide you further on how to do it.

Our tips for the EE:

1. Start early. Since you should base your EE on something interesting (this makes the writing process much more pleasurable), the things you learn during the programme are not THAT important when writing the EE. Starting early means you finish early, and that will be very helpful when the massive workload of DP2 comes around. Besides, since one subject teacher can take a limited amount of students, this lets you secure a spot for the subject you want early.

2. Plan ahead. When starting, the EE workload seems immense. The best way we've found to avoid being

overwhelmed by that is to break down the entirety into smaller pieces. The best way to do this is by planning your work. Start by writing a plan for the structure - what will each section (such as the introduction or a particular paragraph) contain? Once you've done that, it's easier to start writing with the mindset of "I'm just writing a 500-word introduction" instead of "Oh my God I have to write 4000 words on this".

3. Don't stress too much. Objectively, the EE is not as important as your six chosen subjects - each subject can get you at most 7 points on the diploma, while the EE can grant only three. This is not to say you should disregard it - these three points can be the difference maker! It's just that you should remember that the EE is really not that scary when you're overwhelmed or stressed out by it.

- TOK

What is it? - TOK is assessed solely based on two written assignments - the TOK Exhibition and the TOK Essay. As mentioned before, your TOK grade is evaluated alongside the EE grade for up to three bonus points on your diploma. Generally, the criteria here are very descriptive and less clear than for the EE, so we will try to give some tips that will help you fit into these descriptions of a perfect grade.

TOK Exhibition - It's a 950-word piece of writing where you explore three real-world objects in the context of a chosen prompt. There are 35 prompts to choose from (you can find them in the subject guide!) and the objects can be just about anything, so a lot about the exhibition is up to you. There's one thing that stands out in the criteria:

- Be clear. The examiner wants to see you clearly explain the objects you chose and their real-world context. They also want you to clearly and explicitly explain how these objects relate to your chosen prompt. Overall, it's not a bad idea to make the language in your exhibition a little bit unnatural for the sake of being as clear as possible. The examiner also wants to see you clearly justify why your particular objects are here and how they contribute to the exhibition. Any arguments you make here should also be very clear and well-explained, even if it means a small sacrifice in terms of how complex they are.

Overall, the exhibition can give you a maximum of 10 points which will be considered when giving you the final TOK grade on the A-E scale.

TOK Essay - It's a 1600-word essay, where you discuss a topic in terms of two areas of knowledge. The topics change every exam session and some of them dictate which AOK to write about. Some tips:

• Follow a discoursive essay structure. This means introduction, a body with two paragraphs which argue in favor of a claim and two which argue against, and a conclusion. This is because TOK examiners love when you argue with yourself and this structure makes it very easy to do so while also making everything well-organized. It also helps you to address the mention of "clearly evaluating different points of view" in the criteria.

• Use specific examples. In your arguments, they want you to be very specific. This means that, while you can start a paragraph with a general statement such as "mathematics is certain", it should be a short mention and the paragraph should instead focus on a concrete example with clearly supports that claim.

• Focus on the topic. Just like in the Exhibition, make it clear that what you're saying aims to answer the question/address the title. You can for example add a sentence at the end of each paragraph which remarks on what you've just added to this exploration. You should also remember that this means you must focus on your arguments and the context for them (such as the explanation of an advanced example in mathematics) should be as short as possible while making sure the reader can understand what you're saying.

- Avoid extensive definitions. A lot of the example TOK essays that can be found online spend a lot of time defining very basic things. Firstly, these do nothing to address the question. Second, a lot of definitions uses up a lot of words which you could otherwise use to address the topic. This isn't to say that you should never define anything - sometimes that's necessary for the reader to understand your arguments or to clarify how you understand a certain part of the topic. What we mean is that dedicating 300 words to the discussion of the definition of "knowledge" is a bad idea.

The TOK essay also gives you up to 10 points, but due to how these assignments are weighed, your score is doubled in the context of the final grade. In other words, you can get at most 30 points total for these assignments - 10 for exhibition, 20 for essay. With TOK, it's difficult to give universal tips as this subject is a different experience to everyone. Therefore, we want to remind you that starting early is the key to all of IB and recommend you the channel "Get An A in TOK" on youtube as a wonderful resource.

- Internal Assessment

You write an internal assessment for each of the six subjects you chose to study (except for languages and arts). This is by far the most important group of assignments. I repeat, every internal assessment is extremely important. This is because the IA makes up at least 20% of your final subject grade and, since you write at home, you have a lot of time to perfect it. A good IA will serve as backup in case you fumble your exams and can easily boost your grade from a 6 to a 7. We present to you the three holy commandments of the internal assessment:

1. Put all the time you can into perfecting each of your IAs. As we mentioned, the IA is the most surefire way to boost your final grade. Exams may go bad, you may get a horrible

headache on the day of a maths paper, you may see a question you have no idea how to approach. We could go on and on, here are just so many unpredictable factors during the exams and the IA is the one piece of certainty you can have during exam season.

2. Understand what the examiners expect. They say "better the devil you know than the devil you don't". Even before you start writing, we highly recommend researching the requirements for every IA you must write. Generally, every subject guide (you can find practically any of them by googling) has a section dedicated to the IA with criteria and descriptions. Dedicate some time to understanding them as it will really help in the writing process. For example, you can make a cheat sheet where you write down the criteria in your own words. Regardless of how you do it, this is the key to getting a good score.

3. Start early. While most IAs require some knowledge you'll gain throughout the programme, this should not discourage you from beginning the writing process as soon as possible. Start with the second commandment and work your way from there - choose at least a vague area of the topic that interests you, create a plan for your work. As soon as you're able to begin writing, absolutely do it. Remember, starting early is finishing early, which means you will stress less in DP2 when all the deadlines start coming and that you can focus entirely on revising for the final exams. The peace of mind that comes from knowing all your IAs are done is truly worth working towards.

We hope this post gives you a decent idea of what the assignments in the IB are. We know that this seems like a lot, but we promise that it's not as scary as it seems. For the worried ones, a secret note: an acceptable EE takes one weekend to write and you can probably finish an IA in one day. So, don't stress too much about it and remember to start early - your future self will thank you!

5. u/JoaquinRevello

I'm back and here to give some thoughts on your IB summer after getting pinged with the same question dozens of times.
I got a 45 in the IB back in M21 (exam route) and I'm currently studying in the Engineering and Business program at UPenn Wharton (M&T).

Let me start by saying this: there's no magic formula for the best summer, as everyone's circumstances, aspirations, and resources vary. But I'll guide you through two potential objectives: getting into a top university and earning high IB grades (addressed in order below).

What did I do in my summer? I always knew I wanted to enter the M&T program at UPenn, so my summer was tailored to that.

First, I enrolled in the M&T summer course, which was a three-week program that blended technology and entrepreneurship. The course culminated in a project, and our team won an award that provided me with some valuable university connections.

Secondly, I spent a significant portion of my summer writing essays. I completed around 36 essays by the end of the summer, both for early applications to M&T and MIT and regular decisions to seven other universities. Of everything I did, finishing my uni essays before the second year of IB was a game-changer in reducing stress once I returned. With the IB

IAs, tests, and the rest of the IB debacle, it becomes a challenge to squeeze in the time to write accurate essays.

Thirdly, by having my essays out of the way, I was able to fully concentrate on my IAs and EEs. However, I don't necessarily recommend working on your IAs and EEs over the summer. The school environment just makes you more productive due to the deadlines and the stress that comes with you thinking that your life is at the end of a thread. There are exceptions though: I feel starting on my Chemistry IA, Math IA, and EE over the summer would have saved me some stress.

As for my Extended Essay, I chose a physics topic and completed my experiment over the summer right before year 2 began. So that's something I'd do differently: I suggest trying to finish your EE before school starts, based on my experience. Check this video out if you'd like my commentary on my Extended Essay: https://youtu.be/JAduzB19tU8

Regarding extracurriculars, don't be the one scrambling to find a 'wow factor' in Grade 12. It's too late then. Your extracurriculars should ideally be sorted by the end of Grade 11. Grade 12 should be about focusing on your predicted grades, finalizing your applications, and working on your IAs. Now, if you're aiming for top IB grades rather than a top university, my advice differs slightly. It's still not necessary to pre-study calculus or similar subjects in Grades 10 or 11. I would, however, suggest pre-studying a lot of the content and working on your IAs and EEs over the summer.

Finally, understand there are different 'seasons' throughout your IB journey. Learn to adapt to the requirements of each season. Focus on mastering the fundamentals, such as focused work, avoiding distractions, and getting ample sleep.

I see a lot of students asking for some secret strategy for acing the IB. There isn't one. The trick is to focus on the fundamentals, like dedicated work, avoiding distractions, and proper rest. Also, build fundamental habits during your summer that will benefit you during the school year, like daily focused work sessions or ensuring eight hours of sleep each night. Success in IB (and life) is more about these small but consistent actions rather than some elusive 'magic formula'. Good luck, everyone!

The CAS Project

One big part of the CAS programme is completing the CAS project. It is essentially a CAS experience that requires some degree of planning and collaboration between peers, and is supposed to last at least for one month. Completing the CAS project can be tough for some people. Juggling proposals, timelines, and coordinating with your peers on top of keeping up with IB's tough academic schoolwork can really take a toll on you.

During my IB days, I recall seeing a lot of my friends, especially those who were not used to work in an organisational setting, struggle to get their CAS project started. Nevertheless, every IB student is still required to complete at least one CAS project. Thus, this chapter will give you a few tips when doing your CAS project.

Mindset

Have you always wanted to try out coding? Have you always wanted to start a company? A CAS project is actually the perfect place to explore these passions.

This mindset can really help you go through with your CAS project. Just by tweaking your passion to involve more people and serve a community, your hobby can improve your university portfolio whilst acting as a CAS project.

Speaking from my personal school days, I always wanted to teach other kids. However, like many students, I procrastinated on pursuing my interests and passions as I felt overloaded by the hoards of homework and tests. However, when I learned that I had to complete a CAS project as part of my CAS requirements, I was actually ecstatic. I thought that since I had to do a CAS project, I might as well do something that I enjoy that would otherwise take too much effort. This led me to view teaching as any other schoolwork that I had to complete, thus I felt forced but motivated to teach. This eventually led me to create a non-profit that teaches underprivileged Indonesians and Malaysians.

This is just my story on how I used the CAS project as a platform to pursue my interests. You could easily do the same. Want to learn coding? Make a CAS project on making an app that helps the elderly keep track of their finances. Love art? Make sculptures or paintings to decorate an orphanage. The list goes on, just pick an interest and make a CAS project. Your life will be so much easier and you will feel proud of what you have accomplished.

Start Early

As of IB's latest syllabus you should have CAS experiences that span around 18 months of your academic journey. However, as previously mentioned, CAS projects are more intense than your average CAS experience. This is why you should complete your CAS project as soon as possible.

Many schools even force or rush their IB students to finish their CAS project by their first Semester. However, if your school does not enforce this, please take initiative and do yourself a favour by completing the CAS project as soon as possible.

You do not want to be stressing around during exam season looking for partner organisations when you could be resting or revising. I know of someone who put CAS to the very last minute. As a result, while most of his peers were revising and doing past papers, he was busy coding an app with his friends. This made his CAS project less unenjoyable and even worse, his grades took a toll as well.

Doing it with Competent People

This may sound like no-brainer advice but please work with competent people. You would be surprised to find many students don't pick their group mates carefully and end up working with the wrong people. So please spend some time to ensure that the people that you are working with are quite competent.

Also, don't give yourself a hard time by forcing yourself to work with friends that have a bad track record of pulling their weight in group work. I know working with friends can sound appealing but IB is hard enough as it is and you do not want to be wasting extra energy confronting people, especially your friends, to do their work. Alot of people, including myself, find it very uncomfortable to push your friends to do work or to confront them about things you disagree on. So for your own sake, prioritise competency over working with your friends.

Some Extra Tips to Get Started

An easy way to start a CAS project is just by contacting any sort of community centre, old folks home or something similar around your area. This ensures that your CAS project minimally fulfils the 'Service' strand.

Now, ask the organisation what they do? Who do they help? And ask if they are open to getting some help from you. Don't forget to include your CAS group mates in the conversation. After that, you start to weave your passions into the CAS project. Think of how your passions align with what the organisation needs then offer to help. Offer to create art pieces, teach English or create some sort of app to help the organisation, whatever your passion is, offer it. If your passions align with what whatever organisation needs then boom you have just laid out the foundations of your CAS project. Simple as that. All that is left is for you to sort out the details and deliver on your promises.

While this method is not for everyone, it is a pretty straightforward way to get your CAS project started. This is especially helpful if you still are not entirely sure on exactly what you would like to do for your CAS project. I saw a lot of my IB peers starting out their CAS project this way, so hopefully you found this small segment to be helpful.

Working Together

This segment will give some basic tips when working together with other people. This is more for those of you who have no experience working with other people on a big project. No need to fret, this is quite normal for most students this age. Anyways, here are those tips:

1. Make a good timeline with your group mates. Make sure it covers the schedules of meetings and when certain things need to be done eg. Lesson plans or app prototype. Making a timeline greatly helps you not lose track of what and when to do things for your CAS project. Don't forget to create a google calendar and integrate it with your CAS Project groupmates. This ensures that everyone is in the loop
2. Make meeting minutes aka. Assign someone to take note of what is being discussed during the meeting. This is what many people inexperienced with working together tend to forget. They have long meetings, but after such meetings they forget certain key things that were discussed during the meeting. This ensures you do not forget anything important. These days there are many technologies online that will help you make meeting minutes but more on that later.
3. End your meetings with actionables. This essentially means that at the end of your meeting, everyone needs to be sure on what needs to be done next and by when. What happens often, is that meetings end up becoming places for fruitless discussion. As whatever was discussed during the meeting did not really have an effect on what you do. So having actionables ensure your meetings are more useful. This also helps ensure that work is allocated somewhat fairly among groupmates.

While you will still inevitably encounter problems working with other people. These tips should help smooth out the process of working with your CAS project group members.

Maximise your Reflections

Remember that at the end of any CAS experience or project, you are required to write some reflections on what you have done. To recap, the IB syllabus requires you to write at least one reflection for every learning outcome. It is very likely that your CAS project can allow you to write reflections for 7 of the learning outcomes. My advice here is to use your CAS project as a means to write reflections on learning outcomes you were not able to cover using your CAS experiences.

The CAS project is especially useful in covering your 'Global Engagement' learning outcome. Contrary to popular belief, you do not need to engage the international community for your CAS project to qualify for 'Global Engagement'. The IB guide states that you only need to tackle a global issue in a certain way. This could be done locally, nationally or internationally. So if your CAS project is under the 'Service' strand it is very likely that you will be able to write about 'Global Engagement'.

46. Conquering CAS

This chapter will be kept very short. If you are honestly struggling to complete your CAS requirements then I cannot do much for you except shake my head in disappointment. The good thing about CAS is that it gets everyone involved in the community, teaches students to be creative and aims to keep everyone in good health. The sad thing is: if you were really that concerned with community service, wouldn't you be doing it already, instead of doing it for CAS? However, that is not our concern. Your aim is to complete your CAS activities and projects, cover the seven learning outcomes, and finish CAS as soon as you can (preferably in the middle of your second IB year) with minimal difficulty.

As part of your "core" IB requirements (which include the EE and TOK components) you are obliged to complete the CAS program. This means that you must make noteworthy progress in each of the three components: Creativity, Action and Service, partake in CAS activities that cover the seven learning outcomes and successfully undertake one CAS project. All of this needs to be done in the span of 18 months.

Creativity

Probably the 2nd easiest CAS component to fulfil. You don't need to be a young Mozart or Picasso to do a 'Creativity' strand activity. First and foremost, engage in school creativity activities. This includes any play productions, choirs, and art competitions. If that doesn't work out for you, do something independent. Design their website, make a new banner/poster to boost school spirit, teach younger students how to draw/Photoshop/act. It's pretty easy to do 'Creativity' strand activities , just don't leave it too late.

If you don't want to get involved with the school, you can also just do creative stuff by yourself. Paint, sing, learn a musical instrument – the opportunities are really endless. Just make sure that there is some kind of 'outcome' for every activity. This could be a finished painting, a poem or an audio recording of you playing the new song you learnt on the piano. This is crucial, as creative efforts without an 'outcome' (e.g. learning a language) are no longer accepted.

Action

This should be very straightforward. I know what it's like to be lazy and non-athletic more than anyone else, but even I managed to do my 'Action' CAS activities with absolute ease. I joined the school sports teams not only for the sportive factor but also simply because it was a lot of fun. If you go through high-school never having tried out for the football, basketball, swimming, volleyball, tennis or track and field teams then you are missing out on a lot of memorable experiences.

You can't honestly say that there is a struggle to find activities to fulfil your "Action" activities requirement. Even the non-athletic kids at my school somehow found their way to the local gym and at least lifted some weights or did some treadmill running. There is always some solution available.

Also, if your school offers PE lessons, then use that! Physical education is not a part of the IB and is definitely you being active, which makes it eligible for CAS. In addition to that, think about trips you've taken with your family and friends!

Did you go skiing? Biking? Hiking? All of these activities can count as an 'Action' CAS activity.

Service

This is the problem area for most people. I don't think it's because we are all inherently selfish and egotistical, but it is perhaps more to do with a problem in finding service work. If your CAS coordinator (assuming your school has a CAS coordinator) is living up to the expectations then you should be able to get advice and opportunities via him/her. I know schools treat CAS and especially the service component in varying degrees of seriousness. Nonetheless, you need to ensure you did enough to make the IB moderator satisfied if your portfolio is sent off.

The type of service you do will largely depend on where you live, how comfortable you are being outdoors, how fluent you are in the domestic language, and a variety of other factors that would make it too difficult to give you any specific tasks. Like I said before, no one is asking you to create a charity overnight or clean oil spills and create peace in the Middle East. You just need to demonstrate that you care enough about the community and do the activities required. Join your school's student council! Collect some trash!

CAS Coordinator

As aforementioned, the school's CAS coordinator will largely decide the success of your CAS program. When I did the IB, the CAS coordinator was wonderful. Not only did he make sure that everyone did what was required of them, he also made sure that those who tried to cheat the system were sufficiently punished. Your CAS coordinator will either be very engaging and hunt you down if you are lacking sufficient activities (for your own good of course) or he will be easy-going and let you decide what you want to do and when you want to do it. The latter approach is a bit too risky for my liking.

At the end of the day you just have to make the best of what you've got. If your CAS coordinator doesn't seem to care about whether you pass or not, then that just means you will have to work that little bit extra than the student who has a CAS coordinator who does everything for them. Having a poorly run CAS program is not a good enough reason for failing to meet the CAS component requirements.

Tips

Although my CAS advice lacks much detail, I can offer you a few words of advice on the CAS program in general.

Completion – make sure you complete the CAS program as early as possible. I'm not saying you give up on all creative, athletic and community related aspects of your life for the remainder of your IB experience, however it will be more beneficial for you to complete CAS as soon as possible. Since the IB now requires you to complete CAS in the span of 18 months, it's good to start on the first day of your IB programme.

I had friends who were being chased down for a good part of grade 12 and this stress reflected on their other IB work. The lesson here is that the sooner you finish CAS, the sooner you can start to worry about all the other work you have to juggle for the IB. Get this out of the way as soon as you can – even if that means working in hospitals and running marathons every weekend in your first few months of IB.

Planning

As mentioned before, the IB likes to see a good spread of CAS activities over 18 months, so it greatly benefits if you have some sort of plan on what CAS to do. This is to ensure you don't overwork yourself in a few months only to find out that you still need to do CAS afterwards.

As a rule of thumb, it is ideal to have 1 CAS activity or project happening at any point of time in the span of 18 months. This however does not mean that you have to do CAS every day, it just means you have some sort of CAS activity going on at that general period of time.

For example, if you have an activity called jogging, you can jog twice a week for 4 months. This means that this activity is recorded as 4 months. Hope this helps clear things up.

Writing the Portfolio

Make sure you keep a very clean and tidy track of all your CAS activities. To satisfy the IB, you will have to write/record a certain number of reflections for each 'learning outcome'. Do this as soon as you finish the work, otherwise you will just forget what you did. Keep all this information in a very safe place and don't lose it because there will come a day when your CAS coordinator will ask for it.

Faking It

Just don't do it. How bloody hard is it to legitimately do tCAS? If you think you can forge your tennis coach's signature, then don't act too surprised when your CAS coordinator calls him up only to find out you never did those tennis lessons. There's nothing more sneaky and self-centred than claiming you helped your community when really all you did was just cheat. You will probably get caught and feel guilty as you are made an example of in front of your friends. Just do the activity – it's really not that much to ask.

While on the subject of misconduct, please avoid declaring random things as a CAS activity when you know you didn't deserve it. This includes doing paid work, tasks for your family, favours for your friends, and any other clever ideas you might have to get an easy CAS activity. Examples include kids who lie about jogging at home, or those who claim to do unpaid work for their parent's company. Don't end up like this. Not only do you risk being caught, you're also better off just doing the activity and benefiting from the experience.

University

One massive advantage that you will have over other non-IB university applicants (and even job applicants) is that you can use your CAS experience to build up your CV/application. Community service looks great when applying to competitive universities, as do creative abilities and an athletic lifestyle. Make the most of your CAS program at school because it will be of great use in later life. Even in my current CV I still have elements of community service that I did during CAS.

For this very reason, I strongly suggest that you make full use of your CAS program and do service activities that are more attractive than others. For example, organising a concert at the retirement home is a lot more eye-catching on your CV than handing out pamphlets or walking dogs. In fact any service work that requires engagement with people you would not normally work with is very impressive to universities and employers. For this reason you should ensure to do CAS service activities that actually mean something. Similarly, playing for the school football team is more effective than spending an hour a day at the gym because it shows that you can cooperate with others and work in a team. Choose activities that you might want to impress with later on in life.

Failure

If you fail your entire IB Diploma because you did not meet the CAS requirements then there is little hope for you. I have seen some of the worst IB candidates still manage to scrape through their CAS program so for you this definitely should not be a problem. Don't overestimate CAS as it really should not dominate your IB schedule. Then again, don't leave it as the last thing on your to-do list because it will harm your other IB work.

A lot of students dread CAS. I don't understand this. CAS allows you to have a positive impact on your community. I promise you that if you are dedicated and actually spend time once or twice a week on an activity that helps others around you, you will feel like a million bucks. People that simply study all the time can never get the best grades because they eventually burn out and feel too much stress. So it's important you actually do things you like or have interests in.

You should treat CAS as that much needed oxygen that's saving you from drowning. Try to pursue activities that you are genuinely interested in and don't just volunteer so that you can get a CAS activity. Give value to the world, and you will be paid back handsomely in the long-term.

I know for a fact that playing football for the school team had a huge benefit on my life in the IB. After those practice sessions I felt better, my mood was elevated, and it's always nice to be away from books once in a while. What I'm trying to say is that CAS is actually a really, really good aspect of the IB. It turns us into more open-minded individuals and gives us time to pursue our passions.

47. Applying Artificial Intelligence

This chapter will deal with a relatively new addition to the hectic lives of IB students: Artificial Intelligence. With the rise of online services like QuillBot and ChatGPT, tons of kids have begun using (and overusing) AI as an assistant in their IB studies. Although these services can be a life-changing tool, there are a handful of risks that you take by using them, some of which could cost you your diploma. This chapter will give a few tips to help you use AI to its fullest potential without sabotaging yourself and your grades.

How can I use AI?

The uses of AI in the world of academia are truly limitless. Here are a few ways you can use ChatGPT (or any other similar AI generator) to stay on top of IB work:

Brainstorming

Using ChatGPT to brainstorm ideas is a game changer. Now, let's get one thing straight: 'brainstorming' does not mean 'writing the entire essay for you'. Not only will that get you flagged for plagiarism and thus disqualified, it's also just plain wrong. What I mean by 'brainstorming' is asking the engine to generate ideas for an assignment and then incorporating these ideas into stuff you come up with yourself. If, for instance, you're set on exploring a certain literary theme in your Language/Literature EE, you can use AI to propose literary extracts relevant to this theme that you could analyze and compare in your essay. Of course, this idea of brainstorming applies to any IB assignment (even things like CAS), as ChatGPT will give you at least a semi-accurate answer no matter what you ask it.

Time Management

Using ChatGPT is especially beneficial when you want to start managing your time. When I wanted to create a study plan for the final exams, I literally just entered the subjects I needed to study, the amount of time I wanted to study each subject for and any additional information like the weekly time slots during which I was already busy. Based on this information, ChatGPT greeted me with a sleek revision timetable that I ended up using up until the final exams.

Top tip: when doing this, tell the engine to "organize the plan in a table". This will put the study plan in a grid that you can print out and stick on your wall. In addition to the table itself, ChatGPT may include tips regarding study methods and intensity aimed to optimize your use of the study plan, which may be something to take note of as well.

Revision

Not only can you use ChatGPT to create revision timetables, you can also use it to get free exam questions. Cool, right? All you need to do is ask the engine to generate a practice IB exam question, making sure you specify whether you're taking the subject at SL or HL. Although ChatGPT won't be able to retrieve real questions from past exams, it will use syllabus data to emulate IB questions as well as to provide step-by-step explanations on how to get to an answer. This is particularly helpful if you've done all the subject's past papers but still feel you need more practice on a certain topic. Honestly, I was surprised at how accurate the generated questions were especially for math, so it's definitely worth a try if you're at your wits' end!

In addition to this, ChatGPT can aid your revision by crafting study resources like flashcards. I would advise this especially for content-heavy subjects like Economics and Psychology for which you need to memorize copious amounts of definitions and case studies. You can also ask AI to think up mnemonic aids that will help you remember key processes and concepts across all your subjects.

College Applications

AI is an amazing tool for creating outlines, which you can capitalize on during the college application process. If you're lost, you can ask ChatGPT to create outlines for your personal statement and/or college essays. You can then tailor these proposed outlines in accordance with your needs.

Nonetheless, definitely don't put all your trust in AI with this, as universities may have niche expectations of what they want to see in their ideal personal statement or college essay. If a conflict arises between the AI-generated outline and advice given by your college counselor/official university resources, always prioritize the latter when making decisions about writing style and structure.

Are there things I cannot use AI for? Cheating?

Despite popular belief among my M23 year-group, under NO circumstance can you use AI to generate entire essays, IAs or EEs. If you're planning on doing this, you might as well shoot your IB diploma in the foot and here's why.

The main reason for not doing this is pretty obvious: you will get caught. Now that AI is becoming more and more accessible, so are softwares that can detect and flag AI-generated content from a mile away. This is the case even for AI-generated text that has gone through a paraphrasing service like QuillBot. One of my friends thought she was Einstein for running a ChatGPT-generated essay through a paraphraser, only for it to get her a severe warning and failing grade for one of her IB Philosophy essays. It really is not worth it. At the end of the day, you'll still have to gain all that knowledge somehow for the handwritten exam, so you might as well just get on with writing your IAs and EE by yourself as well. There's really no point in putting the diploma you put so much effort and money into in jeopardy over a few hours of work.

Academic Research

I wouldn't recommend using AI as your number one resource when doing academic research for your IAs and EE, as it isn't guaranteed that provided information will be 100% accurate (not to mention that ChatGPT is tricky to source). Instead, I'd recommend using AI as a stepping stone to finding academic journals, published data and other reliable resources that can in turn become the backbone of your essays. These are the main pointers when it comes to applying AI to your IB studies. Of course, there's a lot more ways AI can be implemented depending on each specific assignment and subject, so it's worth consulting your friends and online platforms like the IBO subreddit when finding innovative ways to use AI to bolster your academic progress. If you're ever worried about a gray zone in the use of AI as a part of the diploma programme, talk to your school's IB coordinator, who will be able to give you advice based on official IB guidelines. Happy AI-ing!

48. The Power of Technologies in the IB

Back in my IB days, myself and many other peers were hesitant in learning new technologies. We thought that the time involved to learn how to use these technologies properly would be more of a hassle compared to the help it would give us. I was quite stubborn with this as I did not want to waste extra energy learning something new, when I still had tons of IB content to learn.

One day, my friend saw me manually calculating some numbers for my Chemistry IA and he decided to show me how he used Excel to do most of his calculations. He told me that in about 20 minutes, he was able to do all of his calculations for his IA. Meanwhile, 20 minutes was not enough for me to finish calculating one data set.

This changed my mindset and made me realise how big of an idiot I was for not properly using the technology I have access to. Since then I learned about plenty of digital apps and technologies that easily saved me hundreds of hours of work during my IB days.

Beyond that, it's generally a good thing to develop a habit of making the most of the technologies around you. Knowing your technological tools well can go a long way in your future career, potentially impressing your bosses as well.

This chapter will mainly focus on the common Office Applications such as Word, PowerPoint and Excel along with their Google equivalents (Docs, Slides and Sheets) which are essential apps when writing EEs and IAs.

You may be thinking: "Of course I know about Word, I use it for all of my EEs and IAs", but while you may use Word often, there is a chance that you might not be making full use of its features. Hopefully, this segment can help you learn about some of these application's features and can save you some extra time. If you're sure you know your way around these apps, you can directly go to the next chapter, where I will be talking more about more uncommon applications or websites.

Microsoft Word / Google Docs

This is probably the most commonly used app for any IB student. Every student has probably spent hundreds of hours on Microsoft Word or Google Drafts writing and editing their EEs, IAs and ToK essays. With all this time spent, you would expect people to master this app. Yet, from my experience, I saw many peers who only treated Word as a place to type your reports and did not know of certain basic features. I will be sharing some of Microsoft word or google docs' essential features that can either save you some time or improve the quality of your work:

Table of Contents

Don't waste your time spending countless hours manually typing your table of contents and constantly updating the page numbers and subheadings. Despite how often people use Word, I was very shocked to see many of my IB peers still do this.

Luckily, Word and Google Docs makes it super easy for you to make Table of Contents. You just have to select the headings for each segment in your EE or IA and click the 'heading 1' button in Word or Google Docs. For sub-headings you select the text and click the 'heading 2' button. 'Heading 3' for further subheadings and so on. After this you can instantly generate a Table of Contents by clicking references and clicking the Table of Contents button. Boom there you have it, you just saved yourself hours of time from figuring out how to properly structure your table of contents and manually copying your subheadings. The best thing is every time you can easily update the Table of Contents by just clicking on it and clicking update. This will ensure that your Table of Contents have the correct headings, sub headings and page numbers.

Page Breaks

Ensuring that your EE or IA looks neat can be very annoying if you do not know the right technology. Manually pressing 'enter' until a subheading or paragraph reaches the next page is very time consuming. Additionally, every time you tweak something, you will likely need to change your 'enters' to ensure that your report looks neat. There was also a point where I wasted time entering and tweaking my EE and IA such that it looked nice, this all changed when I discovered the magical function of 'Page Breaks'.

You can find this function in the 'Insert' tab in Word or Google docs. What 'Page Breaks' basically do is that it automatically makes you type your next content in the next page. First of all, this saves so much time from manually clicking the 'enter' key. The beauty of this page breaks is now that your entire document will not move when you change a line or two. New lines won't push whatever you have written downwards, instead whatever new you will write will only fill up the page. If this sounds confusing, try it yourself, it takes a few minutes to learn how 'page breaks' work but you will use and appreciate it the rest of your IB programme and beyond.

Justify

In case you do not know, 'Justifying' your document just means that your lines will be distributed from left to right. There is not much to be said about this. Your teacher should already comment on your IA. It does not do much, but it makes your IA or EE or whatever report you are writing much more professional. Remember, organisation and presentation is part of the marking criteria. So do yourself a favour and justify your documents.

Word Count

Most of you probably already know that Microsoft World has the word count feature. Just so you know, google docs also has this feature hidden under the 'tools' tab.

However, the word count displayed by word or docs does not accurately display the word count of your EEs or IAs. This is because most of the time the word count suggested by the IBO does not include words used for sub-headings, values in a table, appendix and so on. This is why you have to manually select certain chunks in your document and tally them yourself.

A lot of the friends I knew blocked a chunk of their document, looked at the word count, and keyed it into their calculator. This can be tedious especially for EEs as every one or two paragraphs you have something to skip. Luckily, there is an easier solution. Just hold command (for Mac) or control (for Windows) while you block the relevant chunks in your document. This saves you quite a bit of time from tallying your own word count.

On a side note, when checking your word count, do check if it includes footnotes or not. Sometimes, footnotes can add around an extra few hundred words to your document. Thus, making it seem like you have no more word count left even though you have some space to write. So make sure to turn it off when counting your word count.

Equations symbols

This segment applies to not just Math IAs or EEs but any IA or EE with some form of formulas or calculation. Please do not type out equation symbols using normal letters eg. Typing the multiplication symbol using 'x' or writing variables using 'x'. This makes your report seem untidy and can become confusing for report markers. Instead use word or doc's 'equation' feature found in the 'insert' tab. It allows you to type mathematical equations using special maths symbols. You will have access to special maths symbols such as roots, integrals, or fractions which may come in handy. So please use this function in the future whenever you're writing any sort of maths equations.

To add on, this 'equations' function comes with an 'equations alignment function' that allows you to centre equations with multiple lines based on the '=' symbol. This is super useful when you are making formula derivations or are doing complex calculations that require multiple lines of working.

Microsoft PowerPoint / Google Slides

In hindsight, you would think that Powerpoint or slides has no relevance in the IB curriculum. As IB has no projects that directly require you to use PowerPoint. However, the usefulness of PowerPoint actually lies in its tools. To be more specific, PowerPoint or Slides is your best friend when making Graphs or Illustrations.

So every time you need some sort of graph or diagram, maybe an externalities diagram for Economics or just a diagram to show how your chemistry experiment set up works, PowerPoint has got your back. Setup a blank slide and just use their wide range of shapes and icons to create your diagram. Once you're done, screenshot the slide and use it in your IA or EE.

I believe PowerPoint or Slides is the best tool for the IB student when it comes to making graphs or diagrams for two reasons. One, its very easy to use and is good enough for the needs of most IB students. Second, is that unlike paid software such as Adobe, PowerPoint or google slides is free to use.

On a side note, you can use word or docs' tools to make graphs as well. But most people agree that moving things in word can be quite annoying at times, so I still find it better to make whatever graph or diagram I need in PowerPoint then move it over to word.

Microsoft Excel / Google Sheets

For most Science based EEs you will definitely process your data through various calculations before you obtain your desired results. If you are like me, doing these calculations manually feels very tedious.

I remembered how painful it felt to do uncertainty propagation for my chemistry IA. Ensuring I used the correct variables and keyed in the right uncertainty values for my apparatus felt very tedious. While the maths itself is not the most complex, the thoroughness involved and the repetitive nature of the task really took a toll on me. On top of that, I remembered finishing my calculations only to end up with a result that doesn't make any sense. Turns out, through the different processes of error propagation, I keyed in an extra zero somewhere and it messed up all of my calculations. This made what should have been basic maths turn into a really long task.

Anyways, if you thought what I shared was very annoying, do yourself a favour and learn how to use excel or sheets if you haven't. I know Excel or Sheets looks slightly more alien and harder to use than Word or PowerPoint but trust me it's worth it. Don't be one of my dumb friends who insisted on manually calculating all their IA work, you will just waste your time and are more likely to end up with more inaccurate results.

You don't need to master the wide range of Excel/Sheets functions, you just have to understand some basic features and you can easily save hundreds of hours of your time when doing your IAs or EEs. Thus, this segment will tell you Excel's features that are most prevalent to the IB student.

Operations and Functions

This is probably the backbone of spreadsheets.. First, you have to understand how to utilise operations and functions in Excel or Sheets. Its really simple, just click on one of those boxes in your spreadsheet and type in the '=' symbol. This establishes that you are going to use that box or cell to make some calculations. You then type in the coordinates of other cells to use them in your equation. If this sounds confusing go try out excel or sheets yourself, it's really quite simple.

All that's left is for you to know some basic operations and functions. So here's a summary of all the important operators and functions you need to know:

The 4 basic operators: +,-,* (times) and /. This should help you do 90% of your IA calculations.

AVERAGE(): Pretty self-explanatory, but this function helps you find the average of a few cells. This is usually used when finding averages from multiple data sets.

SUM(): A quick way to sum up a range of cells

MIN() or MAX(): Find the maximum or minimum number in the range of cells. Helps you find uncertainty.

These 4 functions are probably more than enough to help you speed through most of your science IA or EE calculations.

So now what? All that's left for you to do is to type in your formulas in your sheets and input your relevant data. After that Excel or Sheets will do all the magic and give you the results that you want. Easy as that. Using spreadsheets easily saved me hundreds of hours of calculations in my science IAs.

Just a side note, it is important to ensure that your Excel formula is correct in the first place. I suggest doing one manual calculation and cross checking it with whatever Excel or Google Sheets is showing. If all is well, proceed to copy and paste the formulas and the relevant data required.

Rounding and Decimals

So another tedious thing I found about doing my science IAs was rounding to a certain amount of significant figures or decimal places. Once again, it is not hard, it's just very boring and tedious. Well, Excel or Sheets can help you with this too:

Decimal Places: You should see some 0 icons with some arrows in your menu, these buttons help you round to a certain number of decimal places. Just select your data and press the 0 icons to add or reduce the number of decimal places

Significant Figures: This one's a bit more complicated to understand. But essentially just copy-paste this function '=ROUND(number, digits-(1+INT(LOG10(ABS(number)))' and you should do fine.

Plotting Graphs

If you have done some sort of research report in the past, plotting graphs should not be alien to you at all. I am just going to give you two other features that Excel and Google Sheets have that will help you plot better graphs:

Trendline - You can generate a trendline from your plotted graph in Excel or Sheets just by adding a chart element. Excel or Sheets will automatically do the maths for you to generate the most suitable trendline. This comes in handy as hypothesising a correlation between two variables is generally a prerequisite to getting a good IA grade for the science subjects

R squared value - Excel also generates this value along with the trendline. For those of you who don't know, its a value that tells you how strong the relationship between two variables is. It's another point of analysis that can be helpful in improving your IA.

So besides saving you a bunch of time, Excel or Sheets will help you gain a few extra marks in your IA or EE.

Planning with Excel

Excel is much more than a tool to help you do your IAs. While I did talk about all the benefits of using excel to do your IAs and EEs, its benefits extend far beyond that. Personally, Excel or Sheets acts as a great planning tool. You can get creative and use Excel for your own uses, but here is how I used Excel to help myself throughout my IB journey:

Past Paper Tracker - I have touched on this in the "The Power of Past Papers [II]" chapter, but here is a recap. Revising for the IB exams can get real messy real quick. This is because due to the hundreds of papers you will have to bulldoze through for practice. So having an excel sheet greatly helps. Why you may ask? Well you can use it to keep track of which papers you have done, but beyond that you can use Excel to see your average performance in each subject or paper. This enables you to focus on weaker papers/topics/subjects, saving a lot of time for you.

CAS Planner - In the CAS chapter, I touched on how planning your CAS properly is really helpful so you don't do too much or too little at the same time. You can use excel to create a list of CAS activities you plan to do. After that you can map these activities in your excel sheet. This ensures you have a consistent CAS portfolio in 18 months.

But these are just the ways I used Excel to help organise myself go through the IB journey. Whatever your circumstances may be, Excel can probably help you organise your life to some extent.

I understand that this chapter covered pretty basic software features. But hopefully, you learned some extra tricks or gained some ideas on how you can use these applications to help you in your IB journey.

49. Academic Dishonesty

If you have come here looking for ways to cheat on your exams then you are out of luck. It's not that I'm an extremely honourable and moral person (although I would like to think so) it's just that there is no point in cheating. The information I have provided so far in this book *is* in a way tricking the system without *actually* cheating. So you are technically not doing anything wrong, you are just abusing certain aspects in order to get a higher grade – something that any clever student would do naturally. It is one thing to plagiarize your essay, but it's a completely different matter to slightly "manipulate" your lab report data in order to get higher marks. This chapter won't give you the best tips on how to cheat. In fact it will do quite the opposite – it will tell you why most methods of cheating fail and what the consequences usually mean.

You have to be pretty stupid to follow a two year program only to then have your diploma taken away for academic malpractice. That's two years of your life practically wasted. If you fail the IB diploma because of cheating then you are pretty much screwed. Why risk two whole years of relatively demanding work so that you can bump your grade up a little bit? The risk is simply not worth the reward. It's even more redundant given that you can easily get a higher grade by simply following the guidelines set out in this book. No matter who you are, there is absolutely no reason for you to even think about cheating.

Although the IB originated in Switzerland, don't expect them to be very understanding, or "neutral". Any form of academic dishonesty is dealt with the utmost seriousness. The vast majority of the time when you are caught and reported you will lose your diploma. Not only does cheating carry serious risks but you will also put yourself under more pressure. The threat of being caught will make you underperform and provide an unnecessary distraction.

Plagiarism

Plagiarizing is probably the most common type of academic dishonesty found in the IB program. I'm not going to go into an in-depth discussion of what constitutes plagiarism and how to cite – your school should have already shoved that down your throat. I merely want to explain to you what happens when you try to do it. Hopefully this way you will avoid "accidently" doing it and think twice before you complete any piece of work for the IB.

Many of you may have heard of the website turnitin.com. This website scans for plagiarism. Depending on what school you are in, you may have it that your teachers scan every single piece of work that you hand in electronically. For those of you that have no idea what I'm talking about let me explain. Turnitin.com (amongst many other more sophisticated websites) scans documents for any evidence of plagiarism. They take your words and check them across a multitude of various sources: websites, paid websites, written books, magazines, journals, etc. The program then composes a very in-depth report that specifies exactly how much of your document is plagiarized and to what degree.

These expensive plagiarism scanners that the IB use are growing in sophistication every year. Almost every possible essay-writing database is now listed, along with written books that have been made into e-books. Even if you paid ridiculous money for someone to custom write your Extended Essay, chances are the scanners at turnitin.com will catch it because they can afford to scan almost every database.

So what does all of this mean for you? This should be a wakeup call for those of you who are likely to plagiarize "unintentionally." I'm talking about those of you who thought it was ok to throw in a few sentences here and there from your textbook because it's not available online. Almost everything is now available online and turnitin.com will scan these archives.

The consequences for plagiarism will more than likely lead to you failing that specific piece of work, and, depending on the degree of plagiarism, maybe even your entire diploma. I trust that you realise the dishonest aspect of plagiarism and will refrain from trying. More importantly however, I want to warn you to make sure that you don't accidently and unintentionally plagiarize either. I know that sentence doesn't make much sense, but it's for your own good that you make sure that none of your work is anyone else's words. So please, think twice before you include any sentence that is clearly not your own.

Why in the world would you even contemplate cheating on the actual IB exam day? If you're at a respectable and honest IB school then chances are that your exam centre is going to have some of the most vigilant proctors making sure that your every breath and sneeze is natural. You and your fellow candidates are going to be like little sheep surrounded by a pack of wolves.

Even before you walk into the exam room your face will tell the whole story. Even the bravest of you that lack any conscience will struggle to conceal that nervous and tense look when you step into the room. Chances are that even before you actually begin to cheat you will get caught cheating. This paragraph (and probably chapter) only applies to a small proportion of candidates out there, but nonetheless it's important to get the message out there that cheating on the exams is near impossible – and stupid.

Almost anything you can think of has already been taken into account. Random pre-exam calculator checks, plastic see-through bags, no talking in the exam centre, assisted toilet breaks, only bottled water. For every cheating method there is already an answer. The only "cheating" left for you to do is to follow the legitimate advice and tips that I have been suggesting. On exam day the only thing you should be thinking of is the exam itself. Anything else on your mind will distract you from doing your best. The IB diploma is not some middle school exam where you can write the answers on the palm of your hand, or slip in a cheat sheet. This is one of the most prestigious and respected high school programs in the world and they are not about to let their reputation slip as a result of academic malpractice.

As long as we are on the subject of cheating, there is one final word of warning. With the recent rise in cell phone and internet use, it has become almost inevitable that students discuss exam questions and answers online and over the phone. Make sure you are not amongst them. Schools have begun paying incredible attention to this and I have heard of cases where students were tracked through Facebook or their cell phone and eventually stripped of their diploma because they broke several rules about revealing exam details before the examinations were completed worldwide.

Given that the IB is an international program there are small possibilities for the manipulation of time zones in order to get exam information. But again let me warn you. Schools have begun to monitor students' cell phone use before and after the examinations. Also more and more papers are being divided into several time zones. There's probably nothing worse than being fully ready for an examination only to turn the paper over and realise you have crammed the last hour on questions that are not there.

The message here is pretty crystal clear: don't even try to cheat during your IB program because you will more than likely get caught and there is very little benefit. You can achieve amazing results without needing to plagiarize or be dishonest.

Cheating will have severe repercussions for you later on in life. You can forget about going to any respectable university if your diploma is taken away because of academic dishonesty. Not only is it a burden on your academic future but it also has serious social and academic consequences.

50. Appeals and Re-takes

Once you receive your examination results one of three things will happen. You may get the grades you were expecting and get what was required for your university. In this ideal scenario your IB adventure is over, and you can finally move on. Alternatively, you may receive your results and find out that you *deservedly* fell short in a subject or two, or perhaps failed something, and as a result your first choice university offer is no longer an option. The final scenario is that you receive your results and find that there are a few subjects where you know you should have done better. You are shocked because, as things stand, you cannot get into your first choice university or perhaps even your backup choice. There are several options that you may choose to take, outlined below:

Appealing

I'll be honest with you. When I first got my IB results in June, I did not get into my first university of choice. I got 42 points but fell short in HL Mathematics because I got a 6 instead of the required 7. My offer from Oxford was 40+ points overall, with 7's in HL Mathematics and HL Economics. I wasn't too surprised because I knew if there was one subject where I might fall short, it was definitely maths. Nonetheless, as things stood, I was not going to get a place at Oxford. I called up my coordinator and told him the situation. He highly recommended I appeal not just the mathematics grade, but also the 6's I got in SL English and SL Physics. The logic behind this was that if I didn't go up in maths, then at least maybe Oxford would reconsider if I got 43 or 44 points overall.

After several weeks I was informed that my English and Physics grades would not improve. This was very disappointing because I felt that my English exams went perfectly and I had superb IA marks for both English and Physics. I felt like there was no chance that my maths grade would increase because first of all I was predicted a 5, and second of all because maths is rather objective – there are right and wrong answers with little room for grey areas and errors by examiners. Well, I turned out to be mistaken. I received the news from my coordinator that the grade had gone up to a 7, so I had met my offer and got a total of 43 points.

The point of that little story is that you should not just try to appeal when you feel like you could have done better. Even in exams where you are 80% sure you cannot improve, it may be worthwhile appealing if your university choice is on the line. Of course this will come at a financial cost, but I would say that if it is affecting your future then the financial cost is worth it. Besides, if the grade does change you will be refunded the full amount. Would I have appealed if I got my first choice of university and could see no direct benefits of a higher IB score? Probably not. I would recommend appealing only if it will affect your university decisions.

Retakes

In the unlikely scenario that you completely mess up your IB exams there is always the option of re-taking them in November. I am not a big fan of this option for several reasons. First of all, re-taking in the winter exam session still means that you will miss out on a year of university unless you can find somewhere that starts after the winter break. If not, you would be better off repeating the year and sitting the examinations in May

Second of all, re-taking exams is only a good option if you genuinely think that things will change. There is no point in redoing the exams if your approach is the same. If something tragic happened that distracted you from performing at your level, then retakes can be a good opportunity for a second chance. If however, you failed to meet your targets because you did not prepare adequately, then chances are this will happen again during retakes.

For these reasons retakes should only be considered as the final resort. It goes without saying that if you missed a university offer by a small amount then you should first appeal your grades before you even consider retaking the exam.

Life After IB

The day of your last exam will be a day that you remember for a very long time. I finished my last exam more than 10 years ago and I still remember that day as if it was yesterday. It will be a strange feeling. You go from having no free time at all, to suddenly having the longest and most carefree summer of your life. When you walk out of that exam room, you will want to celebrate but you will also be so incredibly exhausted that I suggest you go home and hibernate.

The reason I wanted to write a quick chapter on this is because I have seen over the years an alarming number of students suffer almost from a kind of post-IB depression. In the sense that, they just don't know what to do with all this free time they have acquired. Students have even told me they feel like they don't have a purpose anymore, now that IB is finished. They feel empty inside and unsure about moving onto the next stage in life.

First off, know that what you're feeling is very normal. Even if your friends are not talking about it, there are tons of people reading this who feel much of what you feel. I felt it after most major milestones (high school, year by year in college, etc.). There are short-term and long-term things you should do, and I'll detail a few of them and why you should do them:

Exercise – even if you hate exercise, go take a walk. Go play tennis with a friend, or go swimming, or something. Do this at least 3-5 times per week, and you will soon find that you crave the activity. It will do wonders for your state of mind.

Get sunlight. It seems strange, but sunlight causes your body to release all sorts of things it needs, including neurotransmitters which regulate mood.

Read – you've spent the last two years reading mostly what others imposed on you, so you've built up some animosity toward reading. But you probably used to love it, and you can again (and it will make you healthier and happier). If you need suggestions, PM me.

Make others happy. Part of how we define our self-worth comes through service to others. So go make someone's day. Maybe you take a younger sibling to some activity they love. Take your dog for a walk. Go volunteer somewhere not because you need CAS, but because helping people makes you feel better.

Long term, you have goals and a plan. What are small steps you can take toward those goals now? Maybe you read a book or journal article for self-education. Maybe you work on a website. Maybe you browse the syllabi for the classes you're taking this fall and decide to start learning ahead of time?

On the positive side, I do still contend that in the vast majority of cases, life tends to get better after IB. By that I mean, the workload and the stress at university is, by and large, substantially less than the two years of IB. I say this as someone who went to supposedly the best university in the UK. I honestly felt that IB was more stressful and difficult than my three years at Oxford.

Keep yourself busy and try and have some carefree fun!

Conclusion

Just please remember grades do not define you. Remember that this is all about learning and trying to do your best. I have so many regrets because I spent so much time alone in my study procrastinating work, not talking to my family and friends, and missing out on really great events that would have made my final year so special. There is always a way to achieve whatever you want in life so long as you are passionate about it, no matter what IB you get. Again, a number does not define you, no matter how important it seems right now. You are beautiful, smart and capable of anything you set your mind to. Do your best and live life.

And my final piece of advice to you is this, there are days that are going to come where you're going to receive a result that you didn't expect, the important thing is to move on, right now, your marks don't matter a lot in the scheme of things, but they are a major indicator of how well you're doing. So if you fall, get up, dust yourself off, and just keep going.

IB is tough, but you got this.

PSA from an IB teacher:

Your IB exam scores do not determine your worth, value to society, or success in the future.

Exam season is upon us, bringing the yearly allotment of stress, sleep deprivation, and string ties. Before their first exams yesterday, the tension was palpable and many students were nearing a nervous breakdown. It's natural to feel this way in

this season, but I wanted to remind you that who you are as a person is not determined by the numbers you'll see in July.
Put forth effort that reflects your character, and aim for the top. But know that in 5 years, you won't be remembered by the specific scores you earn. A 45 won't be nearly as impressive to the real world as it is on reddit. You may be remembered by your intelligence, but your kindness, perseverance, dignity, and honor will form the lasting impressions.

I've taught IB for about 20 years and love this program and the opportunities it creates, but I also think it's important to separate identity and performance.

Tip of the day: sleep is important. You will perform better after a night's sleep (more than 5-6 hours) than you would if you stayed up studying. Your brain cannot function well without sleep.

Though I don't know you, I'm proud of the journeys you've taken to get to this place. Only you know the challenges you've faced, yet you've persevered and can see the finish line. Don't stop running here, but don't ignore the entire race if you stumble at the end.

Contributors

Do YOU want to contribute to the next edition of this book? We are always looking for talented and insightful IB students (current and alumni) to improve and add onto this book. For more information on publishing your IB material, please visit www.zouevpublishing.com, where you can find our other range of IB books also. We are also interested in obtaining individual chapters on subjects not yet addressed in this book, so don't hesitate to get in touch if you feel like you have something to contribute – we would be happy to collaborate.

For any questions or comments, please email us at zouev.publishing@gmail.com

Special Thanks

Thank you to my parents, who always supported me in whatever I did.

Roman, thank you for being a great big brother and an awesome editor.